MYSTERIES OF ANCIENT SOUTH AMERICA

HAROLD T. WILKINS

Facsimile Edition.

Harold T. Wilkins. *Mysteries of Ancient South America*
First published in 1945.

ISBN: 978-2-925611-33-2
Printed in the USA.

www.ultimatumeditions.com

MYSTERIES OF ANCIENT SOUTH AMERICA

by
HAROLD T. WILKINS

RIDER & CO.
LONDON :: NEW YORK :: MELBOURNE :: SYDNEY
68, FLEET STREET, LONDON, E.C.4

Dedicated to my distinguished friend

MILES POINDEXTER

Senator of the United States, one time U.S. Ambassador to Perú, whose travel-studies on the mysteries and pre-history of the old Inca Empire, and the Ayar-Incas, have made him famous all over the countries of the Andes and won him the Gold Medal of the Sun of Perú.

FOREWORD

"*I have but one object: to bare the mysteries that the jungle fastnesses of South America have concealed for so many centuries. We are encouraged in our hope of finding the ruins of an ancient, white civilisation and the degenerate offspring of a once cultivated race.*" . . .

(The last message sent to London over the Overland Brazilian Telegraph in Rondonia, by Colonel P. H. Fawcett, on April 20, 1925.)

To the above message to Britain, from the first, but, I hope, not the last of the British conquistadores who conquered South America by brains and courage, not by rapine and blood and banditry, the author ventures to add that he has tried as best he may to fill up the lacunae, which fate ordained that this soldier and explorer of the Legion of Frontiersmen, forever pushing forward into the unknown, should leave with a great question mark across them. It seems unlikely to hope, now, for Colonel Fawcett's return from the lost world of Brazil's jungles, nearly twenty years after he and his son and Mr. Rimell vanished. So, having said *Ave et Vale* to these brave British spirits, I express the hope that this book may be found not only entertaining, but to carry farther the trail he, and a long line of Englishmen, Scotsmen and Americans, from Ephraim George Squier to Sir Clements Markham and *el Gran Caballero,* Don Roberto (the late R. B. Cunninghame Graham), blazed into unknown and mysterious South America.

THE AUTHOR.

Bexleyheath,
Kent, England.
Spring 1945

Extract from the 1943–44 volume of *Who's Who in America*:

Wilkins, Harold T.: Author and traveller, born Gloucester, Eng., March 18, 1891, educated Grammar School and Cambridge U.; began as schoolmaster and went into journalism, serving in all grades from reporter to editor; worked in Fleet Street, London; travelled in many parts of Europe . . . has done extensive work in S. American archæology and Brit. and Am. archives for pirate and treasure hunting stories and general adventure by sea and land. . . . Author of more than a score of popular and general interest books, pubd. in New York, Boston, and London, Eng.

CONTENTS

LIST OF ILLUSTRATIONS

LIST OF DIAGRAMS

CHAPTER I

OUR EARTH'S GREATEST DISASTER

"As above, so below. That which hath been shall return again."
Warning of an Ancient Mystery.

A FEW months before the outbreak of the Second World War I was aboard a steamship sailing from Singapore to San Francisco, making her course for Honolulu. The high, cobalt sky of the North Pacific had changed to a strange unearthly grey, and the barometer had fallen. We were, as the radio warned, some miles and an unpleasantly few hours from the vortex of a typhoon. The sky seemed to have descended till our mast trucks and the radio antennae touched what resembled the lid of a flat box or canopy. Below our keel the sea stretched flat and grey. There were no waves; but the waters appeared to drum with the pulsing of a heavy ground-swell above one of the deepest abysses of the North Pacific. There came a sudden flash of lighting and the reverberations of tropical thunder. Then the wind unaccountably died and the sea began to rise and heave. A strange thing now happened. All over the ship could be felt a singing hum. Our steel hull had become a gaint 'cello in the hands of some Titan of a maestro, who was playing a sort of fugue of an apocalypse. The waters responded somewhat in the way a flat disc will do when sand has been laid on it in formless heaps, and the vibration of a fiddle-bow causes the particles to take a pattern.

Looking over the bulwarks, or gazing down from the navigator's bridge, passengers and ship's officers saw that the sea had now become covered with a vast scum of light grey colour. It was pumice-ash from submarine volcanoes erupting in a tremendous convulsion. In port, where the captain had divers examine our keel and propellers to discover what possible damage the ship had sustained, it was found that the steel had been scoured clear and bright from marine foulness and barnacles and the blades of the bronze propellers burnished till they shone. The tremendous submarine convulsion had filled the deep ocean craters till the surface of the ocean had become one vast detergent and abraded whatever metal passed through it that day. Possibly, far down below, there lay, many fathoms under the keel of our ship, some of the highlands of that drowned continent called Rutas, in the old Sanscrit traditions current in the *goparams* of old Hindostan; or, as others call it, Mu, Lemuria or Gondwanaland.

But, some ten or twelve thousand years ago when the Great

Deluge of Noah and Ogyges happened, even worse convulsions of the shuddering earth and sea stretched right round our globe from the Pacific across South America to the shores of Africa, where stood that giant pharos called the Pillars of Hercules, right into the Mediterranean, till they shook the old Levant and a more ancient Greece. In the skies of terrible night shone a giant comet, or aerolite, or wandering star, or planet (we do not know which), but which brought such destruction on the earth that those who survived the disasters regained sanity only slowly, and, in some cases, never. (As in that of the lunatic civilisation of the old Aztecs, to which a definitely paranoiac twist was given, making murder of bestial sort a rite of barbaric religion.)

Comets, of course, are not identical with aerolites. The comet has a tail of deadly and lethal gases, usually too attenuated to poison mankind in the manner described by fantaisiste novelists. But the comet has also a hard core, or metallic nucleus, enveloped by a "coma" that has always, as far back as tradition goes, made mankind fear and wonder. It has a luminous course of its own and flashes across our skies like a dog with his tail behind him, and, past perihelion, may never return, vanishing into infinite space. But the aerolite is as a cosmic bull running amok in a china shop. What it may do—and, luckily for us, we have no record of the falling of such gaint lawless bodies, in historic and recorded times, on *thickly populated lands*—has been vividly seen between the years 1908 and 1937, in North Siberia and in Brazil's hardly explored forests, where a giant body of this sort laid waste hundreds of miles of woods and primaeval jungle and bush, and brought death and destruction upon hundreds or thousands of primitive or savage people in villages within a radius of hundreds of miles of its impact.

I was on my way to South America to try how far I could verify a theory of mine that Atlantis, the famed drowned land, may be looked for in the splendid and mysterious ruins of her old colony in unexplored Brazil and parts of western South America. In that colony, if indications be correct, a very high degree of scientific civilisation had been attained more than 20,000, perhaps, even 60,000 years ago, in a day when modern archaeologists, who have never come within hundreds of miles of these great ruins in the South American jungles, too confidently assert that nothing but lowest savagery existed, and perhaps not even a vestige of humanity was found.

True, we shall have to verify these theories, not by waiting till some iron man of the year A.D. 1960 can dive to the floor of the Atlantic, way beyond the modern Canaries and Cape Verde Islands, in order to grope along carved pillars and splendid temples, clutched in a forest of sea weeds and the lair of deep or middle sea cephalopods, or devil-fishes. I think the late Doktor Eckener of the exploded *Graf Zeppelin* airship has indicated the way to this knowledge; or the exploration may be done in one of those giant three or four-engined Flying Fortresses and Liberators now used to bomb vast cities and munition works, but which, in our new and better age to come, may be put to solve the age-old secrets now barred to us by dense woods and wild uplands, beset with vile insect plagues, and hunger and thirst and legions of fierce unpacifiable savages, such as haunt the now deadly and mysterious Brazilian Matto Grosso and the unknown hinterland of the Andean cordilleras to the east of Bolivia and Perú. Science has much to learn and unlearn, and the path of the air-minded may yet rise to stars where, alas, it now befouls the whole earth!

But, to return to the subject of this giant cataclysm, of the day when South America was the cradle and beacon of the older world's civilisation and the home of a humane and civilised race of white men and beautiful women—as it actually was. This cataclysm is no theory or fantasy of mine. It happened about 9753 B.C., according to the long-lost—if, indeed, they are not merely buried, to be resuscitated in due time—archives and libraries of the ancient temples of the Pharaohs at Thebes and Sais, on the Nile. It was actually witnessed by the remote ancestors of the strange and vanishing race of dwarfs, called Bushmen, still found today in a palaeolithic state of culture, wandering in the dreaded Kalahari desert of South Africa.

In this book, I find it necessary to start at the end, rather than the beginning; since there are many intelligent people who have to be convinced that this cataclysm—told in a rather naïve and garbled form, in *Genesis*, and certainly no myth—actually occurred and was no merely local catastrophe of what is now called Iraq.

Twelve thousand years ago—not more than a short hour in the long history of our planet—the ancestors of the fast-vanishing Bushmen dwarfs of the Kalahari desert of South Africa were cowering in terror behind big boulders or in the darkness of deep caverns shrouded by forest and dense jungle. They were watching the night skies, in awed fascination or shrinking in fright from the hoarse rumbles and cliff-crashing reverberations preceding and accompanying the most appalling earthquake that has ever shaken and convulsed our earth. And well might they be afraid! They were undergoing the greatest disaster that has ever befallen man since he had quitted the monkey trees, straightened his back and become true man, *homo sapiens*. Night and day the ground shook and heaved. On the sea coasts, looking eastwards towards a great island-continent where dwelt a race of men like gods, who had evolved a high type of civilisation, terrific tidal waves were rolling in higher than the highest hills. They crashed on the beaches with immense force and a momentum carrying them very far inland, while colossal league-long rollers came on behind.

Whole countrysides that had never seen the sea were drowned, while the waves, like some gigantic bore or eagre, swept up the sides of mountains and even drove backward the powerful current of deep, wide rivers. Night closed down in terror. There came a rain of fire from the heavens, which set ablaze great primaeval forests, or cut mile-long swathes in them when the searing wave and blast of hot air and gases, preceding the incandescent metallic core of the immense meteorites, scorched over the woods, rolling up earth as a scroll of the past that had now no meaning or validity. As the appalling night wore on the terrifying noises reached a truly diabolical crescendo of crashing detonations. It seemed as if Titans in the skies were bombarding the earth with a deluge of rocks, cleaving earth's skin in order to penetrate to the magma that lies deep below. The watchers began to fancy that the heavens were drawing nearer the earth, which was behaving very much like a planet that has been forced out of her orbit under great stresses and gravitational pulls from without.

Came day, or a slight lessening of the nocturnal blackness, and the light of the sun appeared to have gone out like a candle blown out on an altar. For many days, indeed, night and day could hardly be told apart. A great pall of black smoke covered the vault. No light pierced the blackness, unless the vivid, eye-ball-searing blaze of lightning of an electric glare never seen before even in that sub-tropical country, or the white flare of the sudden fall of an aerolite. At times, when the pall of smoke showed a rent in its veil, the sun hung like a ball of blood, but the penumbra soon darkened all the air, as in time of eclipse. Then, an immense cloud of reddish powder filled the air, and to the terrified Bushmen it looked as if the whole world were now going to blaze up. The powder was followed by a rain of fine cinders which covered the trees still left in the devastated forests and blanketed the vegetation with white.

Now, the watchers and listeners cowered on the earth in the heart-sickening fear of a man who hears the shriek and whistle of a falling high-explosive bomb deepening its pitch, before it crashes near to where he lies. . . . The air was pierced by an ear-shattering shriek—then another, and another, and another. Four tremendous explosions made the ground tremble. Men clinging to trees on the tops of hills were thrown to the earth. Four enormous white-hot globes had fallen from the sky into the forest behind the screen of trees. The river that flowed near by became a cloud of hissing steam which rose into the air of the night and increased the already terrible heat engendered by the flames, springing up from the mass of compressed air, glowing white-hot and incandescent, that is borne in front of aerolites.

Scenes like this were witnessed on a great belt all round our globe, stretching from isles of Java and Malaysia, right across the Pacific to the Andes of South America and the high sierras of old Mexico and the Antillean islands of the Caribbean, on over the South and North Atlantic to the shores of North Africa and the greater Mediterranean basin. They were seen, too, in Northern, but not Central Asia.

One Bushman, more daring than any other of his cowering clan, ventured out from his "air-raid" shelter into the night in a lull of the cosmic bombardment, when the pall of smoke had partly cleared, and saw, as he said, *two moons* riding in the sky, where before there had been no moon! Far out over the ocean, raging in a tumult never before seen by man, a whole vast island-continent in the South Atlantic had vanished, and a highly civilised people in millions—whose pioneers had contacted the Bushmen—had been swallowed up in an abyss which engulfed great palaces and temples and high towers in the depths of the sea. This is a "legend" told among the South African Bushmen even to this day!

(Lest the reader suppose that this is a fantasy of my invention I may point out that the Herreros, or Ova-hereros, a turbulent Bantu people of former German South-West Africa, have an ancient tradition that after a great deluge two *white men* arrived among them, as their (Ova-herero) ancestors were refuging on mountain-tops. They add that these white people became the ancestors of the black Ova-hereros, which doubtless means that the strangers acted the part of apostles of a civilisation from a vanished continent. The Bushmen of the Kalahari are, of course, neighbours of the Ova-hereros. Also, the Namaqua Hottentots, in the west of Cape Colony, report the arrival of what they call a "swimming-house", or Noah's Ark, very long ages ago, aboard which were men and cattle. These men settled in the country and among them was one Heitsi-Eibib, a pioneer of culture who, says an ancient tradition, "came from the east", which may or may not denote an Atlantean colony of the Old World. In the Sahara desert are races with traditions of an appalling convulsion which created the Sahara, and also destroyed vestiges of a very ancient civilisation).

Then torrents of rain, lasting many days—forty, says the story in the Hebrew book of *Genesis*—fell hissing on the hot earth. Across the raging ocean, in far-away Brazil, to the west, aboriginal Indians who had taken refuge on the summits of the Serra do Mar, the eastern coastal range of old Brazil, said there were great and terrible rumblings, both above and below ground. The sun and stars turned red, blue and yellow, and wild beasts mingled fearlessly with men. "A whole month passed and our forefathers heard a roar and saw darkness ascending from the earth to the sky, while thunder rolled terrifyingly and great rain in spouts blotted out the earth, and made day night. . . . People fled to the trees for refuge against the rising waters, and many died of hunger and cold as they hung perched on the highest boughs." (*Vide* p. 18.)

"Human nature was never lost, even in the days when the world perished," says an Aztec *Codex Letellier* "and so the ancients celebrated their feast (called Pilquixta) of the renewal of the human race. . . .

> "Every four years the ancients (in Mexico and Central America) added another eight days in memory of the three occasions that the world perished and so they call it on these occasions, *señor*, because although *this* was lost, *that* did not perish. They call it the Feast of Renewal, and so they say that that fast and feast having concluded, men changed their bodies like children, and thus, in order to represent this feast in the dance, men symbolically led children by the hand." (Translated from the *Codex Letellier.*)

It is remarkable that in far-away Egypt of the Pharaohs there was in the great hall of the temple of Rameses at Karnak (Thebes) by the Nile, a picture, col. 8, with legend of a feast of renewal *celebrating and mourning the loss of a drowned continent* in the Western Ocean. In those days of the Pyramids, it cannot be suggested that ancient Mexicans cut or painted such a picture on the walls or pillars of the temple of ancient Karnak, more than 6,400 miles away.

The ancient Mexicans recorded three great catastrophes, of which the third was the supreme disaster. They were caused, say their traditions, by volcanic fires, tidal waters and hurricanes. They participated together, say the ancient Mexican traditions, in shaking the earth at various times. Each catastrophe was followed by an era of ruin, and the destruction of the human race. Men climbed trees, ran everywhere in their terror, crowding and pushing together, embarked in ships, hid themselves in caves, got on mountain-tops. The few survivors were so far dispersed that they thought they were alone in the world. Every four years a *fiesta* was held in Central America, wherein ancient princes and peoples prostrated themselves before the gods, praying for no return of these calamities. Dances and feasts celebrated the escape of the survivors.

The *Codex Chimalpopoca* speaks of a

> "rain of fire, which followed the 'sun of rain'. All that existed burned and there fell a rain of rocks and sandstone".

The same *Codex Chimalpopoca*, containing the history of the kingdoms of Culhuacan and Mexico from "creation downwards", tells us also:

"The sky drew near the water and, in a single day, all was lost. The mountains themselves sank under water, but the water remained calm for fifty-two springs. At the end of the year, Nata and his wife Nena escaped in a hollow cypress tree, when the waters had drawn near the sky. . . .

"It is said that the rocks that we see, actually, today, were spread all over the land, and that the *tetzontli* boiled and bubbled with a great noise, and that then there also rose up rocks of vermilion colour. There were two repetitions of these terrible celestial disturbances, which followed periods when the darkness covered the face of the earth. One period lasted even unto twenty-five years. . . ."

(*N.B.*) This volcanic rock *tetzontli* is a rock known to geologists as "porous amygdaloid". It was used to build most of the houses in Mexico City. Bustamente, the historian, who commented on the Mexican history of Padre Bernard Sahagun, says that little volcanoes surrounding the valley of Mexico to the south-east formed the *tetzontli*. Native Indian traditions say that this lava-bed spread as far as Acapulco, on the Pacific.

Another Aztec codex has a picture of the Great Catastrophe:

"Now, it was in the year *Ce Tecpatl*, which meaneth 'Flint', on the day *Nahui-Quiahuitl* (which signifieth 'Four Rains'), that men were lost and carried away to destruction in a rain of fire, and were changed into birds. The sun was even burnt and all was consumed with the houses . . . and all the lords perished."

Reminders of this rain of fire are seen near Mexico City, in the great lava-bed, Pedregal de San Augustin. Under the bed are ancient houses and ancient pottery.

The Quiché (Guatemala) "legends", in the book of *Popul Vuh*, paint a vivid picture of men lost in terrible floods and rising waters . . .

"There came a great flood, followed by a thick rain of bitumen and resin, when men ran, here and there, in despair and madness. They tried, beside themselves with terror, to climb on the roofs of houses, which crumbled and threw them to the ground. Trees they tried to ascend, which threw them far away. They sought to enter caves and grottoes and immediately they were shut in from the exterior. The earth darkened and it rained night and day. Thus was accomplished the ruin of the race of man which was given up to destruction."

The effect on the survivors, rendered insane by such frightful phenomena which naturally followed on the violent disturbance of the earth's orbit and the setting-up of an appalling centrifugal force which drove our planet farther from the sun, is possibly suggested in the curious myth of the *Popul Vuh*:

> "The creators preserved a small number in memory of mankind, of men of wood. . . . These are the little monkeys which today live in the woods. . . ."

Some of the Mexican myths repeat, in a different form, what is said of pre-diluvian men and of the later eruption that destroyed Sodom and Gomorrah, and the Biblical cities of the plain:

> "They who came from the east beyond the sea could not cause the savages of the land to work or worship, and so there came a great deluge."

This is a remarkable reference to the coming of the civilised Atlanteans of old Brazilian Atlantis: the men in black, missioners, law-givers, teachers, such as the *men*, Quetzalcoatl, to Central America; Bochicha, to old Colombia; Manco Capac and Viracocha to old Perú.

The Washoan Indians—a small tribe on the eastern slopes of the Sierra Nevada who speak a language quite different from other California Indians—have traditions about foreign invaders landing from the sea, and making them into helots. This happened long ago. (Later in this book we shall refer to similar prehistoric invasions of the South American west coast.) These invaders would appear to have been survivors from some great cataclysm; for, says the myth, they made the ancestors of the Washoans pile up stones for a great temple whereon these "great lords might take refuge". It also appears that a great deluge rushed in from the sea, before this temple or Babel-Tower had been erected, and drowned many of the Washoans and their conquerors. A pharos (fire) burnt night and day on top of this high tower. Then came a great heaving of the earth and a second cataclysm which submerged the Babel-Tower and drowned the lords who had fled to it. Only the top of this great erection remained above the waters. Another curious variant of the same myth says that the Lord of the Universe flung the men who survived the cataclysm on to the summit of a temple-pyramid far away, "as if they were but pebbles".

The Piman, or Papagos Indians of Arizona and Sonora, Mexico, say that a great or divine man, whom they call Montezuma, escaped from some great drowned land beyond the sea and arrived in a ship or ark on the mainland of ancient North America. Some time passed and he built a refuge tower to reach the skies, when thunders from the god of cataclysm destroyed the partly built tower and the sun vanished into heaven along with the Great Spirit, which, of course, may be rationalised as an eclipse.

The west coast Okinagan (Salishan) Indians, now in British Columbia and the Colville Reservation in Washington, U.S.A., have a tradition that, ages ago, when the sun—which may mean the satellite that was to become our present Moon—was no bigger than a star, a female semi-divinity of a race of nephilim—the giants or demi-gods mentioned in *Gen. vi*, 4, and *Num. xiii*, 33, *R.V.*, translated "giants", in the *A.V.*—known as Scomalt, reigned over a large island where her subjects rebelled. She drove them all into a corner, broke off that corner and sank it and them into the sea. (This sounds like a version of the catastrophe that befell the Atlantis of the Plato-Solon story). Again, the Kutchins or Loucheux Indians, an Athabascan Indian tribe of Central Alaska and North West British America, speak of a great flood and the coming of a divine or godlike man—a culture hero, common in ancient myths—who came to them from the Moon and went back there after he had imparted to their ancestors elements of culture.

Nor did other aboriginal Indians of far North America, British Columbia and Alaska escape the catastrophe. The remote ancestors of the Taimshans of the region of Queen Charlotte Island, British Columbia, say that, before the catastrophe and the terrible deluge, "the earth was not as it now is: for there were neither mountains nor trees".

In Alaska, the forefathers of the Tlingits took to their canoes, which were ultimately stranded on the sides of high mountains. Bears and wolves swam off to board the boats and were driven back by clubs and spears. Then comes the story of a curious spectacle witnessed by these ancient Indians, 12,000 or more years ago:

> "Our folk landed right on the mountain-top and set to and erected walls of great height to keep out the rising water. Here, they docked their boats, and watched floating past great trees torn up by the roots, and monstrous devil-fish and other strange and terrible creatures of the land and sea swam and floated past, dead or alive or dying. . . . When the tide went out it tore past like a mill-race . . ."

In the region of the Upper Marañon, or Amazon, the ancient Indians were terrified by a deluge of hot and steaming water which poured down on the earth, burning and scalding it all up, and destroying the great forests. "On earth all was dark as night for many moons. The sun was completely hidden for days."

The Coroados, or tonsured Indians, also called the Kainganags, who live in the country of the Rio Grande do Sul (South Brazil), have the tradition of a great flood that covered the whole earth inhabited by their forefathers. Only the top of the coastal range of the Serra do Mar—the eastern coastal range of Brazil—remained above water. The Ipurina, of the Rio Purus, Upper Amazon territory, tell of a deluge of *hot* water . . . apparently too hot to bring fried fish! This scalding liquid poured down on earth, burning all up, including the forests. On earth all was dark as night, and the sun and moon hidden. Other tribes in the same region of the Amazon—the Parrarys and Abederys, and Kataushys—tell a vivid story of catastrophe, identical with that of Eastern Brazil, *supra*:

> "Once on a time, folk heard a great rumbling *above* and below ground. The sun and moon turned red, blue and yellow, and the wild beasts mingled fearlessly with men. A month passed and our forefathers heard a roar and saw darkness ascending from the earth to the sky, accompanied by thunder and heavy rain which blotted out the earth and made day into night. Some people lost themselves; others died without knowing why things were in so dreadful a state of confusion. The waters rose very high, till the earth was sunk beneath them, and only the branches of the highest trees stood out above the flood. Thither people fled for refuge and perched high among the boughs. They died of cold and hunger, and only Uassu and his wife were saved. When they came down from the height they found not a single corpse or even a heap of bleached bones."

Out in the Arctic sea, off Northern Siberia, are now desolate islands with a vegetation of only stunted bushes and the hardiest mosses. Before the Great Catastrophe these tundra islands were merely mountain-tops rising over a warm and lush country, where great monsters, such as mammoths and mastodons, ranged round feeding on the luxuriant grasses and vegetation of warm pasture-grounds. Then, raging, rising floods drove vast herds of these monsters on to the high grounds where they were trying vainly to seek safety. But salvation there was none! They died by thousands, of cold and starvation, bogged to the necks in marshes, where, today, these huge beasts are found complete in carcases, even to the hide and hair. It is obvious that they were refrigerated before their bodies could decompose. . . . Signs of thick sediments around show that a great and widespread flood came roaring on them from the southwards.

The same thing happened on the slopes of Andean ranges—far lower than today. At almost the same height as are now the ruins of mysterious Tiahuanacu*, the city of the dead, 12,000 feet up on a bleak paramo, at the elevation of Lake Titicaca, Perú, you can

* It is, of course, possible that two epochs and two widely sundered peoples were the victims of these cataclysms on the site of Tiahuanacu.

today see, in a great plain near Bogotá, the capital city of modern Colombia, South America, what are called "the Giants' Fields". This strange flat is heaped with fossilised and petrified bones of mastodons, overtaken by sudden catastrophe, which withered their pasture-grounds, then near the sea and warm and lush. They too died of cold and starvation—and also of rarefaction of the air, wherein they could not breathe. For their death was accompanied by an appalling and sudden rising of their old plains right into the clouds, more than two miles high! That brings us to the strange fate of highly civilised Tiahuanacu and its astonishing megalithic ruins, then located, like the pasture-grounds of the mastodons, close to the shores of the Pacific. (Or it might, even *ages before*, have been submerged under the waters of the ocean!)

That was a civilisation of a reddish-skinned race, with some subjects who had, in some cases, prognathic features—projecting jaws—and black skins, as objects of pottery and terra-cotta ware, dug up from under the ruins, show. So far back is their time, that the images found in the alluvium are fossilised and petrified. . . . So suddenly came disaster on them that none but men who were engaged on duties in ancient mines in the mountains—not then so high as the modern cordilleras and paramos of the Andes—could have escaped the cataclysm. And even so, the appalling raising of the Andes, which certainly followed the great deluge and flooding in of the sea over the land, and upheaved Tiahuanacu and the nearby Lake Titicaca, more than two miles into the clouds and rarefied air, very likely exterminated most or all of the survivors.

Says the most ancient legend current among the modern Aymara Indians of Bolivia—Perú:

> "After a long night there dawned, standing upright to the eyes of our forefathers, the great ruins you now see."

More than 11,000 years *later* came the gold-hungry conquistadores of Don Francisco Pizarro, who smashed the giant monoliths of ancient Tiahuanacu in order to get out the great silver bolts which riveted the 200-ton stones, the silver itself in each bolt weighing half a ton! They also smashed up many fine and very ancient statues of men, women with babes in their arms, "so real they seemed alive", youths and fair maidens, sitting or standing in an ancient colonnade by a stream once flowing under the great walls.

Nor was this the only highly civilised, now dead city to vanish as a dream in the night on these ancient shores of South America, when megalithic Tiahuanacu fell. When I was at Santa Fé de Bogotá, in Colombia, just before the present World War, I met one Señor Muñoz, a *haciendero* who owns an estate on the seashore not far from Guayaquil, Ecuador. He set a diver to fish up statuettes from a drowned and very ancient city lying under water just off shore. (The age of this ancient civilisation is not known.) The diver came up with artistic statuettes of men and of women whose hair was dressed in very Egyptian fashion! They had the same curiously long slanted eyes as you find in frescoes in the tombs of the Pharaohs. On their breasts were jewels carved in stone. The dead and ancient civilisation must have been, even then, very, very old; for some of the statuettes are pornographic—a sign that the makers are of a race that has lapsed from a higher state of culture.

As said Muñoz to me: "Señor Wilkins, it may amaze you to hear that every race in the world is represented in these statuettes, so incredibly ancient, found under water by my diver. There are Aryans, Semites, Caucasians, and even a race remarkably like the modern Japanese! The race had seals like prisms, covered with hieroglyphs. Also, I have found ancient convex lenses, under water, there, and also reflectors. They were made of obsidian. . . . They must have been scientific opticians, even astronomers."

Maybe, the drowned race, like their highly civilised contemporaries the Tiahuanacuans, were ancient American colonists from the vast, sunken, highly civilised continent of the mid-Pacific, called *Rutas*, in the pagoda traditions of old Hindostan, and which, they say, was disrupted by a series of terrific earthquakes and a deluge, sinking it far under the ocean, in a day, "before the Himalayas existed".

Sir James Jeans, F.R.S., the British physicist and astronomer, tells us that, about 2,000 million years ago, a rare event happened in our universe. A second star, unmoored, so to speak, came near the vast incandescent and gaseous mass that was our proto-sun. At perihelion, the pull of the star raised a huge tidal wave of glowing gas on a zone of the sun. So terrific the pressure became, that the sun threw off fragments of itself that ever since have been circulating as planets round our Sun. Modern evolutionists and scientists say such an event has happened *only once* in our universe—and this may be true in relation to the sun. But a modern scientific association meeting in Vienna, some years ago, calculated that, in 9684 B.C., our earth, spinning at the poles, sustained a collison with the head of a tremendous comet. The terrible impact caused the earth—a spinning top or freely rotating gyroscope—to lurch and tilt violently at the axis. Followed a revolutionary change in world-climate—from lush, steamy warmth of a tropical forest, or marsh, to the intense cold of the ice ages, with glaciers covering the north and farther south hemispheres.

In polar Spitzbergen, for example, you find under the present frozen surface of the beaches successive layers of fossilised plants, ranging over the whole gamut from the tropical and equatorial to the temperate and arctic. It is difficult to suggest an explanation unless you visualise our earth, tilted at the poles, under the impact of some body from outer space and slowly swinging through an arc of ninety degrees, *so that equator and poles change place*!

According to another extremely ancient tradition, about 9700 B.C.—this date, as I said, is based on evidence once existing (in the time of Solon, the legislator of Hellenic Athens) in the temple archives of the old Egyptian temples of Heliopolis and Sais, or Thais, on the Nile—a great comet approached the earth. Perhaps it may have been Halley's, which makes its periodic appearance every seventy-six years in our skies, heading towards the sun. Certain astronomic calculations appear to import as much, though none can say with certainty. More likely, it may have been some great, stellar body of a lost or dead world, from outside the galaxy of our own Milky Way of an "island-universe", which approached our sun on a parabolic, or hyperbolic course, and, having caused a grave catastrophe to our earth, vanished, never again to reappear. Or it may have been our present, *dead* Moon!

On earth, the times were disturbingly like the present. Disharmony and disunity reigned over the planet. Live and let live was an outmoded and despised principle. There was a great world war raging. Psenophis, the old priest of Heliopolis, showed the secret temple archives, concerning the story of this forgotten and ancient world war, to Solon, the Greek, visiting the Nile about 573 B.C. The old Egyptian priest said the catastrophe happened 9,000 years before. A race of militarists had sailed out of the Atlantic and invaded all Western Europe and Northern Africa, as far as Libya's deserts. They had a large navy and army. Paying no heed to any nations desiring, in that far-off day, to remain neutral, they overran every country between Gibraltar and the modern Levant, till they finally confronted one army alone: That of an ancient Attican race of probable Pelasgian origin. These ancient men of a forlorn hope of freedom stood in much the same position as did Britain, in 1940, at bay behind her moat, and defying the armies of Hitler, who had also overrun most of Europe.

"The earth was corrupt and full of violence . . . the wickedness of man was very great in the earth . . . every imagination of his heart was only evil continually." (So *Genesis*, drawing on some extremely ancient, pre-Babylonian source, long lost.)

Militarism and rage for conquest had made a hell both of Atlantis and, according to the old Sansar legends, of the land in the Pacific called Rutas (Lemuria), where black and yellow races struggled perpetually. Aelianus Claudus, the Roman rhetor, who died A.D. 410, cites a very curious story about conditions in Atlantis prior to the great cataclysm. It is taken from a vanished book of the great Greek historian Theopompus, who flourished at Chios, in 354 B.C. Only a few fragments of the histories of Theopompus have survived, and in one of them there is a very curious talk between a certain Silenus and Midas. (I give my own translation from the Latin):

> "Europe and Asia and Libya (Africa), islands, are girdled by the ocean. Beyond them are continents of infinite size, which support great animals, and men double our size, and span of years. In the same are great cities, with laws and customs of a life wholly different from ours . . . this land possesses great quantities of gold and silver, which are reckoned by these people as of less value than iron is with us. . . . Among these cities are two greater than the rest: one named Machimus, the other Eusebius. They are quite unlike. Machimus is warlike; Eusebius is pious and peace-loving. The peace-loving people reap the fruits of the earth without plows, or oxen. They have no need to sow or till. As he said, they live free from sickness and die laughing, and with great pleasure. They are so exactly just that the gods many times vouchsafe to converse with them. The other inhabitants are continually armed and fighting, and subdue their neighbours. Sometimes, they die of sickness, but this rarely happens. Most commonly they are killed in war, by stones or wood; for they are invulnerable to steel. . . ."

There follows a story of a great invasion of Europe by the warlike race of this Atlantean continent, and two people, named Marcellin and Avienus, make statements about this great island-continent.

Says Marcellin:

> "In the Atlantic sea, in the European sphere, is a more worthy island."

He is capped by Avienus, *who seems to refer to America*!

> "Fruitful in the ocean stretch lands, and beyond, backwards, *other shores stretch to another world. . . .*"

This battle of Atlantean warriors and "old Greeks" figured on a *peplos*, or embroidered robe, which used to be carried round, in Plato's own day, in the harbour streets of Athens, at a festival of the goddess Athena. One old Greek writer, named Crantor, who lived in 310 B.C., says he actually was shown pillars, in a temple by the Nile, where the Egyptian priests said there was pictured, in hieroglyphics, the history of the drowned continent of Atlantis.

Naturally, however, had the pre-Diluvian-age man been good

or evil, man of a golden age or necromancer of a race of half-demons, he could not have prevented the impact of that wandering, cosmic body from outer space. "What had to be had to be"; for, as the Greeks themselves said, not the gods on the high hill of violet-crowned Olympus can deflect by a hair the decrees of death and destiny.

It may be, as Mr. H. G. Wells contends, that history never repeats herself in an infinitely varied and incessant universe; but, on this occasion, at least, as old Lord Palmerston might have said, she "came damned near it".

Suddenly, without warning, as the two embattled armies confronted each other, there came, as the ancient Egyptian records said:

> . . . "violent earthquakes and floods, and, in a single night and day of misfortune, all the warlike men in a body sank into the ground, and the island of Atlantis . . . disappeared* into the depths of the sea."

The old priest Psonchis, of the Egyptian temple of Thais (or Sais), made a further remarkable statement:

> "There was a rain of fire from the skies . . . caused by a declination of astronomical bodies moving round the sun and in the heavens. The great conflagration recurs at long intervals . . . and those who live on high mountains and lofty places are more liable to destruction than people by rivers or seashore . . ."†

He also spoke of a boundless continent beyond the submerged island continent, which can be nothing but North and South America.

Here, as evidence in the shape of amazing ruins of dead cities in the jungles and on the unexplored plateau between Goyaz and the Rio Roosevelt of modern Brazil today attests—to those who have seen them—there lived between 15,000 and 10,000 B.C., perhaps even earlier, a highly civilised race of handsome, intellectual men and beautiful women with classic Greek features, and often bright red hair like that of Berenice. (But they were *not* Greek in origin, nor any colony from old Greece.) They lived in walled cities—walled not against savages, but the mighty gulf of the Marañon, the older name of the Amazon. They had a gold coinage, fleets, cities of shining white stone, with magnificent plazas, paved with great flags, and exquisitely ornamented temples and great

**Vide* Plato's Dialogues of Critias and Timaeus, apparently quoting Solon, or traditions in Solon's family to whom Plato belonged. It is Plutarch who names the old Egyptian priests as Solon's instructors.

† Ibid.

mansions, with fine fountains. Their coasts were lit by pharos or lighthouses, for mariners. Lenses they had invented, and reflectors they knew—which are the elements of the astronomical telescope. They built peculiar pyramids, rounded at the tops, and their ruins —seen still, today, deep in the jungle, for this is no fantasy of a lost world of fiction—bear many letters identical with those of the Phoenician and Greek alphabet, as well as other forms of bizarre and more archaic shape. Native traditions say they used a light which seems akin to that of the electric bulb.

It is probable that their priest-astronomers had been perturbed by the increasing frequency of violent earthquakes—such as we, in our modern world, have witnessed between A.D. 1938 and A.D. 1944. They had kept a keen watch on the skies, night and day, and sensed the approach of some cosmic disaster. Before this happened, this mysterious race of Hy-Brazil* of prehistoric South America sent forth bearded men in black, of gentle mien and high culture, to civilise the savages and barbaric races of Central America and the highlands of the Andes and Colombia. There is good reason to suppose that the race, like the Carthaginians, hoped to find out some more stable countries, to which they might flee from the wrath they foresaw was at hand. One of these pioneers was named Quetzalcoatl, another, Bochicha and a third, Viracocha. They were sun-worshippers. There was no temple to a moon. Head-dresses of this amazing South American race of the pre-deluge are found, *today*, on totem poles in British Columbia, and these Indians have a garbled version of the name Quetzalcoatl, associated with a legend of an appalling deluge and great catastrophe that shook the earth. They said he and his brother travelled round, working wonders and were magicians of a powerful sort. All were in black robes or tunics.

Probably, over the land-bridge linking Brazil with Atlantis, the motherland, and North-West Africa and Europe, the same Atlantean men in black travelled the vast way to Asia, bearing the same warnings and carrying out the same civilising mission. Says a Burmese tradition:

> "When luxury prevails, fire consumes the world and water washes it away. A thousand years before the destruction of the world a certain *Nat* came from the superior abodes. His hair was dishevelled, his face sad, *his garments were black*. He goes everywhere through the public ways and streets, with mournful voice, warning men of the approaching cataclysm." (*Burma: Asiatic Researches*, Vol. VI, pp. 172–244.)

******Hy* **or Royal Brazil is the name given in the Old Irish legends to a lost golden world. As stated elsewhere in this book, the old Irish, nearest to the Keltic root-stock, maintained a very early connection with a civilised race across the Western Ocean, and in the cordilleras of the Argentine, today, there is actually an** ***Indian*** **tribe speaking** ***Erse*****!—AUTHOR.**

It may be more than a coincidence that the name *Nat*, in the form of *Nata*, is that borne by another Atlantean missioner, who is the Noah in the Mexican *Codex Chimalpopoca* version of the Great Catastrophe. (*Vide* pages 14-15 *supra*.)

Then came the Great Catastrophe which annihilated this strange and mysterious civilisation of old Hy-Brazil, the royal colony or empire of Atlantis.

The day of the world's judgment was also about to fall on a strange island with a mausoleum* and temple where mighty rulers and warriors with Caucasian features met in a sort of Valhalla with the spirits of their dead. This eerie island, on which hardened travellers of today, who are sceptical of most things under the moon, say rests an aura or spirit of ancient evil, we know as Easter Island. It lies 2,000 miles westwards into the eye of the sunset's fires from the South American coast and the other mighty civilisation represented by Tiahuanacu, the mysterious. Here all round were tall cliffs on the top of which ancient but very skilful architects and engineers had designed and erected a colossal platform made of megalithic stones, laid beautifully together without the bond of any cement or mortar. The imperious race who made this strange island-mausoleum were like the Egyptians of the old Pharoahs: they conscripted, for the work of raising these mighty stone blocks into position, slave-labour.

Right round the towering cliffs stretched these gallery-platforms. They rise tier above tier, terrace on terrace. Each terrace, at dignified intervals, was occupied by the towering figures of colossal men in stone gazing in calm disdain, or frowning menace *inland*—and not out to sea where lay the Fatherland of their great Southern Sea Empire. A queer "red top-hat" beetled over the great brows of each colossal man. One figure is thirty feet high and so huge and spreading that thirty of the English sailors of Captain Cook's day easily dined in the shadow of its form, at noon!

The "wrinkled lip and sneer of cold command" on the faces of these imperious colossi seems to menace anyone approaching the great amphitheatre from inland. Behind the grand platforms of cyclopean blocks the thunder of the great Pacific surges crashes on the beach, while the rude bourdon of the music of the South Pacific winds roars like an organ above the heads of these Ozymandiases, kings of kings. There are no fewer than 550 of these tremendous images of martial men and rulers, mostly without feet. Almost every face is arrogant and masterful—men of a race of world-con-

---

* But so obscure is the chronology that the cataclysm which destroyed the great Pacific empire, of which Easter Island may have been an island-outpost, might have occurred many thousands of years *before* the *Hy*-Brazilian-Atlantean disaster, and contemporaneously with the cataclysm which, if it did not raise Tiahuanacu from *the bed of the ocean into the clouds*, two or four miles above, assuredly, on geological evidence alone, raised it two miles into the sky from the sea-shore of old South America!—AUTHOR.

quering imperialists and militarists. Yet every face is different and individual. Indeed, it is obvious that they are portrait faces of actual human beings, and not gods or *nephilim*. A few have a merciful, or contemplative look—philosophers, or physicians, or teachers, or sages—but in nearly all the jaw is big, and the chin juts out like a rock.

This island is a Valhalla-graveyard of very strange sort. The master-race does not live in it. No; their empire island-continent lies far over the Pacific, and the slaves and skilled craftsmen of the corvée, along with their task-masters and the supervising engineers and architects, and the priests of the Valhalla-temples down the majestic causeway, inland, are fed, clothed, munitioned and supplied by food-ships arriving periodically from the Fatherland.

Inland from the giant megalithic platform goes a tramway, supported on bags of leather-hide which are inflated, to act as ties or sleepers, as the British call them, to the "railroad" track. Down this tramway come those giant red toppers made of red tufa from a volcanic crater, inland, to be fitted on to the brows of the colossal images, on the sea cliffs, on which the crimson top-hats are wedged with white stones! Arriving at the feet of the images (represented stylistically at the end of the great trunk), the toppers are rolled up an inclined ramp, where slaves have the job of fitting them on the cyclopean heads.

Four splendid stone causeways radiate inland from the platforms. They are magnificently paved, and lined at intervals with splendidly carved statues of men. They pass on to an open plaza of great extent where towers up into the sky a domed temple, many-sided and polygonal, with statues at every angle of the building. The sign of the female vulva on some of the stones suggests that a form of the oldest worship on earth is carried on by this strange race: that of reproduction, of which this is one of the phallic symbols. But another symbol, a circle, sometimes cleft with a rod, and on some of the images themselves engraved in series on the necks or backs, imports that they also worshipped the sun; perhaps, an emblem of a central mystic sun: the unrevealed God.

Close by the cyclopean cliff-platforms are seen queer half-pyramids, with rounded tops; but another even more amazing thing is seen carved on the walls of strange catacombs hidden in the cliffs, and whose pedestal stones were, with great difficulty, found 12,000 years later by American "gobs" of the U.S.S. *Mohican*. It took them two days' hard work to force a way into these hidden catacombs. They discovered niches with human remains in them and, on the walls, frescoes or carvings of a *queer animal of prehistoric sort, which has a cat's head and the curved form of a man with a bent back and long thin arms*. Zoology and geology know of no such prehistoric monster; but it was also found on pieces of very ancient pottery dug up on the shores of South Perú by U.S. Paymaster Thomson—who, in Easter Island, directed the opening of the cunningly sealed and hidden catacomb. Nothing could more graphically testify to the great age of this unknown race.

The menacing stare of these cold-lipped, stern-eyed colossi of the cliff-platforms must have played some mysterious, if not sinister part in whatever queer or occult rites, or ancestor-cults were celebrated in this island graveyard. *Else, why do they gaze inland and not out to sea?*

A woman's cyclopean statue has also been found, lying face downwards in a crater of the island. It was the last to be set up. But mostly they are of men with oval faces, great eyes and a short upper lip.

Drawings in the rocks suggest that the race sailed three-masted ships, and knew of four-footed birds. In some cases, they have ears with enormous lobes, singularly reminding us of the *Orejones*, or long-eared warriors of the old Incas of Perú. How they moved these mammoth blocks of stone, many tons in weight, often twenty feet thick at the base and fifteen feet high, is still a problem unsolved—except for the suggestion of the ancient tramway. The foundation stones of the colossal platform are of such hard basalt that even modern tools, with specially tough alloys, would be blunted.

One day, while the slaves and slave-artisans, under the eyes of their taskmasters, were putting the finishing touches to a number of heads of great figures lying in a vast quarry-crater of a workshop to which the avenues lead from the cliff-platforms—there are 500 colossal human heads in carved stone lying on the sides of this great amphitheatre, and more or less covered in grass or bush, today—a stern-faced supervisor, cracking a hide-whip, had just stepped forward to flog the back of a craftsman who had been detected scamping the work on the back of one of the images, where he believed it would not be noticed. While the crack of the heavy thong still resounded in the hot air of a windless day, a black cloud seemed suddenly to cover the face of the sun. It spread very rapidly to the horizon. The ground heaved violently in tremendous tremors that lasted many minutes. The whole island shook to the rim and tops of the crater. Mountainous waves of an ocean infuriated and maddened by some tremendous force swept right over the tall cliffs and crashed on to the feet of the colossal images. The light of day went out. The night of total eclipse had come. A heavy black pall covered the vault of the heavens. Strange rains of blood-red water and white ash, mingled, cascaded on to the causeways and covered the dome of the great temple of ancestors and ghosts. The terrified slaves in the quarry-workshop threw down their tools, heeding not the whips and curses of the taskmasters, who, themselves, white to the very lips, began to stammer and to follow the headlong rush of the panic-stricken workers to the safety of caves in a neighbouring hillside.

At the end of the tramway, a gang of many hundreds of slaves had just hauled a cyclopean statue on to the platform where it was to be set up, when the island shook and the vast tidal waves swept right over the mighty balustrades. In the unearthly darkness, as of a last day of earth, the terrified slaves cast off the hauling-ropes and the great trunk and head of the statue crashed on to its face, with the head looking out to the maddened ocean, raging as under the force of a hundred typhoons. They fled, seeking safety and harbour, as they raced, many being crushed under the weight of mighty masonry and great carved stones, toppled over by the violent quakes. The quarry was abandoned, the keeper of the sacred mausoleum-temple fled with the rest, the architects, the officials, and the engineers. May be, mephitic gases overtook them on their way to shelter in the secret caves of the cliffs on that dreadful island night; but those who managed to survive the long days and nights of cosmic cataclysm ran out on the cliffs to wait for the relieving food-ships that were never to come. (The master-race's policy did not permit the slaves to grow food in the island.) For the mighty Pacific island-continent of Rutas-Mu-Gondwanaland had toppled from her foundations deep, deep down into the hell of the abyss, and the boundless, heaving waters of the ocean now covered a whole vast land where life, legend whispers, had been one long dream of paradisiacal bliss, peace and prosperity, until one of its races, the men of blood and brawls, had turned it into almost continual fighting internally, with wars of ancient conquest abroad.

But who were these strange people who left the amazing number of 550 colossal images in Easter Island, of whom not even the unquiet sea whispers tales of old, unhappy things and battles long ago?

May be, the answer is to be found in the book of *Genesis*:

> "There were giants on the earth in those days; mighty men who were of old, men of renown . . . and God said the earth is filled with violence through them, and behold I will destroy them with the earth."

The old Goths, in one of the Eddas, say the giants were drowned in the deluge. (I shall, later, in this chapter and others, refer to the undoubted existence of giants in prehistoric South America.) Eupolemus, who wrote a long lost history on the Jews of Assyria, says the ancient Babylon was founded by giants saved from the Deluge. It was they, he says, who built the celebrated Tower of Babel which thunderbolts overthrew, and they were dispersed all over the earth. (This is a Near East version of the famous storming of the gods in Heaven by the Greek Titans.) Euhemerism, which may be right or wrong, may suggest the story took its rise in the invasion of all Western Europe by the old Atlantean militarists; for the story of Eupolemus is that these giants were plunged into the central abyss at the time of the great catastrophe. But it is curious that Pedro de los Rios, Dominican missioner, in Nueva España, in 1566, sets down an Aztec tradition that, *before* the Great Catastrophe and deluge, the land of Anahuac—old Mexico—was inhabited by giants, one of whom escaped to build a great pyramid at Cholula, made of bricks, passed from hand to hand by a file of men. The gods in wrath at these Titans scaling the skies by the staircase circling their tower, sent down fire on it. As this tower-pyramid of Babel was subsequently dedicated to Quetzalcoatl, if my theory be correct, the giants must have invaded the land of Anahuac, after that gentle man in black had returned to his eastern homeland—Atlantis, motherland, or imperial Atlantean Hy-Brazil—from which he said he would one day return.

Fragments of other astounding memories of the Great Cataclysm are crystallised in *Genesis*, such as the Deluge story derived from lost and very ancient books, older by far than the Babylonian legend of Gilgamesh on brick cuneiform tablets. It is found, too, in the old Aztec codices of Mexico. The Indians of the high savanas of Colombia, South America, say the Great Catastrophe befell the Earth before the *Moon shone in the skies*! And this part about the Moon is no childish myth of a primitive race. The old Arcadians, a Pelasgian race of the Mediterranean, also said a great Deluge overwhelmed their ancient land—the Deluge of Ogyges—before the Moon accompanied the Earth! Their ancestors were thus called, by the Greeks, *pre-Selenites*, which means what it says and is not a corruption of pre-Syllani, or pre-Hellenes, as a too ingenious nineteenth-century commentator made out. It is curious that the ancient Mexicans spoke of the planet Venus as lighting the eastern skies, *and not the Moon*. May it be that these stories, so widely sundered by the oceans, commemorate the strange fact that 12,000 years ago our present Moon wandered into the Earth's gravitational field and was made captive?

Beyond much doubt, the Moon played an immense, but *not* the only part in causing the Great Catastrophe.

But what is even more remarkable is the insistence in the *Genesis* story of the Bible, the Babylonian legend on the Gilgamesh tablets from Nineveh, and in the traditions of very ancient date, current in Perú of the Incas, that, after the Great Catastrophe, something was seen in earth's skies that was not there before: the *Rainbow*!

If rainbows were not seen in the ancient Earth it is obvious that rain must have fallen in the night hours, when the sun's light was not there to give the prismatic effect of rays in water-drops. If you had a planet as near the Sun as Venus is, you would find, as in Venus, that rain, in torrents, falls only in the night. When our Earth was hit by a wandering comet, or other cosmic body, 12,000 years ago—and one admits the heavy mathematical odds against such a collision—there was, probably, a terrific force exerted that tore it from its old orbit, far nearer the Sun, and drove it outwards into space! If that happened, the year would be lengthened from, say, 250 days to the present 365 days, and this may account for the incredible years of the patriarch Methuselah—which make a modern compiler of mortality tables smile in his beard—or those of the Kings of ancient Sumeria, which so puzzled the late Sir E. Wallis Budge, of the British Museum. (He was an Egyptologist and Assyriologist.)

Fantastic as the theory sounds, in the ears of the more crusted sort of astronomers, it is very curious that both the ancient Mexicans and the old Roman writer, Varro, between whom there can have been no contact, say that, at the time of the Great Catastrophe, an amazing sign appeared in the skies:

> ". . . the star of Venus . . . changed in colour, size, form, shape and course, and never before or after was the like seen."

What had really changed was not the shape or course of Venus, but the orbit of the Earth reeling backwards into space, as the axis at the poles tilted and lurched with extreme violence. It would have driven survivors mad, and might have been responsible for the horrible cults of human sacrifice, and propitiation of harvest-gods, found in ancient races after the Catastrophe, and reaching a degree of aberration that approached paranoia among the Aztecs and Mayans of Central America.

The ancient Chinese annalists record startlingly similar phenomena of this same cataclysm. A learned late seventeenth-century Jesuit missioner, Padre Martin Martinius, in a very rare volume of his *History of China*—in black letter Latin and not in the great library of the British Museum—says that the ancient Chinese say that, before the Great Catastrophe to the Earth, there was a golden age:

> "Four seasons succeeded each other regularly and without confusion. There were no impetuous winds, nor excessive rains. The sun and moon, without ever being clouded, furnished a light purer and brighter than now. The five planets kept on their course without any inequality. Nothing harmed man, nor did he harm anything. There was universal concord and amity reigned all over the earth. . . . Then the second heaven began . . ."

The word "heaven" seems to be the equivalent to the "sun" of the Mexican codices . . .

> " . . . The pillars of heaven were broken. The earth shook to its foundations. *The sky sank lower towards the north. The sun, moon and stars changed their motions.* The earth fell to pieces, and the waters in its bosom uprushed with violence and overflowed. . . . The system of the universe was totally disordered. Man had rebelled against the high gods. The sun went into eclipse, the *planets altered their courses,* and the grand harmony of nature was disturbed." (*Hist. Sin.* lib. I., p. 12.)

Another Chinese myth says that at the Great Catastrophe the whole Earth tilted violently and sank into the sea off the China coast. It adds, what sounds like eye-witnesses' testimony, or ancestral memories, that the waters of the Great Deluge streamed off *south-eastwards*!

The Jews, too, a race of world-wide wandering, have a curious, and in this cosmic connection, significant myth that the Great Deluge was "caused by the Lord God changing the places of two stars in a constellation." (*Vide* Josippa Micha ben Gorion: *Sagen Juden.*)

North American Indians have rites, celebrated today, which show that their ancestors, ages ago, knew of a time when rainbows in Earth's skies were *not.* The Acoma-Pueblo Indians of New Mexico yearly perform a play in which they climb a ladder to reach the rainbow. It is a play created round a Deluge myth. Again, in the highlands of modern Colombia, South America, there existed in the time of the Spanish conquistadores a native myth of the Chibcha race—I shall refer to this again, later in this book—according to which Bochicha, the pioneer from Atlantean Brazil, as I call him *infra,* suddenly appeared on the plateau of Cundina-Marca when there was no moon in the sky, and mountain walls hemmed in the tableland. He was tall, white-skinned and bearded, and bore a golden sceptre. After his time, Chia—the Moon-goddess—rode in skies of earth. A variant of the same myth says that another evil god caused a Flood, and that Bochicha, appearing in a rainbow, ended the Flood.

The ancient Mexicans had a feast, celebrated as late as the day of Cortes, the Spanish conquistador, commemorating changes in the condition of several of the constellations—including the planet Venus—after the time of the Great Catastrophe. . . .

> "*She* (*Venus*) *caused death to the world,* and is one of the six constellations that fell from the sky at the time of the Great Deluge."

These "six stars" that fell from the sky may have been disrupted parts of some large asteroid or giant aerolite (meteor). They had, perhaps, been broken up by the pull of the earth's gravitational field. On the other hand, Mr. H. S. Bellamy, an authority on Myths of the Moon in the ancient world, supposes that the book of the Revelation of St. John the Divine is really a history of the Great Cataclysm, and enshrines, in mystic and cryptic language, some ancient story of an earlier, pre-Lunar satellite of the earth approaching close to the earth and being destroyed by it. He cites the theory of an Austrian engineer, Hans Hörbiger, of Vienna, about the ultimate destruction of satellites by the parent planet. When the satellite drew near the earth, it shone with a brilliant light reflected from the sun, falling on a thick coating of ice—the glaciosphere. This split and fell on the earth, exposing a layer of red earth, which, in turn, fell on the earth in a rain like blood. Then the metallic core stood bared. It split into tremendous slabs, crashed on the earth, in the Pacific and Atlantic and submerged two great island-continents. The slabs shivered the earth's crust and penetrated to the magma under it. This appalling impact of these cosmic "bolts" knocked out the supports from the continents, and so Atlantis and the Pacific continent of Mu-Rutas-Gondwanaland were engulfed in a terrible abyss into and over which the maddened ocean poured its water, mountains high!

In the ancient world, the priests and prophets had a saying: "As above so below. What has been shall be again." Censorinus, the Roman chronologist of the third century A.D., said that, at the end of every great year of six Babylonian *sars* (a period of 21,600 years), our planet undergoes a complete revolution. Polar and equatorial regions gradually change place, the tropical vegetation and swarming animal life moving towards the forbidding wastes of the icy poles. . . .

> "Catastrophes attend the change, with great earthquakes and cosmical throes."

The old Greeks had a saying that every world was a transcript of a former world, and the same persons reappeared and played once more the same part they had played in each successive cycle.

The ancient Greeks also said that, at the end of every 12,000 years, the beds of the oceans are displaced, and a semi-universal deluge takes place. Their priests of the sanctuaries kept in strict secrecy any notions of how long such a catastrophe might last, and all about its details. They called the period the Great or Heliacal Year, the "winter" of which was called the Cataclysm or Great Deluge, and the summer, the *Ecpyrosis*. So, by turns, the world was to be drowned and burnt!

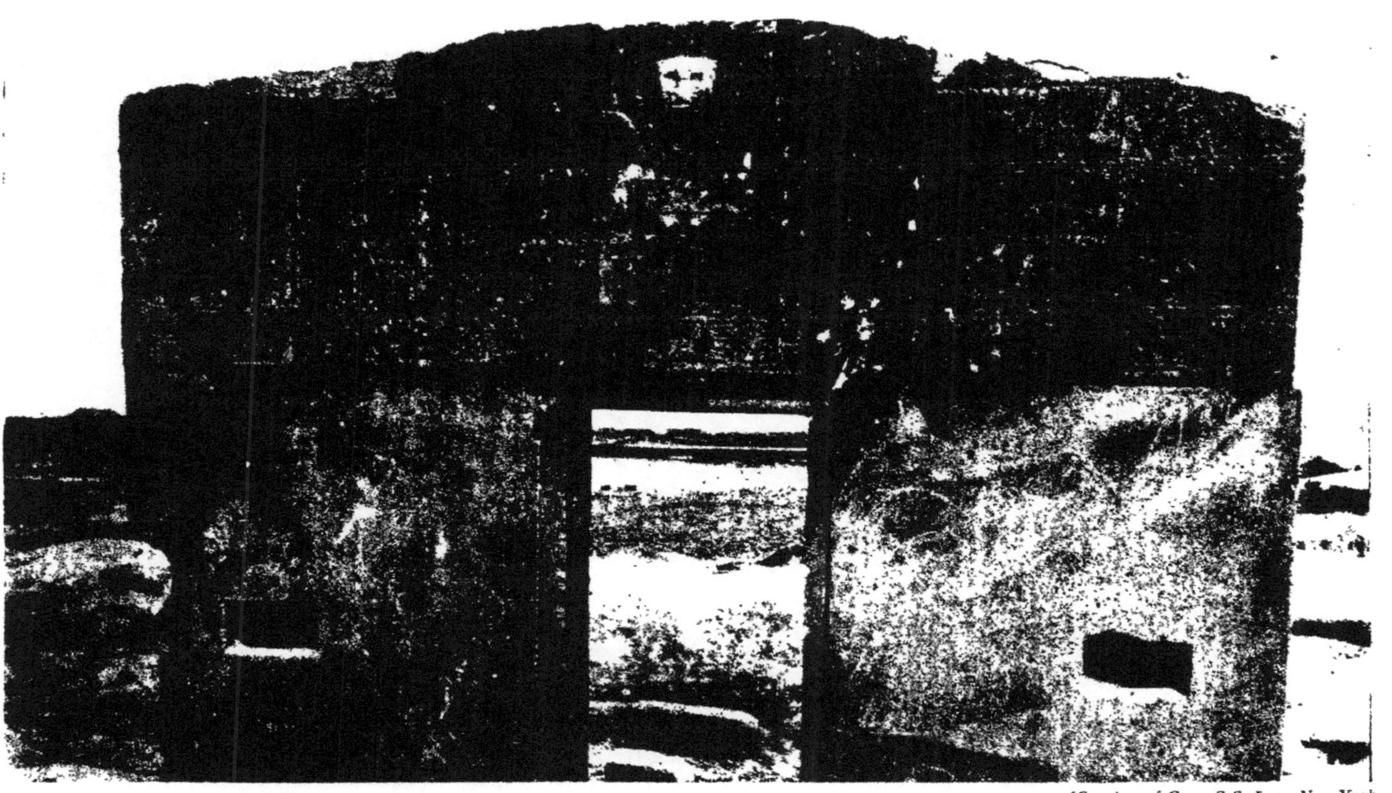

[Courtesy of Grace S.S. Line, New York

Gateway of the Kalasasaya (Sun-Temple) at Tiahuanacu. Central figure of the Sun (top) is served by winged messengers.

Reputed tomb of last Aztec Prince-Emperor Guatemotzin, where great treasure is said to have been cached, on frontier of Chiappas Province, Mexico.

These traditions seem to have come from the sky-towers of the ancient Babylonians who said that ancient Babylon was founded by giants who escaped the Deluge. These giants were great astrologers who had received from their ancestors secret learning, which they imparted to the high priests of Babylon, along with all records that dated before the Great Catastrophe. And before dismissing these stories of giants as moonshine and fairy stories of the childhood of our race, be it remembered that ancient Perú was invaded by giants who built cities and sank wells, that their skeletons have been found in a cave near the railroad at Manta, Ecuador, and that skeletons with headbones of monstrous size and a lower jaw twice the size of civilised man were found in conical mounds on bluffs in Western Missouri (by Judge West), as long ago as 1875. Indeed, ancient Mexican records, reversing the story, in *Genesis*, of the Tower of Babel, says that Giants escaped the cataclysm and built a Tower of Babel, whose site was to be seen in Cortes' day. (One of the South Sea islands has also a cyclopean tower built by "giants who were curious to peep into the moon".)

These ancient predictions, by the way, are no more fantastic than the statement made by Dr. H. Norris Russell, director of Princeton University Observatory, in February 1939. He says our earth will grow hotter as the sun grows colder. Earth is warmed up by one degree each 100,000,000 years. Eventually, he says, the climate and temperature at the equator of the earth will be like a blast from an open furnace door, and a mass migration of humanity will start out for the poles.

Since it is now round 12,000 years after the last Great Catastrophe, what may be the fate of the earth at the end of this cycle? Are we on the eve of another Giant Disaster?

No longer ago then October 25–30, 1937, our Earth was in grave danger of collison with a small planet astray in the solar system. In that month, we were very near a Great Disaster:

> "There was great excitement . . . the planet was rushing towards the Earth almost in a straight line. Had it hit us, the international system might have been altered. . . . The planet missed us by only five and a half hours. It is the narrowest escape the world has ever had in the period of astronomical observations." (*Dr. H. E. Wood, astronomer at Cape Town Observatory.*)

Meantime, it may be recalled that the late Sir Arthur Conan Doyle, who died in 1930, sent round to friends in England (in 1928) a remarkable letter based on certain mystic revelations received by his wife, Lady Conan Doyle, at a family séance, in 1923. These automatic writings, it is said, foretold the rise of the Nazis in Germany, the coming of raging fires by night over Britain, and an attempted invasion, but they were but the prelude to tremendous happenings no man may control. Conan Doyle said that the predictions "from beyond" foretold that "soon" a great disaster would come on the earth, following on Armageddon. It would happen very suddenly, without warning, and the general upheaval of civilised life would be of appalling character. The catastrophes—a series—would last three years, during which a number of countries (five) in the Mediterranean basin would be swallowed up in the convulsions of the earth and sea. The bed of the Atlantic would rise and tremendous tidal waves would surge on to the American, the British, and the Irish low-lying shores, causing great disasters to people living near the shores. Apparently, the disaster would be brought about by some cosmic body in collision with our polar axis and causing it to tilt violently.

Of course, it has been said you may refuse to argue with a prophet but may disbelieve him.

"But when is the next cataclysm due?" the shuddering or scoffing reader may ask me. I can but return the famous answer of the late Premier Asquith, on another occasion, my own prophetic soul exercising its vaticinatory powers on occasions of which my conscious mind is unaware.

The answer, indeed, is one that would be more congenial to "Woe, Woe", Signor Ansaldo, the mouthpiece of Mussolini's radio, than to any of us. It has even been predicted, in other mystic quarters, that the final Armageddon will be followed by the emergence from the bed of the South Atlantic of the drowned continent and cities of Atlantis.

Be that as it may, never has a more graphic forecast of the end of the solar system—not merely of the earth—been made than by the ancient Brahmans of the temples of Hindostan, thousands of years ago:

> "Strange noises are heard proceeding from every point. They are the forerunners of the Night of Brahma. Dusk rises at the horizon and the Sun passes away behind the thirtieth degree of the Zodiacal sign of Macara and will no more reach the sign of Pisces (Minas). The gurus (watcher-disciples) of the goparams (pagodas) appointed to watch the ras-chakr (Zodiac) may now break their circles and instruments, for they will need them no more. . . . Gradually the light shall diminish and pale. Heat shall get less, and uninhabitable spots multiply in the earth. Air become more rarefied. Springs of water dry up. Great rivers see their waves exhaust themselves, the ocean now shows her sandy bottom and plants die. Daily, men and animals decrease in size. Life and motion lose their force. Planets hardly can

gravitate round the Sun in space. One by one they go out as a lamp which the hand of the *chokra* (servant) has not replenished with oil. *Sourya* (the Sun) flickers and goes out. Matter falls into dissolution. Brahma, the demiourgos, merges back into Dyaus (Deus, the unrevealed God), and, his task accomplished, falls asleep. Another day of 4,320,000,000 human years is past. Night sets in and lasts till the next dawn. All germs (souls) are re-absorbed into the Infinite which sleeps till dawn."

My reader has thus a sketch of the final act in one of our old Earth's most appalling dramas, which formed my mental background when I stepped off the liner in Rio de Janeiro's wonderful harbour. I started in that city of colour, warmth and beauty to try to recreate the earlier scenes of this ancient civilisation of Atlantean South America. For, in this, reconstruction of a prehistoric world, it is useless to bury one's self in European, or even American libraries and university schools or museums, wherein South American life and proto-history are subjects as remote as if they were happening in the planet Mars, away beyond the ken of radio and airships. The dogmatic arrogance of so many modern archaeologists is due for a severe shaking; for they, like some of our modern medical scientists, are apt to forget what real scientists and inventors well know: that the bounds of knowledge are often advanced not by professionals or savants in learned societies and associations, but by the less dogmatic and generally undistinguished amateur and lay and modest or humble investigator. *Nous verrons ce que nous verrons*—perhaps, before this chequered twentieth century ends, in the revolution of world history which will come from discoveries in the now buried jungle cities of dangerous South America.

CHAPTER II

DEAD CITIES OF ANCIENT BRAZIL

"And the land shall become burning pitch. They shall call the nobles thereof, but none shall be there, and all her princes shall be nothing. From generation to generation it shall be waste. None shall pass through for ever and ever. A possession for the bittern and pools of water . . . swept up in the besom of destruction . . . and thorns shall come up in her palaces . . . a habitation of wild dogs and bats. . . . He hath utterly destroyed them."

In modern Brazil, I did not find any great enthusiasm about the mysteries of the remote past in a great land which some American observers believe is destined to outshadow Western Europe, at the close of the Second World War.

"There are no ancient ruins in the *serras* and *sertão* of Brazil, *senhor*. No vestiges of ancient culture, no ruins such as you have in Mayan Yucatan, or the jungles of Honduras and Guatemala. All that was here, when Dom Pedro Cabral sighted what is now Rio de Janeiro, in the year A.D. 1500, all that we have here now are primitive Indians at the fishing and hunting stage. They live in huts and clearings in the jungle and *matas*, on the banks of the rivers, in Amazonas and the Matto Grosso. In our *sertão* are scrub, heath, wilderness, but no monuments like those of Perú."

That was the reply to me, when I asked about the ancient Brazilian ruins, of a professor of economics and geography who holds a chair in a famous Brazilian university.

I met another charming gentleman whose father had been one of the *fazendeiros*, or patriarchal landowners of the older Southern type of the colourful days of the Brazilian Empire. He sat in a cane chair, on his verandah, bathed in the light of the bright moon, while fireflies flashed across the velvety darkness cast by tall trees under a brilliantly starry sky. Waving his beringed, white hands towards the gently plashing waters of Rio Bay, he deprecated the foolish waste of energy by restless, inquisitive people who will *not* take the gifts of the gods as they find them. He smiled at the freaks of *estrangeiros*—Englishmen or Americans—who must needs push their noses into the *mata* and *sertão* of interior Brazil, with their sabre-toothed insects, horrible ticks, malignant fevers, clicking mandibles of hideous tarantulas, pathogenic-germed probes of *os barbeiros* (the barber-surgeon beetles of wooden shacks in the Goyaz), the fierce oncas, the snakes, and the unpacifiable Indians—sometimes anthropophagous, often head-hunters—who resent and visit with sudden death, if the intruder persist, any penetration of their jungles.

I found the same lack of interest in the south. It has gone so far that men who concern themselves in recreating the ancient world of Brazil are, with slight contempt, styled *Indianistas*. True, they are often of Indian descent. There was, for example, Senhor Bernardo da Silva Ramos, native of Amazonas, with traits of Tapuyo origin. He sold a collection of rare and ancient coins in order to raise funds to embark on travels all over North and South America, and to Africa, Europe and the Middle East. He became keenly interested in the ancient mysteries of Brazil—in *prehistoria*, which has a literature of its own in Brazil. Comparing the ancient inscriptions in the lands of the "Old World" with those he found in Central and South America, Senhor Ramos filled large folio volumes. The central authorities of Brazil have examined those works, and expressed polite appreciation and interest. In 1928, they voted public money to have one volume published. Both he and Senhor Frot have found in the Matto Grosso many inscriptions in the Phoenician, Egyptian, and even Sumerian scripts and hieroglyphics. Senhor Ramos points out that his Indian forefathers had many traditions of ancient date about a very ancient culture and advanced civilisation, flourishing thousands of years ago, to the north and west of the Central Highlands of Brazil.*

Now, in the archives of the great public library of Rio, which embodies the large and valuable libraries of the old Kings of Portugal and the emperors of Brazil, and also the records of generations of Lusitanian viceroys, I have found a strange MS. written in Portuguese, and scarcely 200 years old, but bitten by the *copim* and badly mutilated in some most fascinating and enthralling passages, which holds a secret that, in some day not far distant, will revolutionise the fixed and settled theories of college professors of ethnology and archaeology, and the field museum workers of New York, Chicago, London, Paris, Rome and Berlin. Especially will it make hay of their cherished theory that writing was unknown in pre-Columbian South America. For, if the story of strange adventures of hardy and uncultured men which it tells, be true—and I think it is—what we call the old world of Asia and Europe is a mere parvenu by the side of this New World of South America. Our professors and archaeological historians are one day going to be forced to call in this New World to redress the balance of the Old!

I stress the lack of culture of these men who were the well-known *bandeiristas*—land-pirates of sixteenth- and seventeenth-century Brazil—because they could and would not have invented the story they tell. Their one object was the hunt for gold and virgin mines of silver. Under the banner of a leader called the *bandeirante*, they started out from the province of São Paulo, in Southern Brazil, abandoning the trading-channels of the rivers and the most outlying settlements, and heading straight into the forbidden territories of the bad Indians (*Indiós malos*) of the *mata* (dense forest) and *chapada* (wilderness). The leader of these *bandeiristas* was usually a man of that older Portuguese stock which had made Lisboa (Lisbon) and the Motherland in Lusitanian Portugal a fine sea-power, from Goa, in India, and the Moluccas and Spice Islands, off the waters of far Cathay, across the unknown seas to Rio de Janeiro and Bahia.

Far north and west wandered these hardy *bandeiristas*, pushing the frontier ever forward into the unknown. They reached places in the Brazilian *sertão*, 400 years ago, that white men, even today, have not penetrated and returned alive to tell the tale. Age

* In August 1944, by courtesy of the British Foreign Office, I received a letter from H.M. Ambassador in Rio de Janeiro informing me that Senhor Bernardo da Silva Ramos had died. It is to be hoped that learned circles in Rio or São Paulo will see to it that his works and records of strange researches into the pre-history of Brazil and South America do not perish utterly, either by the teeth of the *copim* insects, or neglect.—AUTHOR.

after age went by, and the *bandeiristas* made themselves a power dreaded by the colonial governors in Rio, São Paulo and old Bahia.

Came the year 1591, and a galleon from Lisboa crossed the bar of the roadstead of Bahia, then called sonorously and most religiously: *Bahia de São Salvador de todos os Santos* (Bahia of our Holy Saviour of all the Saints). The galleon from Portugal brought the new governor and captain-general, Dom Francisco de Souza, who carried with him, in his trunks, a title, conferred by the court in Lisboa (Lisbon), of *Marques das Minas* (Marquis of the Mines). It was to be conferred if certain very rich mines of silver were discovered to the Portuguese colonial authorities, as promised by one Roberio Dias, one of the oldest and richest inhabitants of Bahia. A bauble for a billion!

Rumour ran in Bahia that this Roberio Dias had silver plate for his own tables, and that the vessels on the altar of his private family chapel were of the same metal of the very finest and purest quality. Folk in the province of Bahia said that this silver came from secret mines located in lands, held in the interior, or *sertão* of Brazil, by this same Roberio Dias, a grim and determined man. Now, Roberio was rich; but not satisfied. He was a commoner. He wanted the titles of nobility and an emblazoned shield with quarterings that he could affix to the stone walls of his *mansão* in the countryside of Bahia. Some time before, folk whispered, Roberio Dias had actually taken ship and crossed the Atlantic to Cadiz, in old Spain. There, he had journeyed to the Escurial palace of the King of Spain, in old Madrid, who then governed both Spain and Portugal.

Said Dias to our Lord, el Rey Don Felipé: "I offer your Majesty all the riches of splendid, but secret mines. There is more silver in those mines I know of than you have of iron in the mines of Bilbao in your Spanish province of Biscaya. All I want, in return, from your Majesty, is the title of Marquis of the Mines."

But, now here, newly arrived from Lisboa, in old Portugal, was this governor and court popinjay, Dom Francisco. *He*, this governor, was to have this title of Marquis of the Mines, while the promised one, Roberio Dias, the finder of those mines, was merely to have the place and title and honour of *administrador das minas* (the superintendent of mines)—his own mines!—with other promises, which meant precious little to a man who had been tricked with a promise of ennoblement.

Dias was in the city of Bahia when the governor stepped ashore on the quays. The governor sent for him. Dom Francisco was haughty and arrogant in manner, and Dias, in a rage he had difficulty in dissembling, agreed to show the governor where these mines lay. However, what he did was to lead de Souza, a true exemplar of the Lusitanian viceroys, on a wild-goose chase into the interior. The mines always seemed to elude the hunters. At last, the suspicious de Souza put spies on the trail of the guileful Roberio Dias, who had led the hunters on every track except the one that led to the mines. The governor's spies were spied on by Dias's men, and still the mines lay lost! Then governor Dom Francisco de Souza showed his teeth. He clapped Roberio Dias into a foul dungeon in the bowels of the old castello and fort on the bay of Bahia. He kept him there, two years, rotting among all the bugs and fleas and toads and lizards, and the worse, dripping damp; but Roberio Dias was of the *bandeirista* type. He might be broken; bent, he would not be. He refused to say where were the rich silver mines. The governor complained home to old Spain, and the King, our Lord, Don Felipé, sent an order for the punishment by death of the contumacious and evasive commoner, Roberio Dias. The galleon duly arrived in the harbour of Bahia; but on the very day that the seneschal of the castello came to unbar the massive iron-bolt-studded door of the dungeon, and read out the royal cedula to Roberio Dias, he found him lying dead on the stone floor. A grim smile clenched the dead man's strong, white teeth. He had left the secret to his heirs, who would not speak, under pain of a dying father's powerful curse.

These mines became known as the "Lost Silver Mines of the Moribeca".

In the next 150 years, many hardy and unscrupulous Portuguese adventurers set out on dangerous trails with the avowed purpose of locating these lost mines of the Moribeca. These *bandeiristas* wandered through dense forests, camped in clearings on the banks of unknown rivers, with fierce Indians lurking in the shades to send forth showers of poisoned arrows. They defied every danger of man, fever and insects, the jungle devils, and the famine and demon ticks of the *catinga*; but the mystery of the lost mines remained unsolved.

Now, came the year 1743, and a native of Minas Geraes—whose name has perished—started with other *bandeiristas* (five of them Portuguese), two *samboes* (negro slaves), and 300 Indians on the trail of these lost mines of the Moribeca. What cared they if a buffoon and *jogral* in Rio, by name of P. Silverio da Paraopeba, had gibed at them, in a little poem about the adventures of crazy *bandeirantes* and *bandeiristas*, "bitten by gold bugs"? Anyhow, *they* never read poems, even if they could read at all. So, let him and his japing fellow-scribblers take a Brazilian *cabaça* of yerba-maté, and go to Hades!

This mid-eighteenth century expedition was well armed, and intended to live on the country. No pack animals, or even the toughest and most leathery-stomached of mules could be taken into the Brazilian *sertão*. It was, as it is today, land of snakes and cougars and of the snarling, prowling *el tigre*, with water for fever-stricken men only to be found in the depths of the sandstone gorges through which turbulent rivers, cluttered with fallen boulders, flowed to dash and foam over *catadupas*, or cataracts.

This expedition was away for ten long years, enduring incredible hardships and braving great perils. Their very memory had been forgotten by the most caustic-tongued of satirical scribblers in Rio and Bahia, when, one day, in the year 1753, an emaciated remnant of the band staggered in from the unknown and halted at a *fazenda* in some little and obscure *povoação* in the province of Bahia. They were almost dead with hunger, fatigue and misery. Reduced to rags and bones! There, in the cool of the evening of a hot day, one of these *bandeiristas*, sitting under the eaves of the verandah, wrote an astonishing story of their travels and adventures. The implications of his story were too amazing to have been realised or perceived by so unlettered a man, though he had a picturesque style of writing. Nor may one wonder at that; for only in very recent years have they become known to historians or scholars, few or none of whom are native Brazilians, or even North Americans.

When this soldier of fortune and man of action took up the quill pen in his stiffened fingers in the backwoods of old Bahia, he never dreamt that he was drawing aside a veil from a *Lost World*, drowned in the waters of the ocean, split, rocked and exploded by titanic earthquakes and tellurian and submarine convulsions, many thousands of years before the ancient Egyptians were building their very early and most ancient step pyramids, at Sakkarah, on the Nile, more than 6,800 miles over the South Atlantic Ocean, eastwards.

This manuscript of an old *bandeirista* eventually reached the Portuguese viceroy in Rio de Janeiro. He clearly thought it held the secret of great riches, and some long-lost mines; for someone in the entourage hid it in the official archives and steadfastly denied that it had ever existed, or had been received. They hoped to make a great and exclusive discovery, aided by this *derrotero*, as the old Spanish treasure hunters called such documents in Quito (Ecuador) and other parts of the old Spanish South American Empire. The manuscript became lost to sight and memory, and all trace of it vanished, from the year 1760 until 1841, when a Brazilian historian and archivist, Senhor Lagos, found it hidden in the archives of the old royal public library in Rio de Janeiro, where I, myself, saw it in 1938–9.

It is unfortunate that the insect called the *copim* has attacked the old parchment, so that many valuable leaves, significant words and parts of words are missing; but enough is left to indicate the startling nature of the discoveries and the fascinating and rather eerie adventures of these *bandeiristas* of 1743–1753.

In the autumn of 1939 I obtained a transcript of the document, thanks to the courtesy of Mr. W. G. Burdett, American Consul-

General in Rio. Thereafter, I spent many weeks translating from the Portuguese and studying this amazing document, and also others, not known to American archivists and historians, but found in official archives in the provinces of São Paulo or Rio, and concerned with these stories of abandoned cities of unknown date and history.

Herewith, for the first time in the English language, I set down this remarkable story of men who, unknown to themselves, were peering into a dead world of the most ancient civilisation we know.

> "Relação historica de huma occulta, e grande povoaçoe antiguissima sem moradores, que se descubrio no anno de 1753.
>
> (Historical Relation of a hidden and great city of ancient date, without inhabitants, that was discovered in the year 1753).

Em a America (in America)..............................
nos interiores (we inland).................................
contiguous aos (next to the) ....
Mestre de Can (Master of Can)..........................
and his band (*commitiva*), having for ten years journeyed in the wilds (*sertões*) to see if we could locate the famous silver mines of the Great Moribeca (who, by the wickedness [*culpa*] of a Governor, was not granted letters patent, because the Governor wanted to take the silver mines for himself and the glory thereof, and he, the Moribeca, was kept prisoner in Bahia, till he died, which was done to worm out of him the location of the silver mines. This account came to Rio de Janeiro, in the beginning of the year 1754 . . ."

(The blanks in the introduction and the text, following, are, as I stated, caused by the gnawing of the *copim* insect. In both West Indies and South America, archives and old newspapers are annihilated by insects.)

"After long and wearisome wanderings, incited by the insatiable lust for gold, and almost lost in the many years we wandered, in these wilds of Brazil, we discovered a cordillera of mountains, so high that they drew near the ethereal region (*chegavão a região etherea*), and served as a throne of the winds, under the stars; their lustre, from afar, excited our wonder and admiration, principally when the sun shining on them turned to fires the crystals of which the rocks were composed. The view was so beautiful that none could take their eyes from the reflections. It began to rain before we came near enough to take note of these crystalline marvels, and we saw above..The spectacle was bare and sterile rocks, the waters precipitated themselves from the heights, foaming white, like snow, struck and turned to fire by the rays of the sun, like thunderbolts. Delighted by the pleasing vistas of that........blended........ shone and glistered........of the waters and the tranquillity ......

of the day or weather (*do tempo*), we determined to investigate these prodigious marvels of nature, spread out before us, at the foot of the mountains, without hindrance of forests or rivers that would make it difficult for us to cross them. But when we walked round the foot of the cordillera we found no open way or pass into the recesses of these Alps and Pyrenees of Brazil. So there resulted for us, from this disappointment, an inexplicable sadness.

"We grew weary and intended to retrace our steps, the next day, when it came to pass that one of our negroes, gathering dried sticks, saw a white deer (*hum veado branco*), and, by that accident, as it fled away, he discovered a road between two sierras, that appeared to have been made by man and not the work of Nature. We were made joyful by this discovery and we started to ascend the road, but found a great boulder that had fallen and broken all to pieces at a spot where, we judged, a paved way (*calçada*) had been violently upheaved in some far-off day. We spent a good three hours in the ascent of that ancient road, being fascinated by the crystals, at which we marvelled, as they blazed and scintillated in many flashing colours from the rocks. On the summit of the pass through the mountain, we came to a halt.

"Thence, spread out before our eyes, we saw in the open plain (*campo raso*) greater spectacles (*demonstrações*) for our vision of admiration and wonder. At the distance of about a league, as we judged, we saw a great city (*povoação grande*), and we estimated, by the extent and sight of it, that it must be some city of the court of Brazil; we at once descended the road towards the valley, but with great caution........would be, in like case, ordered to explore ....by quality and........if so well as they had noticed ....smokes (*fumines*[?]), that being one of the evident signs or vestiges of the place (*povoação*).

"Two days we waited, wondering whether to send out scouts, for the end we longed for, and all alone, we waited till daybreak, in great doubt and confused perplexity of mind, trying to guess if the city had any people in it. But it became clear to us there were no inhabitants. An Indian of our *bandeirantes* determined, after two days of hesitation, to risk his life in scouting by way of precaution; but he returned, amazing us by affirming he had met no one; nor could discover footsteps or traces of any person whatever. This so confounded us that we could not believe we saw dwellings or buildings, and so, all the scouts (*os exploradores*) in a body, followed in the steps of the Indian. . . ."

"They now saw for themselves that it was true the great city was uninhabited. We, all, therefore, now decided to enter the place, our arms ready for instant use, at daybreak. At our entry we met none to bar our way, and we encountered no other road except the one which led to the dead city. This, we entered under three arches (*arcos*) of great height, the middle arch being the greatest, and the two of the sides being but small; under the great and principal arch we made out letters, which we could not copy, owing to their great height above the ground.

"Behind, was a street as wide as the three arches, with, here and there, houses of very large size, whose façades of sculptured stone, already blackened with age; alone..........inscriptions, all open to the day (*todos abertas*)........decreases of........ observing, by the regularity and symmetry with which they were made, that they appeared to have one owner only, being, in reality, very numerous, so that [they stood] with their terraces open to the day, without one tile; for the houses had, some of them, burnt floors; others, large flagstones.

"We went, with fear and trembling, into some of the houses, and in none did we find vestiges of furniture, or moveable objects by which, or whose use, we might guess at the sort of people who had dwelt therein. The houses were all dark, in the interior, and hardly could the light of day penetrate, even at its dimmest, and, as the vaults gave back the echoes of our speech, the sound of our voices terrified us. We went on into the strange city and we came on a road (street: *rua*) of great length, and a well set-out plaza (*uma praça regular*), besides, in it, and in the middle of the plaza a column of black stone of extraordinary grandeur, on whose summit was a statue of a man (*homen ordinario*: not a god, or demi-god) with a hand on the left hip and right arm out-stretched, pointing with the index finger to the north pole; and each corner of the said plaza is an obelisk like those among the Romans, but now badly damaged, and cleft as by thunderbolts.

"On the right side of the plaza is a superb building, as it were the principal town-house of some great lord of the land; there is a great hall (*salão*) at the entrance, but still being awed and afraid, not all of us entered in the hou........being so many and the retre...... ed to form some........ed we encounter a........mass of extraordin........it was difficult for him to lift it........

"The bats were so numerous that they fluttered in swarms round the faces of our people, and made so much noise that it was astonishing. Above the principal portico of the street is a figure in half-relief, cut out of the same stone, and naked from the waist upward, crowned with laurel, representing a person of youthful years, without beard, with a girdle (*banda*) around him, and an under-garment (*um fraldelim*) open in front at the waist, underneath the shield (*escudo*) of this figure are certain characters, now badly defaced by time, but we made out the following:

"On the left side of the plaza is another totally ruined building, and the vestiges remaining well show that it was a temple, because of the still standing side of its magnificent façade, and certain naves of stone, standing entire. It covers much ground, and in the ruined halls are seen works of beauty, with other statues of portraits inlaid in the stone, with crosses of various shapes, curves (arches[?] *corvos*) and many other figures that would take too long to describe here.

"Beyond this building a great part of the city lies completely in ruins, and buried under great masses of earth, and frightful crevasses in the ground, and in all this expanse of utter desolation there is seen no grass, herb, tree, or plant produced by nature, but only mountainous heaps of stone, some raw (that is, unworked), others worked and carved, whereby we understood........they ....because again among......of......corpses that........ and part of this unhappy........and overthrown, perhaps, by some earthquake.

"Opposite this plaza, there runs very swiftly a most deep (*caudaloso*) and wide river, with spacious banks, that were very pleasing to the eye: it was eleven to twelve fathoms in width, without reckoning the windings, clear and bared at its banks of groves, as of trees and of the trunks that are often brought down in floods. We sounded its depths and found the deepest parts to be fifteen or sixteen fathoms. The country beyond consists wholly of very green and flourishing fields, and so blooming with a variety of flowers that it seemed as if Nature, more attentive to these parts, had laid herself out to create the most beautiful gardens of Flora: we gazed, too, in admiration and astonishment at certain lakes covered with wild rice plants from which we profited, and also at the innumerable flocks of geese that bred in these fertile plains (*campos*); but it would have been difficult to sound their depths with the hand, in the absence of a sounding-rod.

"Three days we journeyed down the river, and we stumbled on a cataract (*uma catadupa*) of such roaring noise and commotion of foaming waters, that we supposed the mouths of the much talked of Nile could not have made more trouble or booming, or offered more resistance to our further progress. Afterwards, the river spreads out so much from this cascade that it appears to be a great Ocean (*que parece o grande Oceano*). It is all full of peninsulas, covered with green grass, with groves of trees, here and there, that make...... ....pleas.............. Here, we find.................... for want of it, we...................................... the variety of game............many created beings without hunters to hunt and chase them.

"On the eastern side of this cataract, we found various subterranean hollows (*subcavões*) and frightful holes, and made trial of their depths with many ropes; but, after many attempts we were never able to plumb their depths. We found, besides, certain broken stones, and [lying] on the surface of the ground, thrown down, with bars of silver (*crevadas de prata*) that may have been extracted from the mines, abandoned at the time.

"Among these caverns (*furnas*) we saw some covered with a great flagstone, with the following figures cut into it, that suggest a great mystery. They are as follows:

"Over the portico of the temple, we saw, besides, the following forms:

"Distant a cannon-shot from the abandoned city is a building like a country house (*casa de campo*), with a frontage of 250 feet. It is approached by a great portico, from which a stairway built with stones of various colours is seen to be leading into a great chamber (*sala*), and from that there lead out fifteen small rooms, each with a door communicating with the said great chamber. Each room has its waterspout (or fountain: *bica de agua*).................... the which water meets......................in the exterior courtyard...............................colonnades in the sur..............................squared and fashioned by hand, overhung with the characters following:

"Thence, leaving that marvel, we went down to the banks of the river to see whether we could find gold, and without difficulty, we saw, on the surface of the soil, a fine trail promising great riches, as well of gold, as of silver: we marvelled that this place had been abandoned by those who had formerly inhabited it; for, with all our careful investigations and great diligence we had met no person, in this wilderness, who might tell us of this deplorable marvel of an abandoned city, whose ruins, statues and grandeur, attested its former populousness, wealth, and its flourishing in the centuries past; whereas, today, it is inhabited by swallows, bats, rats and foxes, that, fed on the innumerable swarms of hens and geese, have become bigger than a pointer dog. The rats have the tails so short that they leap like fleas and do not run or walk, as they do in other places.

"At this place, the band separated, and one company, joined by others, journeyed forward, and, after nine days' long marchings, saw, at a distance, on the bank of a great bay (*enseada*) into which the river spreads, a canoe with some white persons, with long, flowing, black hair, dressed like Europeans........................
a gunshot fired as a signal to..
for they escaped. They had...
shaggy and wild.......................................their hair is plaited and they wear clothes.

"One of our company, named João Antonio, found in the ruins of a house a piece of gold money, of spherical shape, greater than our Brazilian coin of 6,400 reis: on one side was an image, or figure of a kneeling youth; on the other, a bow, a crown, and an arrow (*setta*), of which coins we doubted not to have found many in the abandoned city; since it was overthrown by an eathquake, which gave no time, so sudden was its onset, to take away precious objects; but it needs a very powerful arm to turn over the rubbish, accumulated in so many long years, as we saw.

"This news is sent to your Honour from the interior of the province of Bahia and from the rivers Pará-oacu and Uña, and assuring you that we shall give information to no person, whatsoever; for we judge the villages are empty of people and boat owners. But I have given to your Honour the mine we have discovered, reminded of the great deal that is owed to you.

"Supposing that from our band, one of our company went forth, at this time, with a different pretence....he may, with great harm to your Honour, abandon his poverty and come to use these great things for his own benefit, taking great care to bribe that Indian [therefore], so as to spoil his purpose and lead your Honour to these great treasures, etc..................................
....
...................would find, in the entrances..............
.... flagstones...........................
...."

Here are found, in the Portuguese MS., the strange, unknown characters following. They appear to have been engraved on the great stones, sealing the vault of treasure, or the mausolea (?), whose apertures and fastenings the *bandeiristas*, using all their strength, could not force wider, or open:

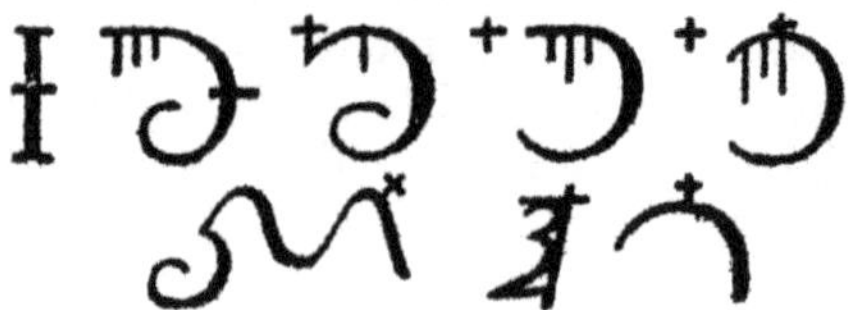

So ends the strange story of the *bandeiristas* of Minas Geraes.

It may strike the reader, as it did myself, when I saw this document, that, out of these forty-one characters, no fewer than twenty are almost identical in form with the letters of the Greek alphabet: kappa, upsilon, zeta, phi, iota, gamma, beta, omicron, sigma, omega, lambda, chi, epsilon, psi (?), theta, nu, while two of the signs are remarkably like Arabic numerals. The startling significances of these amazing identities are, I propose to show, not accidental in their relationship to the Phoenician-Greek alphabet. These strange inscriptions on the flagstones of the vaults (?), found so far apart as Ceylon and the Brazilian highlands (as will be seen, *infra*), must be the oldest existing in the whole world.

Thirty years later—on March 23, 1773—the archives of the governor of the Southern Brazilian province of São Paulo record another accidental discovery of a dead Brazilian city of unknown age. It was found in the *sertão*, or unknown wilds, of the Rio Pequéry. The commandant of the fort of Iguatémy reported to the governor in São Paulo that a fisherman, jumping ashore on a sandbank in the Rio Pequéry, in order to plunder a grove of wild limes and sweet oranges, found a curiously shaped stone of large diameter. He said it was like a *mos de moinhos* (grindstone of a mill-wheel). Near by were the ruins of a house and an ancient stone wall. The commandant of the fort sent out from the garrison a *canoa*, manned by a sergeant and two ensigns, or soldiers, who penetrated the thick and unexplored forest and found vestiges of a city of unknown date.

> "This ancient city is regularly laid out, and is of large size. It had a street that is half a league long. The city stood on the banks of two rivers and had a walled suburb. *Moats* stood between the city and the suburb . . . we unearthed two more of the strange mill-wheels, while we were making a stockade. All round are dense forests . . . the old men of the countryside have traditions that a city stood on this spot which was called Guayra." (*Moats* are said to be a feature of cities of *Atlantean* origin.—*Author.*)

This report will be found filed in the archives of the governor of São Paulo. The soldiers tried to break a way through the dense forests in order to find if any descendants of the people, who once lived in the dead city, survived. What luck they had does not transpire; but it may be said that *bearded white* Indians of the sort testified to in the above story of the year 1753—*not* albinoes—were seen, as recently as 1932, by a German missionary who was wandering along the edge of the unexplored forests in Eastern Perú.

More than once, Jesuit missioners, as Father Juan Lucero, reported meeting white Indians on the banks of the Rio Huallagua, a head-waters' tributary of the mighty Rio Marañon, or Amazon. The German missionary, in 1932, found he could not approach the strange "white Indians". They were shy, timid and furtive and met the forest Indians at the edge of a lake deep in the forests, where they bartered. Fray Juan Lucero, who heard of them in 1681, called them the Curveros, and said they had for King a descendant of the Inca Tupac Amaru, who, with 40,000 Inca Peruvians, fled far away, eastwards of Cuzco, through the unexplored woods, away from the cruel Spanish conquistadores. He—the friar—seems to identify them with the other mysterious white race of *El Gran Paytiti*, who were ruled by a "Tiger-King" (*Paytiti* meaning jaguar), in a "white house" by a great lake. This is a very moot point, and I shall say more of this Paytiti mystery, in a following book. Tupac took with him a rich treasure which two rival bands of Castilian banditti, in Perú, got wind of and decided to pursue Tupac and his Inca Indians. The bands met and fought to the death in the forests, the survivors being finished off by the savage Chuncho Indians. Father Lucero says he had himself seen plates, *half-moons* and ear-rings of gold brought from this mysterious nation.

It is curious and may be a more than accidental coincidence, that this sign of a *half-moon* figures among the inscriptions on the monuments in the abandoned Brazilian prehistoric city.

A colony of these white and bearded Indians, long before the time of the Inca empire, fortified an island in Lake Titicaca, where they were exterminated by the pre-Inca chief Cari of the Colloas, which had migrated to Perú from old Mexico.

Another of these old Atlantean cities was visited by Fray Pedro Cieza de Leon, Spanish soldier-monk, who died in A.D. 1560. It was called Guamanaga, and is and was located on the great cordillera in lat. 12° 59′ S., long. 73° 59′ W. Cieza was tremendously impressed by the great edifices he saw there, all in ruins.

"Who built them?" he asked the natives.

"*A bearded, white people*, like you Spaniards," said a cacique.

> "They came to these parts many ages before the Incas began to reign and formed a settlement here. . . . They do not seem to me Inca buildings; for they are *square*, not long and narrow. It is also reported that certain letters were found on a tile in these buildings. . . . The Indians also speak of bearded white men in the island of Titicaca." (*Cieza de Leon.*)

As travellers know, the native and aboriginal races of South America are a *beardless* race! It is remarkable that one of the colossal stone statues found in the mysterious dead city of Tiahuanacu

[*Courtesy of Dr. Alexander Scott, F.R S*

Pre-Inca wooden figure with curious head-dress.

One of five colossal Atlantean (?) heads found in jungle, Tabasco Mexico, 1940. They may be heads of a band of men.

[*Courtesy of Mr E. D. Rice, Auto-Giro Co., of America.*

Quetzalcoatl's Temple of a Thousand Columns at Chichen Itza. (A rich, ancient treasure said to have been cached here.)

wore a beard—always the mark of a very ancient race in South America, until the coming of the Spanish conquistadores.

Says Cieza de Leon:

> "in the greater island that was swampy (*palude*), in Lake Titicaca, the Colloa chieftain came across white people with beards (or whiskers), whom he fought in such a manner that he killed them all."

That extermination of a South American, pre-Columbian, white race occurred many centuries before the first Inca emperor of the Sun held sway in old Quito and Cuzco. It is probable that descendants of this white empire exist, *today*, in more than one part of unexplored Brazil, and among the Andean outliers, in regions rich with gold, on the confines of the Amazon's headwaters. A chance encounter—if it be chance that guides, seekers towards a solution of ancient mysteries!—made in what used to be the "yellow-jack" port of Ecuador, threw (for the author of this book) the first light on this riddle of a very old world of America.

In 1932 I was waiting for a steamer of the Grace Line, calling at the port of Guayaquil, Ecuador, when I met a Colombian, native of Medellin, who told me a very strange story about a lost world of this kind. He shook with malaria, and his body was badly emaciated, but what most impressed me about this sallow man was the fixed gaze from his dark bloodshot eyes—the stare of one who had seen a vision of the unknown and was mastered by the awe and mystery of what he had seen. According to my informant he had been a member of an expedition led by a mysterious German doctor of science or philosophy, who hailed from Hamburg. In the year 1926, or 1927, this expedition had quitted Obidos, in Brazil, bound for an unknown country in the Brazilian *sertão*. After many days, they found themselves in canoes well up a tributary of the Rio Negro, on the way to an Amazon tributary's headwaters territory. I gathered that this expedition was somewhere on the unknown borders of North-Western Brazil and Southern Venezuela, or the upper Orinoco country.

The man of Medellin was purposely vague in his topography, and for a good reason: *gold* had been found, and a lot of gold, too! He mentioned various tribes of *Indiòs bravos* (wild and unpacifiable Indians) whose territories they touched. Tribes such as the Uapes, Guaipunyos, Metas, the Cirecois, the Eperemenos, and the redoubtable Caribs whom not even the early conquistadores were able to subdue; and my own knowledge of certain dark byways of South American history made me suspect that he had somehow got into a mysterious country once traversed by an Inca Way, leading through territories of pygmies and "white Indians" towards Quito. (It may be still used, today, and by the same mysterious, white "Indians" mentioned in this book.) It was in this very region that the far from mythical women warriors of South America—the white and beautiful Amazons, women of the oldest race of European and Mediterranean navigators, the Carians—had *one* of their colonial empires, as late as Sir Walter Raleigh's day. But the Colombian said nothing of them.

> "After we quitted the rivers, *señor Inglese*, the landscape changed. No more green hells of verdure and lofty forest aisles where gloom and death lie waiting at the feet of giant trees. We left that *inferno verde* behind, and the country began to ascend. In a land of dry scrub, with few brooks or springs, we left far behind us, too, the booming drums of the wild Indians we never saw, who were signalling our passing through their territories. I noticed, one day, that all deer and wild animals we met fled from us at sight. It looked as if they feared something in this mysterious country—something unknown. This was many days after the last vestiges of the forest had faded into the dim, blue distance far back towards the Amazon. Then, one day, we came on a strange, stone object shrouded in bush and creepers. It was a stone monument, looking like this, *señor* . . ."

The Colombian dipped his finger in his glass of aguardiente and drew a diagram on the dirty table in the wharf bodega. The shape was like a cut through the shorter axis of an ellipse.

> "Our leader, the German doctor, said it was an ancient pyramid, and began to look around for inscriptions, ancient writing, or what he called *hieroglificos*. . . . Some weeks later, I remember, we stood in a deep gorge through which raced a tumultuous current of deep, crystal waters, pure as though newly born from the snows of the giant Andes. Looking up, our leader, glancing through his Zeiss binoculars, pointed out to us, where, far up on the farther wall of the *cañon*, an ancient paved road ran. It cleft a wall of the upper cliff, from which it issued, and then it came to an abrupt end on the shelf of a precipice, as if, in a far day, some giant earthquake had toppled the rest of the road into boulders of the stream bed we stood gazing at.
>
> "We camped in the gorge and spent some days exploring. A week later, we built a bridge across the gorge, by felling a tree growing on our side, and passed over to explore the ancient road. It was well paved with finely masoned and squared blocks of a stone, hard as granite. We followed the road

into a long tunnel cut through the cliff-walls, and, once in the sunlight, found ourselves on the hither side of a tremendous gulf, on the dim floor of which, far below, we faintly discerned some strange objects like queer buildings of no sort we had ever seen before. The paved way went ever climbing up the side of the precipices and, at last, brought us to where we could look down into another tremendous gorge or ravine. What we saw here took our breath away. . . . A dead city of towering palaces, splendid ruins, temples, with more of the carved pillars and strange pyramids, mostly covered up with ages of trees and jungle. There were magnificent gardens where stood broken and agèd fountains which once must have spouted with cool waters. Below us was an ancient wall, so high up, that trees of the forests below barely reached its summit. We walked further along the ancient way and came to where two queer thin towers, one shaped like the ——"—(he meant the virile member) —"the other had a top like a pear very rounded at the base. Close by, at the foot of two other walls were many small stone houses. . . .

"Here we ambushed and caught a dwarfish man, about four feet tall, with very red eyes. He had a thick bushy beard that reached below his waist, but his arm muscles were fat and big. Round his waist was a queer leather belt with gold—pure gold buckles of some sort. Otherwise, he was nearly nude. We met others of these pygmy men, and all had a most sickly sort of white skin. . . . Yes, *señor*, white as yours, and not like an Indian's or a greaser's! It was the white of old yellowed ivory. . . . We found they had women and they with beautiful faces, long hair, and either red or bluish eyes. They, too, were nude and their hair reached almost to their feet. The German said they were Greek in type—ancient Greek. They wore gold bracelets on their arms, and gold necklets. But their strange red eyes shone like a jaguar's in the firelight. What scared them were the reports of our guns. They'd never seen such things before."

The man of Medellin—and you may believe his story, or not—told me that he and the others explored a great pyramid-temple whose interior fairly blazed with gold. It sheathed the pillars, the roofs and the walls. Strange letters were engraved on the gold plates. Some parts of the dead city were inaccessible. In fact, it would seem that only the suburbs of the dead city were entered by the roamers. The white men with the red eyes had become degenerate—like Mr. H. G. Wells' Morlocks in the *Time Machine*. If they were not merely degenerate descendants of some very ancient and civilised South American race, then may be, said the German leader to my

Colombian informant, they were the remains of a helot class of the same race. They lived on goat's flesh, cheese and milk. *Quien sabe?* said my informant.*

"In some of the pyramid-temples we entered, we saw deep, blue-veined marble altars (?) stained with ancient blood, or rust (?). Perhaps of ancient sacrifices, or, may be, of some horrible cult of the decayed remnants of this very ancient civilisation. . . . But the *gold*, *señor*, not even the Incas had so much to hide when Don Francisco Pizarro killed the Emperor Atahualpha. High overhead, there were alcoves or galleries actually stuffed with splendid gold objects, vessels, chains, chalices, insignia, and shields and plates engraved with the strange *hieroglificos*. Some of these plates were three or four inches thick—all solid gold, tons—kilogrammes—of it, *señor*. I took one of the gold knives in one of the temples. Eight or ten of them had been attached to one of the pillars. The hilts and the blades were marvellously chased and engraved, as by the finest goldsmiths ever known. Looking up, in another splendid ruined stone building, which cut into the side of a hill, I staggered with amazement to see eight glorious suns, of pure, shining, blazing gold from which rays were made to shine out like stars. Groups of handsome men, beautiful women, naked youths and maidens were carved on the walls of this mausoleum, and over their heads and shoulders, like the halo or nimbus round the head of the Virgin, and the Saints or God, shone stars or moons of pure, shining gold. Chains hung down from the alcoves and pillars, and friezes were inscribed with the strange signs in rows. . . . Did I tell you, *señor*, that each of the dwarfs in the outskirts of this dead city, living either in tunnels, or rooms in the rock, or the little stone houses we saw, carried a long curved knife of pure gold? It was not valued here. I could tell you a lot more . . . especially about a queer sort of lock, like a stick with 9 rings, each ring forming one of the queer letters or *hieroglificos*, which we found on a gold chain in one of the queer pyramids. Apparently, you turned it to form a combination to open or lock the fetters. . . ."

---

* A little-known race of white "Indians", styled *los Paria*, live in a village significantly called *Atlan*, somewhere in the virgin forests between the Rio Apure and the Orinoco. They have traditions about a cataclysm which destroyed their ancient Fatherland, in Brazil, and also of a large island in the eastern ocean where dwelt a rich and civilised race (Atlantis?). They have never mingled with the Venezuelan Indians, but their women being white and beautiful, were often seized by surrounding caciques and taken into *harems*! The Spanish chroniclers of old Santa Fé de Bogotá, where was located the audiencia governing these vast territories, say that these women were kept in a strict purdah of half-darkness, all their lives, and, like Welsh pit ponies, became blind. Señor H. B. Nuñez, the well-known archaeologist of Caracas, says great monoliths, incised with hieroglyphics, and carved pillars of ruins, are found in the forests of the little-known Orinoco headwaters of Venezuela. One day, I may repeat, these ruins will be explored and startling and revolutionary facts about the great white race of ancient rulers of South America will come to light.

I gathered that the members of the expedition took as much gold as they could when they quitted the Lost World city; and that, on their way out this heavy burden led to the death, at the hands of hostile, North Brazilian *Indiós*, of more than three-quarters of the members.

So much for the stories of the existence of strange white people, today—handsome bearded men and beautiful white, nude women with symmetrical Greek features—in the unknown *sertão* of the central Matto Grosso and the Brazilian highlands, and northwards and north-westwards in the mountains beyond the headwaters of the Amazon and its tributaries.

One must now return to the strange story told by the A.D. 1743–1753 *bandeiristas* of Minas Geraes and Bahia.

A few months after the remarkable Manuscript of their *Relatorio* had again come to light, in 1841, in the former royal archives in Rio de Janeiro, a certain Senhor Conego Benigno José de Carvalho e Cunha, a canon and professor of a theological college in Bahia, conceived the idea of using his three months' annual vacation to seek this abandoned city of the *bandeiristas* of A.D. 1750. Whether or not the canon's motives were purely archaeological does not really matter. He was destined to experience the hardships that have usually attended the exertions of men seeking to advance the bounds of knowledge and receiving little more than tepid encouragement and fine, florid words from governmental and administrative authorities.

Benigno carefully studied the *bandeirista's Relatorio*, and about this time he met a seventy-three-year-old man, in a village in a remote part of the province of Minas Geraes, who had journeyed into the wild and unknown region of the Brazilian *sertão*.

Scoffers abounded in the canon's day, as they do now. Says he, with justice:

> "There have not been wanting people who have ridiculed my diligence in this affair. They say the *Relatorio* of 1753 is fabulous; but I find it impossible to discover any reason of self-glorification and self-interest that could stimulate the invention of such a piece of fiction. The story has been written by rude, unlettered men, without order or sequence, just as it came back to their memory."

Benigno comments on the *caracteres gregos ou runnos* (Greek letters, or "runes", copied, about A.D. 1750, by these *bandeiristas*, from the stone walls and vaults of the dead city. I shall state my conclusions about these remarkable inscriptions later in this book.) But what puzzled the canon is the mystery which has led to the loss of many lives—including, perhaps, three well-known English explorers in the year 1926. . . . Just where does this abandoned city of gold and mystery lie? It is the Brazilian Golden Manoa of 1944!

Says the canon:

> "I note that the 1753 adventurers descended a river that runs in front of the abandoned city, and, in nine days of hard marching, reached a cataract. They wrote their story immediately after their coming down the rios Paraguassú and Unna, in the province of Bahia."

He arrived at the conclusion that the dead city of gold and mystery lay behind the unknown Serra do Cincorá in the *sertão* of the province of Bahia. . . .

> "That is the highest and most inaccessible range in the interior of the province of Bahia. It burns with crystals set in. great rocks of the cliffs. Always, a thick mist covers it until noont On the northern side, a zigzag *tromba* (a paved way of ancien. date) climbs to the summit, and one can reach it in three hours That way has been hewn by force of human arms, and not by Nature. Today (the year 1841), the people of this village of Cincorá have neither resolution nor vigour enough to explore the unknown country of this *serra*. On the left bank of a river, called the Braço da* X, a league and a half from the *tromba*, must be located *desta antiga cidade* (this ancient city of the dead). I need money to hire men and mules, for a forced march of 10–11 leagues, from a little village to the road of the *tromba*, at whose summit I hope to sight the walls of the abandoned city."

The rains, however, came on, and made all tracks impassable. So the canon had to content himself with interviewing the people in a little village, called Valença, located on the edge of the unknown Serra do Cincorá. A cattle-dealer told the canon that he had once penetrated to the cataract called the Braço da X:*

> "but according to this statement I knew that, to the east the dead city was hidden in woods, and that he did not dare to penetrate the wilds. When he climbed above the waterfalls,

---

* Author's Note: I have made a slight elision in place-names in this narrative—for reasons that I deem sufficient. The *bandeirista* of 1743–53 does not mention the name of the cataract in this connection. In his *Relatorio*, he says his comrades reached the *catadupa*, or cataract, in *three* days' journey down the river. The *nine* days' journey seems to have taken place on a different occasion; when the *bandeiristas* split up and made an overland trip, till they reached the wide lagoon, where they saw the "white Indians" in a canoe. A slip, like this, would cause an appreciable error in replotting the *bandeiristas*' probable course and distance from a known river.

to the Braço da X river, he found that the Braço da X waterfall dashes tumultuously down from that high cataract by different channels (*boccas*), with great roaring of waters, and spreads out into various peninsulas, which are covered with verdure; and that, on its eastern bank are many and very deep mines, some with gaping openings in the rocks of the mountains (*abertas em penhas*), that formed an arched vault (or arched roofs: *abobada*) underneath which he travelled to the beginning of the plain (*plano*); and then came to a stop, at an unfathomable cavern (*furna*) or pit. He told me of a phenomenon he saw in those workings (*socavões*): a horrible noise is emitted from its mouths. He attributed it to the presence of a great quantity of gold and silver that it contains. And the reason for this phenomenon is very clear: these gold mines stretch under the bed of the river, and have been broken down and caused to subside, in the lapse of time, weight and the movement of the waters. The water enters by the cavernous holes that the river forms in all that extensive basin, after its tranquil flowing, and suddenly impels the air with violence. It shoots out from these caves by the mouths of the mine-workings, roaring like a tremendous cannon-shot."

The canon adds that he has been told that, through the unexplored forests, hiding the city of the dead from the summit of the mountains, there have been cut ancient lanes (*picadas antigas*), "opposite to the paved road found by the *bandeiristas*, and which led them to the ancient city of the dead". The cattle-dealer said he estimated it would take the canon fifty days to go and fifty to return, with pack-mules. "If I hire mules and a guide, the cattle-dealer is ready to accompany me, about November 1, 1841."

Old men, in villages of this part of the *sertão* of Bahia, had told the canon of traditions about an ancient city, under a mountain, that had been overwhelmed by an earthquake, and a flood. "He who went there never returned . . . a long and perilous journey, beset with serpents and jaguars (*oncas*) . . ."

"And there are savages, not wild (*mansos*), who went with me, two days above the rapids of the river which runs in front of the city of the dead, and they told me of all this. I resolved to raise a troop of armed Indians, in the village of San Fidelis, who will remain with me on that road."

But money was wanted to finance the canon's search, and, at that day, money flowed to, not *from* the Royal and Imperial Government in Rio! A scientific institute in Rio de Janeiro appealed to the General Assembly to provide the canon with a subvention, but all they sent him were the most charming good wishes and promises—to operate *mañana*.

Nevertheless, the canon was a man of courage and energy. In his veins, ecclesiastic as he might be by social accident, ran the blood of the older Lusitanian stock of the great age of Henry the Navigator, and not a spirit engendered by *canna*. His ancestors had not mixed their European blood with the rather timid or docile strain of Tupi, or Guarani.

On December 23, 1841, after the rains had ended, the worthy canon, on his vacation, started out from Bahia city, on the trail for the dead city of the *bandeirantes* of 1753. A month later, he hitched the bridle-rein of his horse to a post of a *fazenda* whose owner knew the region of forest, scrub and *chapada* and *serra* for which the canon was bound. The *fazendeiro*, it was true, owned that he had never heard of this abandoned city of the dead; but somebody else told the canon about a colony of runaway blacks—escaped slaves or *samboes* in that region,—who might be reckoned on to bar any gold seekers' way to the dead city. But something else now arose to bar the canon's way to riches and renown.

The procrastinating Government sent no funds for the canon's exploration trip, and the local governor refused his aid . . .

> "I hired a horse to ascend to the *barra* of the rio Parassusinho. I had them burn the scrub and the *catingas* (undergrowth) so as to kill off the horrible ticks who plague travellers in these wilds. I hired a guide and was about to ride towards the *catadupa* (cataract), and, thence, go on to the *coquilombo* (log hut) of the fugitive blacks, when a malignant fever seized me and brought me to death's door."

The luckless canon lay ill for five months. Fevers developed into pleurisies. As soon as he could sit up in his room, at the *fazenda*, or manor-house of the farm, he sent out two negroes with orders to explore the wilderness; and, in fifteen days, they returned with a story about an abyss (*sumidouro*) from which the river gushed forth. But they had seen no cataract such as the cattle-dealer had found. (This cataract was one of the landmarks of the *bandeiristas* of 1743–1753).

All round was dense forest. The blacks went on to a place called Timbo, on the Rio Grande, where they met travellers who told an odd story about the *sertão* (interior) of the Cincorá country.

> "These men, bound for a wedding, had opened a new horse, or mule track by which they came to Cincorá. Last March 1841, they had reached the Geraes, where there is an old highway from the interior, and they lodged on the slopes of the hills (*morros*),

leaving their baggage, horses and mules, below, and saw a good road by which they might ascend the hills, noting the crystals on the face of the rocks. They went on foot to the top, and observed that the road was furnished with snares for wild beasts (*murdéos*). Arrived at the summit, they saw, in the distance, about a league away, a great city, in which a drum beat, and in the hour of the Ave Maria, they saw ascend from it many fireworks (or rockets: *foguetes*); they withdrew, and when they arrived at the rancho, alone, they met the packhorses, and the negroes had burnt all their clothes and provisions. They again took the road and did not come near any game when they reached the Cincorá; so that, in truth, they had died of hunger if they had not reached that place."

The canon gathered, from what these men told him, that the fugitive blacks had made themselves "lords of the abandoned city", behind the mountain-tops, and kept all others away from it. He made one more appeal for financial help from a learned society in Rio de Janeiro. There were good Samaritans who had helped him when he lay sick in the remote *fazenda*. He wanted to pay them back. "I plan," he added, "to set off, again, on September 15, 1842," but feared that the blacks in the *coquilombo* would prevent his own negroes from penetrating beyond the *serra*, and would prevent him from examining the ancient monuments in the abandoned city. . . . He ends with a piteous plea. The aura of misfortune, blasting the bodies and withering the hopes of seekers long before and long after the canon's day, had emanated from the dead city of mystery and gold. It had lighted on the canon of Bahia, even as it had descended and would descend on many others long before and after that day, August 20, 1842:

> "I beg the authorities for a loan to satisfy my worthy creditors, seeing that, out of my slender income, I have already spent over 200,000 reis. I want only to bring the affair to an end. I used the money of the Institute in Rio almost entirely for the purchase of saddle and pack-horses, two of which were of no use to me; for the horse died of plague and the mule broke its back. God keep you for many years!"

However, the worthy canon was *not* to reach the dead city. The old gods of the land had spoken. The fevers and the pleurisies wasted him away to a skeleton, and for many weeks he lay at death's door in the room at the *fazenda* on the edge of the trackless forests. When he recovered, he was overwhelmed by financial difficulties, and to his appeal for help the authorities in Rio, as before, returned only promises.

Yet was the canon luckier than many others in this adventure. For they lost life as well as treasure.

And that is the last one hears of the canon of Bahia and his unlucky attempt to locate and penetrate to the lost city of the *bandeiristas*. Today, in 1945, the Serra do Sincorá, wherein the canon believed the dead city, which might have been 60,000 years old, was located, is surrounded by dense forests through which *picadas*, or tracks, lead to open glades. Sincorá, which may be reached on a branch of the Bahia South-Western Railway, is a place of weeds, dirt and decay. Like one of the ghost towns of Nevada and California, it once hummed with wickedness and colourful blackguardism and activities—which was when it was the centre of diamond diggings.

It does not seem ever to have struck the canon that it was a problem like unto the riddle of the Children of Israel wandering for forty years in a peninsula the size of New Jersey, to account for the fact that the *bandeiristas*, starting out in 1743, contrived to end up, ten years later, in a place so comparatively near their starting-point as the interior of Bahia province. Might not the *bandeirantes* have struck the dead city at a place farther to the west, or south-west, in the unknown *sertão* of Brazil?

That was certainly the opinion of expeditions in the more scientific nineteenth and twentieth centuries. There was the famous Krupps of Essen—German armament makers—for example. They supposed that it was in the western province of the Matto Grosso that the dead city lay. In the 1900s, they organised a large expedition of armed men, guides, Indians, pack-animals, transport financed to the tune of £100,000. It was one of the finest expeditions ever started into the unknown of Brazil; but, at its approach, the wild Indians vanished into thin air, reappearing only at night, and revealing their dangerous presence by showers of poisoned arrows, discharged from the dense bush. By day, the distant drums of the "bush telegraph" beat, smoke signals announced afar the presence of white strangers. Many of these *Indiós bravos* of the Matto Grosso are cannibals and head-hunters, some of whom see better in the dark than a prowling feline. Bleak foothills of the *chapada* and the barren scrub of the *catinga*, and miles of marsh and swamp bar the way to the "White Mountains", where, say the Indians, live a race of superior white beings. The geologist Troussart says this wild region was one of the first to emerge from the primaeval floods of the Miocene Age, of the Tertiary epoch. It is about the oldest land on the globe.

However, what beat the Krupp expedition was not the Indians, or the bush dangers; but the fact that their men and animals could not live on the country. Commissariat beat them!

My friend, Admiral Bertram Chambers, C.B., who spent many

years on the South American station, in the British Navy, and has travelled extensively in South America, raises a point that I had better deal with here. He writes me that, when he was in Perú, he was shown, by a physician, photographs of Indians of that state, and of the Andean regions, who were white *albinoes*. May not these elusive white Indians of Brazil and the Amazon headwaters' territory be albinoes, he asks?

The answer is *NO*!

The old British buccaneers of Sawkins' and Barty Sharp's day knew of white Indians with blue eyes and auburn hair. They said they were "moon-eyed" and could see in the dark. I here cite a curious passage from an unpublished MS.—except in a book of mine, here quoted—of the late seventeenth century, which MS. is in my possession. It was written in 1683 by an unknown buccaneer:

> "They have among them (the Panama Indians) them they call Doctors, that can raise the Divill at their Pleasure; they knew of our comeing, and att what time we should be their". (Extract from the MS. of an unnamed lower-deck man aboard the buccaneering ship of Captain Coxon, in the Spanish Main, and off the coast of "Castillo del Oro," in the years 1680–2. It is cited from a MS. published in my book: *Panorama of* (*South and Central American*) *Treasure Hunting*, published by E. P. Dutton and Co., Inc., of New York City, in 1940. It is the earliest reported case of the existence of the "bush telegraph" in unknown Panama.—*Author.*)

Short, in his *North Americans of Antiquity*, says that among the Menominee, Dakota, Mandan, and Zuni (North American Indians) were many with auburn hair and blue eyes, and with a prevailing white tint of skin. The queer, Lancandones *Indiós*, on the borders of Western Guatemala and the bush of Chiappas, Mexico's frontier state, are also white, though degenerate and dwarfish. May be, they, too, are survivors of a once ruling white race of South and Central America. I here subjoin a passage from a monograph of mine on American "white Indians":

> Theories are various about these "white Indians" of unknown Darien. The buccaneers of Wafer's day spoke of their milk-white skins covered with short down. They said they saw best in the moonlight, and ran skipping round like wild bucks. Among the Cunos Indians live Indians with reddish hair and grey eyes . . . "Entre ellos los albinos no son raros, y algunos hombres de piel casi blanca y cabello rojo dan testimonio del paso frecuente y larga permanencia de los piratas por aquellos lugeres". (So, Ramon M. Valdes). ("And among them albinoes are not rare,

and some men of skin nearly white and red hair give testimony to the frequent passage and long sojourn of pirates in those places".)

But suppose these degenerate white men are the survivors of a lost colony of old Atlantean Hy-Brazil? A colony established near Palenque, by the wise man Quetzalcoatl of Hy-Brazil, whom a catastrophe of nature may have prevented returning from Brazil? *Quien sabe, señores?*

CHAPTER III

JUNGLE LIGHT THAT SHINES BY ITSELF

"The dead also look on and help."
D. H. LAWRENCE.

Now, as we peer into this mysterious ancient world of South America, let us once more consider the strange "runic" set of inscriptions—as the worthy *conego* (canon) of Bahia would have called them, quite erroneously—which the *bandeiristas* of A.D. 1750 found engraved on the great sealed flagstone, sealed with the cement of immemorial time and weathering. As we see, they could not, using all their strength and the tools and weapons at their command, lever up one inch even of the end of the flagstones sealing vaults of what they believed to be either strange talismans, or treasures. Here, again, are these bizarre and incredibly ancient signs, at least 30,000 and probably even 60,000 years old, so incredibly ancient is South American civilisation and so far are men, posing as authorities thereon, from realising the truth, instead of maintaining hoary fallacies:*

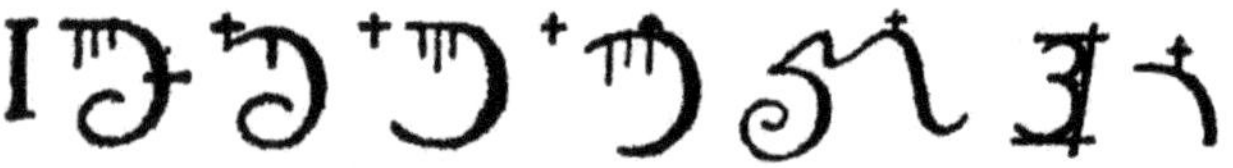

Signs in the dead city of Brazil.

I have been able to find only two ancient *Asiatic* letters in any

* See Chapter V for comparative study of the unknown, South American Atlantean inscriptions.

way corresponding to two, only, of these strange signs. They are:

TIBETAN	KANHERI INSCRIPTIO (India. *c.* 877 B.C.)
5 5	5
Value: *ta.* Value: *da.*	Value: *u.*

What is the origin of these queer signs? What is their meaning? Let us see how far we can cast a ray of light into the dark mystery of thousands of years. (Why I say *Asiatic* will soon appear.) The light will come from a youthful experience in the life of a famous Englishman who has recently himself become a mystery of Brazil's unknown wilds.

One morning, in the year 1893, a young British officer—a gunner-lieutenant—stationed at Trincomalee, Ceylon, was taking his annual leave, starting out, accompanied only by a jungle-wallah, on a trip into a wild and little-known part of this mysterious and romantic island of strange secrets. Its jungles and mountains are as mysterious, today, as in the time of M. Annaeus Seneca, the Roman rhetor, father of the more famous Seneca, the philosopher, who wrote: "Beyond India is the island of Taprobane, the end of the world; after which begins eternal night."

The young officer was keenly interested in archaeology, and accustomed to long tramps and solitary journeys into places remote even from native jungle tracks. Two days later, while he was engaged in researches of an ethnological and botanical character, he was overtaken, deep in the forest, by a storm of such violence and tropical downpour, that he soon saw that he and the wallah would have to spend the whole night under the trees. The terrific intensity of the lightning flashes, searing the black darkness in which not even a bird rustled or monkey chattered, served merely to show that he had completely lost his way. All night, he and the scared jungle-wallah cowered in the shelter of trees and bushes, drenched to the skin, while the incessant thunder rolled in crashing reverberations which made the silence of the forest even more eerie. Towards dawn, the tempest began to let up, and the tattered clouds wisped across the sky; but a hot, white and clammy ground mist hid the surroundings. Slowly it cleared away, and then the officer started in astonishment and some awe. Here, deep in the old home of the mysterious gods of ancient Seleidiva, the unknown was unveiling itself. He found himself confronting an immense rock, covered with parasites and lianas. A tendril of one of the creepers had fallen aside and disclosed what looked to be some very ancient inscriptions of quite unknown character and meaning. The wallah started to cut away the clinging vines and then the young officer saw that the ancient rock was indeed covered with unknown inscriptions, in very large characters, which seemed to be letters of an alphabet, or a syllabary, or glyphs, more than half as old as Time himself.

He took a copy of the inscriptions, and when he got back to civilisation, again, eagerly questioned a learned Sinhalese priest, who said that the writing was a form of Asoka, of the old Asoka-Buddhists, and in a *cypher* which only those ancient priests understood. This assertion, ten years and more later, was repeated by a Sinhalese scholar in the Oriental Institute at Oxford, who added the not very comprehensible statement, that he, the scholar, was the only man living who could read the strange inscriptions, but that even so, he would need to visit the rock himself, and take a careful rubbing, because "the meaning of the characters would be changed in accord with the incidence of the sun's rays, at certain times of the day". Even after reading, the cypher would need to be decoded, said the palaeographer.

(In actual fact, or what the Sinhalese palaeographer averred was the case, the bizarre inscriptions record the cacheing, in a time of great dearth, or famine, of an immense treasure laid under the great, mossy, time-worn boulder. The cache must be thousands of years old.)

Twenty-two years passed by, and the young gunner-officer had become a distinguished colonel and D.S.O.—Colonel P. H. Fawcett—well known all over South America for his services in the cause of science and his expert work in the very difficult task of delimiting frontiers in the wilds of Perú, Ecuador, Bolivia, and Brazil. In 1925 Colonel Fawcett, accompanied by his son Jack, and a young cameraman, Raleigh Rimell, the son of a retired British naval officer, set out from Cuyabá, the frontier town in the province of Rondonia, of the Matto Grosso (Great Woods) of Brazil, on the trail of a dead city, of unknown age, in the mountains of Brazil, on whose walls and pillars and porticoes had been found inscriptions, fourteen out of twenty-four characters of which are identical with those he had accidentally discovered, more than thirty years before, in the jungle-forest of Ceylon.

From that time, in April and May 1925, there have come out of these unexplored jungles and *chapadas* of Brazil little more than rumours and legends about the unknown fate of the Fawcett expedition. True, they are rumours that rustle among the leaves of the Brazilian forests like ghostly whispers heard beneath and among the trees of a "haunted wood" on All Hallowe'en, but now and again, at rare intervals, the careful listener hears an authentic echo of the sound of of a living voice.

The Sinhalese priests and the Orientalist at Oxford spoke of a "secret Asoka cypher"; but this chapter tries to prove that those strange writings—syllabary rather than hieroglyphs, and assuredly *not* Amero-Indian pictographs—are something far more remarkable than even hieratic cypher-script—*if* it be that—of an esoteric, Hindu cult.

The next person known to have reached the dead city of the old *bandeiristas*—if we except the ubiquitous and often courageous and devoted mission priests and monks of the Jesuit order—was a British officer, former British Consul-General in Rio. He was Lieutenant-Colonel O'Sullivan (referred to *infra*), and had acquired old Portuguese documents, either from the Biblioteca Nacional, the repository of the former Lusitanian viceroys' archives, or from Fawcett direct. O'Sullivan,* accompanied by a Brazilian-Indian guide, set out for the unknown *serra*, but in order to put inquisitive trackers off his trail, gave out that he was merely a *garimpeiro*, or diamond-digger bound for some old diamond-workings. That was in 1913, and O'Sullivan had been given, by Colonel Fawcett, a nearly blank map in which he was to fill in his route through this part of the Bahian *sertão*, where our worthy canon came to grief, in 1840. In 1921 Fawcett used his route map and it was so accurate that, alone without even a guide, he penetrated to this dead city. He subsequently wrote to a friend in Rio:

> "I went alone; for I knew I should have much less need to fear the Indians, who will not attack a man alone who meets them fairly. I reached the *catinga* in the *serra*, northwards of Bahia . . . and in the midst of primaeval woods, stood before a mass of jumbled ruins. The city had been a walled one of ancient date. Here, wreathed in jungle and bush there stood a giant monolith crowned by a weather-worn figure, carved in stone . . ."

Colonel Fawcett, however, never indicated its location, as I have done here, and said very little about what he saw. It would also appear that Fawcett did not identify this dead city with the one he was seeking when, in 1925, he set out into the unknown wilds of the Matto Grosso, and was lost about the region between the Rios Xingu and Tapajos. He makes some very interesting remarks about these dead cities which must indicate their tremendous age. He says:

* O'Sullivan died in hospital at Belem, of cancer. He was a healthy man. Others who have gone on the trail of these dead cities have died of mysterious diseases, or been stricken with inexplicable blindness, or met dire misfortune. May be, it would be a case of *post hoc ergo propter hoc* to suggest anything more.

"There was no jungle against which the walls of these ancient cities served as defence. Those walls must have acted as breakwaters in a far-off day when the sea reached far inland. The openings in their walls are arched, filled in with masonry and have no doors. So they feared no attack from any jungle, but from encroachments of the sea. Each city was destroyed by an earthquake. . . . All the Indian tribes in South America have traditions of their ancestors being ruled by men of a white race, very far advanced in the arts of civilisation."

The amazing, possible age of these dead cities of the Brazilian highlands is suggested in what the German geologist, Friedrich Katzer, says:

"The old highlands of Brazil must once have extended eastwards into the Atlantic, and were largely built of materials derived from the destruction of a drowned Atlantic land. . . ."

Professor J. W. Gregory, the distinguished geographer who was drowned in the rapids of the Upper Urubamba river, in 1932, when he was putting the seal to his life-long work: the discovery of the age at which the Andes uprose from the bed of the Pacific, said, years ago, though he was not referring to these lost-world theories:

"The wide, lowland plains, in S. America, were doubtless once occupied by the sea, which then divided this continent into two distinct parts, or lands. These lowland plains hold the basins of the Amazon, the Orinoco, and the La Plata." (*Vide: Geography: Structure, Physical and Comparative.*)

I have mentioned above the two attempts of the Germans to find these dead cities of Hy-Brazil. The first, sponsored by Krupps of Essen, lost many animals and much transport at the hands of the wild Indians of the Matto Grosso; but it was, as I said, commissariat, in a land where white men and mules, or tough burros in a large expedition cannot live on the country, that really beat them and their characteristically thorough organisation. Doktor Eckener also proposed to by-pass the difficulties by flying over the appalling territory in his *Graf Zeppelin*—previously used, it is now admitted, to photograph military details of London's defences.

Colonel Fawcett believed he might succeed where a highly organised expedition would fail. He had good reasons for thinking so; for no man knew and had greater personal experiences of the dangerous tribes who bar the road to these dead cities of Brazil. Fawcett had also pioneering visions of a new Kenya colony type of pastoral state being set up on these highlands of the Matto Grosso.

He had a remarkable knowledge of the arcana of South American pre-history. Books of wonderfully executed hieroglyphic paintings, he said (quoting von Humboldt's story of Narcissus Gilbar, the white friar), were found among naked savages in the Peruvian *montaña*, at Ucayle, near the Amazon headwaters. The *ancient* Peruvians, as Jesuit missioners discovered, used both painting and characters; and all over South and Central America are traditions of white-bearded men who, in the persons of Quetzalcoatl and Bochicha, taught laws, agriculture and religion to primitive races, who said these men came from the *east*.* The dresses pictured on bas-reliefs in the dead cities in Brazil were, he said, found on totem-poles in British Columbia, and in unknown parts of Amazonas there were tribes actually worshipping Wodan, or Odin, god of magic and war—and no archaeologist can explain why this is so! (I have offered a solution of these enigmas, in a chapter following.) But as Colonel Fawcett more than once pointed out, in his lecture given, in 1911, before the Royal Geographical Society in London, nothing will ever be found out by pottering about among debased savages (contaminated by white men's vices) in the known rivers. To solve these riddles and effect a revolution in our ideas of whence arose civilisation—perhaps, in the so-called New World, in the highlands of Brazil, thousands of years ago, rather than in the Old World, so-called, of Europe and Asia—the explorer must follow the hard path of the pioneer, live on the country, eschew luxuries, emulate the hardy Portuguese *bandeiristas*. He believed that Englishmen, "perhaps the race most respected of any in South America", would lead the way in this new advance of the human spirit. (The late Sir Arthur Conan Doyle, present at this lecture, gained from it the inspiration for his entertaining novel: *The Lost World: the Adventures of Professor Challenger.*)

It is pointed out in Brazil that an aura of evil fate today, as in that of the conego of Bahia, in 1841 (*Vide* pages 57, 63 *supra*), or much earlier, has seemed to hang over all expeditions, whether organised by scientists or explorers, or the missionary journeys of Jesuit or Franciscan monks from the sixteenth century to our own day, which have made personal contact with these dead cities in old Brazil. So many of those who have returned—and more have perished without trace—have died untimely, or of lingering and painful diseases. It was in 1926, when Colonel P. H. Fawcett, D.S.O.,

---

*Author's Note: Quetzalcoatl, the civiliser of pre-Mayan Yucatan, Mexico, and Central America, was *not* a god. He was, as my researches show, one of the race of Hy-Brazil, some 30,000, or fewer, years ago, before the time of the great cataclysm that upheaved the Andes and sank Atlantis. When portents threatened the existence of Hy-Brazilian civilisation in South America, Quetzalcoatl was one of the band of wise men in black, including Viracocha and Bochicha, who went out to find lands not so menaced by vulcanism and quakes. How far Quetzalcoatl's own missioners went, some 30,000 or 20,000 years ago, is shown by my own curious discovery that the Thompson Indians of British Columbia have a story of the Great Deluge-Cataclysm in which Quetzalcoatl actually figures, under the name of *Qoaglgal*, as a "man who, with two others, worked miracles and transformed things".

and his son Jack, and their friend, Raleigh Rimell, of English descent, left the frontier township of Cuyabá, in the Western Matto Grosso, to try to penetrate to the lost world of these Atlantean dead cities. Fawcett was sponsored by British and American learned societies and museums, including the Royal Geographical Society of London. He took a radio instrument, and at one time planned to use a hydroplane to help him descend from the headwaters of one of the rivers flowing to the mighty Amazon from this land of the unknown. Indians had told him of dead cities in the Brazilian mountains, behind ramparts of forest and marsh, and of a strange fixed light, burning night and day, on ancient pillars. "It never goes out," said the Indians.

Just before he went aboard the liner for Rio, Fawcett had a talk with Dr. Clark Wissler of the New York Historical Museum. The Colonel seems to have told Dr. Wissler that he (Fawcett) had been told by a dying man of the location of one dead city in the "White Mountains". No one else knew anything about it.

Says Wissler:

> "Nobody can say what may, or may not be found in the Matto Grosso. Colonel Fawcett was convinced that he knew what was there, and where to look for it; but he told us no more than he has told the public."

Coming from a scientist of the calibre of Dr. Clark Wissler of New York, this warning about the mysteries of the Matto Grosso deserves marked attention. About the last persons on earth to know, or even care about these mysteries are, with rare exceptions, the Brazilian professors and scientists in Rio, Bahia and São Paulo.

Fawcett's friends speak of other strange tales brought to the Colonel by wandering Indians, whose tribal lore he had so thoroughly studied in the Matto Grosso and on the borders of Brazil and Bolivia, Perú and Ecuador. Few people knew more than he of the ways of the untamed Indians. There were cities in the Brazilian wilds and Amazonian headwaters, he said, dating back to 50,000 and 60,000 B.C.! White Indians with beards and blue eyes; a light burning without smoke or fire in jungle cities; words akin to Sanscrit; legends of the worship of the old Norse god Odin, in Brazilian wilds; of the *existence, today*, of the famous woman soldiers called the Amazons who fought against the Spanish conquistadores, under Don Francisco de Orellana, in 1542; and of a "tremendous hoard of gold and jewels" made "by Quetzalcoatl (?)" the Mexican god-man of the Aztecs and Toltecs.* (Quetzalcoatl, say old Mayan

* Quetzalcoatl, the ancient Central American missionary from Atlantean Brazil, would hardly have relished these (our) days of the 20th century! He stopped his ears with cotton-wool, when there was talk of war and warriors. His images show him enhaloed with the disc, or half-disc, of the sun.

traditions and Mexican legends, was a *white* man with a flowing beard, who came from the east—*across the ocean*—originated letters, taught arts of civilisation, and sailed away again, *to the east*, in a canoe of serpent skins!) (*Vide: also Author's note*, page 65 *supra*.)

No one knows what happened to the Fawcetts—father and son—and young Mr. Rimell. In fact, the Matto Grosso swamps and jungles are such queer places, with records of white men detained by Indian tribes for twenty-five or thirty years and then returning to civilisation, that one would not deem it impossible, if improbable, that Colonel Fawcett himself is still alive, perhaps in the recesses of the mystic White Mountains, or the hinterland of the Serra do Roncador, even, today, 1945.

No doubt some English or American folk will say that it is a thousand pities that the British Government, or some authoritative body, or learned society has made no effort to send out a special expedition, *ad hoc*, to solve this mystery of the vanishing of the Fawcett party into the unknown, especially as they are, or were, all of British origin. These people may say that it is regrettable that such a task was left to private enterprise where, necessarily, the questions of finance and recoupment have had to be made subsidiary to the main task—one difficult enough in all conscience!—the acting of the H. M. Stanley to this Brazilian Livingstone.

However, that would not have been the view of Colonel Fawcett himself, for, on the authority of one close to him, I am informed he said, just before leaving for the unknown:

> "If there is any attempt to send an expedition after us, to discover our fate or fortune—and we expect to be right away from civilisation for two or more years—for God's sake, stop them! England has nothing to do with this quest. It is a matter for Brazil, entirely."

I have said that out of all the dark clouds of rumours that have, in the last fifteen and more years, drifted out of the unknown wilds into the frontier settlement town of Cuyabá, in Rondonia, at the other end of the Brazilian overland telegraph line, very rarely has one heard come the echo of an authentic living voice. Most of these stories are not worthy of credence or examination, but, in April 1933, the silence of the dead was broken. A missioner of the Dominican friars told the Italian embassy in Rio that an Indian woman had said:

> "The Fawcett party are held prisoners in a camp between the Rios Kuluesene, Kuluene, and Das Mortes. Colonel Fawcett has been forced to marry a daughter of an Indian chief (so said the Indian woman)."

About this time a curious story reached the Royal Geographical Society, in London, from Monsignor Coutouran of the Salesian Mission Fathers of Lageado, in Matto Grosso. The ecclesiastic enclosed a statement from Signor Virginio Pessione, who said that on July 30, 1933 he had visited an estate on the Rio São Manoel, north of the Rio Paranatinga, which lay many miles to the northwest of Dead Horse Camp, Fawcett's last camp on the edge of the unknown. Here, the owners said:

> "An Indian woman of the Nafucua tribe of the Cuycurú captaincy had been living for a year. She had learnt a few words of Portuguese and conveyed the news of white men living for several years with the Aruvudus. Helped by a Bakairi Indian, who spoke Portuguese, Pessione got a statement from the Indian woman, made partly in sign language. She said: 'When my son was still at the breast, there arrived in my village three white men and Indians, descending the Kuluene in a large canoe. One white man was tall, old, and blue-eyed, also bearded and bald. Another was a youth, said to be the son of the first; the third was of greater age. The elder wore a felt hat and colonial helmet. . . . About a year ago, I saw them last. They were well and spoke the Aruvudu tongue. The man with the long, white beard was now chief of the tribe; his son had married the daughter of the chief, Jeruata. They had a plot of land, but moved from village to village, continually watched by the Indians, who would have killed them had they tried to escape. The white men had no bullets to their guns and were very near to such wild tribes as the Suyas and Cayapos.' "

Pessione said the Indian woman's son must now be 9–10 years, the white men having arrived in 1925–26.

However, it must be pointed out that *there is no proof that these detained whites were the Fawcett party*, despite the story of the American missionary, Paul W. Guiley, of the Inland South American Mission, who says that, in September 1934, in a village of the Kuikuris (or Cuycurús) he was shown a young boy with a white and not brown skin, blue eyes and close-cropped hair, whom an old chief said was a son of one of the Fawcett party and an Indian girl, a daughter having died. The Kuikuru Indians told the missionary that Colonel Fawcett stayed with them a year, and left in the direction of the Rio das Mortes.*

* A similar story is told by Miss Marthe L. Moennich, an American woman missionary She, in a book published at Grand Rapids, Mich., in 1942 (?), says she is convinced that "Providence has enabled her to solve the mystery of Colonel Fawcett's 'vanished party'. The half-caste boy (who she thinks is Jack Fawcett's son by an Indian woman) is named Dulipe. The Indians 'killed the Fawcett party, out of pity', shooting great arrows at them to save them from the worse fate of pushing into a country of the unknown where lingering death inevitably awaited them." However, here again, one is forced to bring in a verdict

It is known that Colonel Fawcett took great care to destroy all traces of camp-fires in the woods of the *catinga*, so as to leave no trail to be followed up by adventurers and reckless *garimpeiros* (diamond-diggers). He also, I was told in Rio de Janeiro, took with him an old Jesuit chart and a written account of one of the missioners who penetrated to a dead city in the central Brazilian highlands.

Then came a remarkable discovery. The Brazilian deputy of the state of Matto Grosso, Colonel Aniceto Botelho, found in the jungle of the Matto Grosso, near the camp of the Bacaari Indians—about the region where the Fawcett party disappeared into the unknown —Colonel Fawcett's theodolite compass, in perfect condition, *with no sign of mildew on the glass.* The Colonel might almost have laid it down in the bush on the day when it was found—in April 1933! At this stage, I cannot refrain from quoting from a remarkable letter written to me in February 1940 by the Colonel's devoted wife, Mrs. Nina Fawcett—his constant assistant in his scientific undertakings. Mrs. Fawcett, then in her seventieth year, is (or was recently) living in Perú where she had gone, partly in order to be within aeroplane flight of Brazil when—and who knows how soon that may be?—authentic tidings of Colonel Fawcett comes out of the unknown jungle of the Matto Grosso:

> "To me that (the discovery of the theodolite-compass) is reason to believe that *Colonel Fawcett was alive and working with his surveying instruments*—in the Matto Grosso jungle—*as recently as April* 1933. My husband was then alive and working, and probably had a certain amount of freedom, though under constant surveillance of the Indian tribe which, I believe, captured them about 1926 or 1927, and with whose people they were obliged to remain. This tallies with information received by a party of Italian surveyors, working for the government. That information came from native Indian sources and was sent to the president of the Royal Geographical Society in London, with a letter from the head of the Salesian Mission, who had good reason to believe the story—as I do also!"

Mrs. Fawcett told me (in 1940) that she was ready at any moment to fly to Brazil by air, in order to investigate what she would deem to be authentic tidings of the Fawcett party:

> "I came to Perú two years ago, to spend the rest of my life . . . I firmly believe that, at any time, someone may find one or

of non-proven, as to the *identity* of this party. Things may perhaps have happened, as the Indian told Miss Moennich; but the mystery is still unsolved; albeit Miss Moennich's story has been given a picturesque and pathetic "twist" by some Indian in a Xingu jungle. *N.B.*—I quote merely from a review of Miss M.'s book, in the London *Times Literary Supplement*, August 1, 1942.—AUTHOR.

other of the *watertight aluminium cases* containing Colonel Fawcett's diaries, or the watertight metal tubes containing his maps. The diary cases would be about six by four inches, and the region where I believe all three men, the two Fawcetts and Raleigh Rimell, spent many years, was on the Kuluene river, between or near the points where several affluents meet and join the Rio Xingu. According to an Indian story, which sounds *true* to me, the tribe with whom they stayed during many years are known as the Aruvudus, and the woman who gave the story to the Italian surveyors in the interior belonged to the Cuicurus, the tribe nearest in locality to the Aruvudus. I tell you this in case you might be making another journey into the interior of the Matto Grosso, when it would be well worth while your making inquiries and keeping eyes and ears open for traces of the lost diaries or maps in metal cases—to say nothing of traces of the lost men themselves. Of course, I should be anxious to hear any news . . . or, if I am no longer alive, you could communicate with my son . . ."

The last message sent to London by Colonel Fawcett contained the warning that he might not be heard of for two or more years. The approaches to the dead city in the mountains, were, he said, guarded by a strange race of troglodytes—small, squat negroes of ferocious disposition who were cannibals. They lived in holes and caves in the swamp country on the edge of the unknown land, some 100 miles' distant from the dead city. This race of aborigines were contemporary, perhaps, with the mysterious white people who built the dead cities of Brazil. May be they were the *autochthones* of the old Brazilian island. Though armed only with clubs, they were extremely dangerous, said Colonel Fawcett, and contact with them might prove out of the question.

This race of troglodytic aboriginals may be identical with, or akin to, the short, squat, hairy and negroid people who live in holes in cliffs and caves in the still unexplored and unknown region of the Rio Uapes, on the north-western frontiers of Brazil and the south-eastern borders of Colombia. Jesuit missioners are said to have encountered them in the 1920s in this very region. That they are dangerous and savage is certainly true, and very little, indeed, seems known about them among savants in Rio and São Paulo. Mr. Lewis Spence cites a letter he had from Colonel Fawcett, in 1924, when Fawcett says these cave-men intermarried with the Tupis and Caribs, their progeny being the negroid Botocudos of Brazil and the Aymara Indians of Bolivia.

Fawcett seems to have told no one where he located the dead city for which he was making. I have met people in Brazil who assert that the location was the *Serra do Roncador* (Snorer's or

Blusterer's range), which is marked, on some, but not all, maps as running in a northerly direction from the Rio Kuluesene towards the country of the Gorotiré and Tapirape Indians—an unknown and dangerous territory inhabited by savage tribes. The *Serra do Roncador* which maybe the snowy, or "White Cordillera" of the tradition of the Indians, would certainly have lain along the route taken by the Fawcett party, in April and May 1925; but the *serra's* actual location is very uncertain. No one, I have been told, in Cuyabá "ever returns alive from these *serras*. The approaches are guarded by *Indiós malos*, who beat drums and use the bush telegraph to signal the coming of intruders."

Few white men knew more than Fawcett about the habits and ways of strange Indian tribes living in unexplored forests and on the edge of primaeval marshes, months away from the remotest outpost. These tribes, he said, are not "the debased types of savages, found on the Andean slopes, contaminated with the white man's vices". He told the Royal Geographical Society, in a lecture, in London, in May 1910, about the Morcegos, or "bats", who sleep in great hollows in the ground, closed by wickerwork lids. All day they sleep, and emerge to hunt by night; but they can scent the stranger from afar. All bush through which he has passed will be burnt to the ground.

"Fire they know," he said on another occasion, talking to a friend in Paris (the late Dr. Arthur Lynch, soldier for freedom and Philosopher), "and they are armed with enormous bludgeons. Their keenness of vision is intense, but they cannot endure the rays of the sun. As for their powers of scent, the finest bloodhound falls below them." From another source in South America, the writer of this book heard of a remarkable adventure which Fawcett had with these "bats", who, resembling the curious troglodytes mentioned above, are about the lowest of the human race, and live in the wild country of forests, bush, scrub and marsh guarding the approaches to the strange White Mountains, where, perhaps, he had been told the dead city lay:

> "One day, we suddenly and unexpectedly found ourselves right in the middle of one of the bush villages of the *bats*. There were about two hundred of them sleeping in their holes, closed in by the basket lids; but our sudden approach had been made known. Our situation was extremely perilous. I kept as calm as possible, my face and bearing appearing as unmoved as I could make them. Tearing branches from trees in the forest, I soaked them in a spirit made from certain other trees. Then I set a light to the torch and danced towards the *bats*, shouting, at the top of my voice, a chorus from a famous music-hall song of the late 1890s: *Ta-ra-ra boom-de-ay!* The effect was almost magical. The Indians came out of their holes in the ground, and, regarding

me as a strange white god, bowed low to the ground. That happened in the morning. Before the fall of night, and the coming of the time when the *bats* hunt under thick boughs of the virgin forest, we had put the greatest distance we could between them and us . . . I had, not long before, met a man who had fallen among a Matto Grosso tribe a little less degenerate than the *bats*. This Brazilian was hunting for nuggets and gold dust. One day, on the bank of a forest river, he was rushed by a horde of these Indians, who had laid an ambush in the jungle. They trussed him up and tied him to poles laid across men's shoulders. His fate had no element of doubt in it. The Indians smacked their mouths and rubbed their naked stomachs, as they eyed him gloatingly. Arrived at the forest village, a woman of the tribe, who had lost her husband and whose charms had become a little faded, so that she could not secure another matrimonial partner, took a fancy to the whiter-skinned man. He was adopted as her paramour and taken into her hut; but he was so keenly watched he could not escape into the forest. His captors hunted at night, and slept in the day. They, too, had a sense of smell keener than a bloodhound, and could track men and animals by it. Months passed, and the shades of the tribal cooking pot loomed perilously near. His dulcinea had grown tired of him. What could he do? If he fled on foot, through the forest, unless he kept it up night and day, with no halt for food or sleep, these night-hunters would surely recapture him. A plan came into his mind.

"In the middle of the morning, when the Indians were fast asleep, the captive stole out of his hut, unseen and unnoticed by the bored fair one, and slung himself into the branches of a tree on the edge of the forests which stretched endlessly into the far distance. From tree to tree he went, like a monkey, until he had put about a mile between him and the camp. That was all he could manage in a day's strenuous work. Came night, and he lodged himself in the fork of a tall tree in the forest. The howlings of the monkeys and shrill noises of the insects, could not drown out another sinister sound below him: the Indians were on his trail. Next day, he resumed his flight through the tree tops, living on what fruit and nuts he could gather on the way. When darkness fell, he ensconced himself again in a tree top, and once more heard the Indians in full pursuit after him. For ten days he stayed in the tree tops, till he could safely put foot to the ground. Yet he spent two months wandering in the virgin forests before he met our party."

On his projected expedition to locate the dead city of the *bandeiristas*, Fawcett well knew that mules, carrying maize, would not get far into the *chapada* and the *catinga* of the Matto Grosso. There was little fodder in the forests around, and soon the men of the expedition would have to carry their own baggage, and jettison all that was not absolutely needed. (That jettisoning probably accounts for the instruments, gear and odd objects in the hands of Indians on the trail followed by Fawcett into the *sertão* of the Matto Grosso.)

About food Fawcett was not too fastidious:

> "There are plenty of snakes, and when your backbone hits against your ribs, a plate of snake-meat, under your famishing jaws, is not to be despised. Three miles a day are all we can cover in this wild country, until we reach more open landscape in the highlands of Brazil. After that, I hope we may find a stream which will take us to the Amazon. I find I can't take a radio transmitter, so shall have to be content with a receiver. It will help us establish our longitude in the unknown. Next time we come here, I'll take a hydroplane with me to travel the streams."

The Colonel and his son and friend, Rimell, passed away like a leaf on a stream, and concerning their fate, only rumours from the whispering gallery of one of the world's strangest lands have since been borne on the winds and waters of this unknown and dangerous wilderness.

The American explorer, Commander George Dyott, attempted to solve the mystery of the fate of the Fawcett party; but apart from the fact that Dyott's main purpose had necessarily to be concerned with securing literary and cinematographic material to pay for the cost of his trip, he could not play the part of H. M. Stanley to this Livingstone. For one thing, there was no Gordon Bennett, of the *New York Herald*, to finance him, and, for another, disgracefully little support and no financial aid has come from the British Government, in an affair of *real* exploration which a British national, Fawcett, had undertaken. Perhaps Fawcett was right, when he told the British Royal Geographical Society, in London, in March 1910:

> "Exploration is a matter of fashion, and South America is not in fashion. Here, however, in these days of luxurious equipment and perfection of organisation, the explorer of unmapped corners must return to pioneer methods and be content with his hammock and his rifle and what a kindly Providence will send him for food. I hope it will be Englishmen . . . who will follow the traditions and show the way."

Dyott, too, was gravely handicapped by entire lack of knowledge of Indian tongues in the Matto Grosso; so that he was not in a good position to check the stories told by chiefs of tribes through whose lands the Fawcett party may have passed on their way to the unknown.

After Dyott's expedition, other stories filtered through to the station of the Brazilian telegraph line crossing the Great Divide, south of the Matto Grosso.

For some reason, the British Foreign Office made a great mystery of the report of the Fawcett party's detention by the Aruvudu tribes on the Rio Kulusene, and hushed it up. In March 1934, a native Brazilian dog taken by Fawcett into the wilds to give warning of the nocturnal approach of wild animals, or prowling Indians, returned to the *fazendeiro* who owned him. The dog carried no message, but was emaciated and worn out, indicating lengthy travels. (But is it necessary to say that other reasons than the death of Colonel Fawcett might have caused the dog's return?)

About this time, a film actor, Albert de Winton, who had spent nine months in the Matto Grosso, trying to trail Colonel Fawcett, came back to Los Angeles, Cal., with only vague Indian stories about the Englishman. "But my belief is that he is still alive," said de Winton. Next, some *fantaisiste* in Moscow, who, perhaps, had grown tired of the Italian fable about the late Colonel Lawrence of Arabia accused of doing secret service work for the British Government in Arabia, Afghanistan, and Abyssinia, made an absurd statement about Colonel Fawcett:

> "He is a British secret agent in Brazil, and regularly sends radio reports to the Foreign Office, in London." (*Moscow Radio.*)

Later, reports were cabled and radioed to London and New York about a Spanish expedition with machine-guns, bombs, aeroplanes and dynamite, all set to solve the famous Brazilian mystery; but the Brazilian Government nervously demanded "safeguards" from that expedition. That year (1934) closed with newspaper stories about the well-known German, Doktor Eckener, planning to fly the *Graf Zeppelin* airship over the Matto Grosso from a base in Rio. He meant to survey the Rios Xingu and Tapajos, a colonel of the Brazilian General Staff accompanying him in the gondola. Unfortunately, that piece of romantic Jules Verne did not "come off"—for, as contemporary history records, lightning fired the hydrogen in her hull and destroyed her on U.S. territory.

Then General Rondon, the well-known champion of the Indians of the Matto Grosso—he is a Brazilian of pure Indian blood—told the press of Rio, in April 1939, that a chief of the Bacairy Indians told him that Colonel Fawcett had been killed in 1926 by the Anaqua Indians who had ambushed him in the region of the jungle of Rio Kulusene.

Were the mysterious mountains, called the *Serra do Roncador*—which, as I have said, above, I was told in Cuyubá, were the hidden objective of Colonel Fawcett—also the grave of his hopes and his party?

At this time, none can say.

The brothers Ulyatt, however, tell a curious story which purports that Colonel Fawcett's quest lay not on a hill-top, or bleak plateau, but in a valley. The story seems to be based on authority, and whether accurate or not, must mean that there are more than one of these dead Atlantean city ruins in unknown Brazil. These two brothers came in from the north-west, in the direction of the mysterious Rio Roosevelt. They avoided the other, western route into the Matto Grosso, which strikes over the Cordillera de Parecis, from Bolivia. Deep in the forest round the headwaters of the Rio Roosevelt and the Rio Branco, the brothers were one day startled by the growling of a dog they had with them. When they looked out of their tent, they found they were hemmed in by powerfully built Indians, armed with long bows and arrows. There was no mistaking the mien of these Indians. It was unfriendly. The chief clearly meant that the brothers Ulyatt were not to stand on the order of their going, but to make themselves scarce at once. By signs, it was indicated to them that if they were found to have returned, the Indians would kill them at sight in the dense forests. Everything they had was taken by the Indians, and the Ulyatts at once broke camp and got out of the region.

Said one of them (at a house in Rio de Janeiro): "The legend of this long-lost city of an Atlantean white race is that it lies on top of a hill; but really it is under water in the bed of a turbulent river, strewn with boulders that have fallen into it from towering cliffs. Mrs. Fawcett very kindly helped us with details of the Colonel's plans. I am sure the only practicable way of reaching the territory, where I believe Colonel Fawcett and his party still are, and where is the lost city, is by the route we came: from the north-west. We met Brazilian bushmen in the forests who are not in good odour with the Brazilian authorities. These bushmen are rubber-gatherers, but they never quit the rubber camps. They know about the missing Colonel; but not who he is."

With the Ulyatt story may be contrasted that of Signor Vialine. It is one more singular token of what a whispering gallery of rumours, seeming fantasy, strange romance, or myth is in the great South American cathedral of mystery. (Vialine's story was told in summer 1938):

"Signor Vialine, an Italian explorer, trying to locate the Serra do Roncador, which some folk say is the site of a dead city sought for in the Brazilian Highlands, by el Coronel Fawcett,

> says he saw skeletons of three white men, whom he supposes to be the Fawcett party................Mua Indians, says a Dominican missioner, at a station on the Rio Araguaya, killed Coronel Fawcett."

Mrs. Nina Fawcett, the Colonel's wife, is, I think, not only intuitively, but factually justified in holding that this seventeen-year-old mystery is still unsolved. As late as 1934, it was said that she had received telepathic messages from her husband, who, she thinks, was then still alive, but in captivity. The fate of the son of Colonel Fawcett and the young Raleigh Rimell has not been indicated in these messages, so far as one knows.

What was Fawcett's *main* purpose in taking this dangerous trip into the unknown?

Nothing less, as this narrative should have shown, than the discovery of an outpost of the drowned continent of Atlantis, in the wilds of unknown Brazil!

"Atlantis?" queries the scoffing and orthodox historian or archaeologist, with a sceptical lift of his eyebrows.

"It sounds like a fantasy by Mr. H. G. Wells, set in Brazil."

Well, let us see what is the evidence.

The reader may have noted that about half of the amazing inscriptions copied by the *bandeiristas* from ruins in the abandoned city of the Brazilian highlands, are identical with letters in the Greco-Phoenician alphabet. Nor can that resemblance, or identity, be merely accidental, or a coincidence. Unless the robust sceptic be prepared to take the hazardous step of suggesting that the Brazilian *bandeiristas* of 1753—who, after all, were rough, hardy, scarcely scholarly men whose object was the finding of gold and silver—were liars and forgers, for no conceivable purpose connected with self or any other interest, he will find it difficult to explain away these strange inscriptions. (The evidence rules out that the dead cities were Phoenician.) He has done his best to *ignore* them, ever since they were re-discovered by a Brazilian historian, burrowing in the royal archives at Rio de Janeiro, in 1841; but the time for tacit contempt or a conspiracy of silence has gone by, or will be, by the time this narrative appears in print. It will, and I ask my reader to pardon me for repeating this, make hay of his cherished illusion that *writing* was unknown in South America, before the arrival of the Spanish conquistadores and the Portuguese navigators, in the early sixteenth century.

The writer of this book has found some very curious links between the so-called "Old World" of Europe and Africa and the "New World" of Brazil. Some of these links may have been known to Colonel Fawcett, but at least one of them surprised so well known an authority on the "pre-history" of South and Central America as

Miles Poindexter, the Virginian senator and one-time American ambassador in Lima, to whom I showed it and them in the autumn of 1939.

The first link occurs in one of the books of the Sicilian geographer and historian, Diodorus Siculus, who flourished about 44 B.C. Diodorus, who is known to have visited Egypt, Carthage and the Near East, with which lands his histories deal, tells us how, thousands of years ago, Phoenician traders of the Mediterranean found a large island in the Atlantic Ocean, several days' sail beyond the Pillars of Hercules (neighbourhood of Jebel Musa (Abyla), North Morocco, and (Calpe) modern Gibraltar, Spain), and the western country of Africa. It was *from this continental island that the Phoenicians obtained the elements of their phonetic alphabet*, used, later, by the Greeks of Athens. Some thousands of years earlier still, and long before the Nilotic dynasties were recorded by the priests of Egyptian Heliopolis, Manetho the Mendesian (about 261 B.C.) said the Egyptians derived, from this now drowned continent, the elements of their hieratic hieroglyphics. May be, survivors had travelled overland to the Nile from North Africa, or the ancient Egyptians had had direct contact with the Atlanteans, said to have been a white, black and red-skinned people. It is more than likely that the lost books of Manetho, written largely from records and journals preserved in the temples of Egypt, would have thrown some light on the nature of this contact. (Since Manetho asserts that all the gods of Egypt had once been mortals and lived on earth, one may guess that the loss of his great and rationalist history is irreparable. And the like applies to the twenty-five lost books of Diodorus, which took him forty years to write and were partly based on vanished records of the priests of old Carthage and Egypt.) Diodorus says that he heard, in old Carthage (?), that the Phoenician traders founded a trading city at Gadeira* (modern Agadir, at the coastal end of the Great Atlas range in French Morocco), and while they were exploring the coast outside the pillars of Hercules, they were driven by strong winds a great distance over the ocean, "and, after many days, were carried on the island (of Atlantis?)".

Diodorus adds (Lib. V., p. 74):

> "Men tell us . . . that the Phoenicians were not the first to make the discovery of letters; but that they did no more than change the forms of the letters; whereupon the majority of mankind made use of the way of writing them as the Phoenicians devised."

---

* The place-names Cadiz, Agadir, and Gadeira are probably eponymous. Some colony from Atlantis to the mainland of old Europe and Africa therein commemorated the name of an old king of Atlantis—a man, not a god—whose name was *Gades*. (*Vide:* Diodorus Siculus.)

Since the walls and monuments of one of the dead cities, of unknown age, in the Brazilian highlands, bear letters, many, but not *all*, of which are so strikingly Greco-Phoenician in form, it is, perhaps, permissible to ask whether it was by the ocean-route that these same forms were carried, on the one side, to Brazil; on the other (by *Phoenician traders*) to the Mediterranean?

Diodorus, speaking of Atlantis, says:

> ". . . it is an island of considerable size, a number of days' voyage to the west . . . the dwelling-place of a race of gods, not men. In ancient times this island remained undiscovered, because of its distance from the other inhabitants of the world. . . ."

Then, Ammianus Marcellinus, a Greek geographer contemporary with the Roman emperors Julian and Valens (fourth century A.D.), while enumerating the different sorts of vulcanism, says:

> "It was by a *chasmaties* (in which the force of the commotion opens gulfs in the earth and swallows a whole country) that there was engulfed, in the profound night of Erebus, an isle in the Atlantic sea that was more spacious than all Europe. . . ."

Elian, the Roman sophist and compiler (died A.D. 140), quotes from Theopompus, a Greek historian of Chios, of the fourth century B.C. who, says Elian,

> "speaks of a continent, infinite and immeasurable, which the ocean circumscribes. The men who dwell there have more than twice our stature and days. . . . Two cities are there, one peaceful, the other warlike. The warlike city sent ten million men to invade Europe."

Both the pious city and the warlike had plenty of gold, which "is of less value than among us".

Theopompus was a contemporary of Plato and may have drawn on some lost source wherein legend and folk-lore is intermixed with some vanished truth of pre-history: the fly caught in sea-amber.

But something saved from what has been lost about the history of Atlantis, as well as the ancient continents of South and North America, is found in what the Greek Plato tells of the travels of Solon, the legislator of Athens, and of whose family Plato was a member. (Solon wrote a poem about Atlantis, which was preserved for many years in Plato's family papers, but has long been lost.) Solon visited Egypt about 548 years before the Christian era. In the dialogues of Plato (especially in *Timaeus*), it is said that the island-continent of Atlantis was greater than both Libya and all the Near

East. "It was easy to pass from Atlantis to those islands, and thence to all the countries bordering on the Atlantic Ocean." The dialogue tells how Sonchis, an agèd Egyptian priest of Sais, or Thais, in the Nile delta, deplores to Solon that when the Greeks and other nations began to have letters and the elements of civilisation,

> "after the usual interval the stream from Heaven like a pestilence comes down and leaves only those of you who are destitute of letters and education and know nothing of what happened in past times."

The old priest went on to say that the sacred registers in Egypt had been founded 8,000 years before, and the early Athenians', 9,000 years before Solon. The Egyptian sacred registers, perhaps kept by the priest Psenophis, at Heliopolis, told of a great navy sailing out from Atlantis, transporting an immense army of Atlanteans on an expedition which was planned to achieve a world-empire. This militarist expedition from the Atlantic ocean continent reached as far east as Egypt, and as far north-east as the coast of ancient Italy, in Etruria. One nation alone finally opposed these ambitions of world-domination: the "ancestors of the Athenians". . . . Then there occurred "violent earthquakes and floods, and in a single day and night of misfortune, all your warlike men, in a body, sank into the earth, and the island of Atlantis in like manner disappeared into the depths of the sea".

The old priest of Sais, or Thais, referred to those sun-stone people of heliolithic culture which the late Professor Sir Grafton Eliott-Smith speaks of as existing about 15,000 B.C., in regions of the Mediterranean valley, long since submerged. The ancient Egyptian priest adds these remarkable words, which must point to the existence of South and North America as recorded in the sacred registers of the old priests of Egypt:

> "That other sea beyond what you call the straits of Heracles is the real ocean, and the surrounding land may truly be called the boundless continent."

Remember that these words were spoken by an old priest of Pharaoh's Egypt, some 2,530 years ago; and that the catastrophic events he describes had happened about 9,000–10,000 years before that! All this, as one hopes to show, has its bearing on what these *bandeiristas* of the year A.D. 1753 found in the *sertão* of modern Brazil. It has, also, one hazards, some connection with the traditions of the Toltecs (Ana*tol*ians), the ancestors of the Aztecs, that they came from Atlan, or Aztlan. The great storehouse of Mayan and Central American legend and mythical history, the *Popul Vuh*, tells of a happy land of the golden age where ancestors lived in great peace and happiness, speaking the same tongue, till they migrated east and west. The *Popul Vuh* also tells of three sons of the King of the Quichés, of old Yucatan-Guatemala, who visited

> "a land in the *east*, on the shores of the sea whence their fathers had come, and whence they brought back, among other things, a system of writing. . . ."

One of the South American colonies of Atlantis may, probably, have been the land called Brazil, and Brazil, indeed, was actually the ancient name of the land and one borne thousands of years before the arrival at Rio de Janeiro of old Pedro Cabral, the Portuguese navigator. That occurred in A.D. 1500 and has given rise to the sheer legend that King Emanuel of Portugal named the land Brazil, because the dye-wood, brazil-wood (*Biancaea sappan*) was found there. As a matter of very curious fact, the name Brazil was known to the old Irish Kelts,* and an Irish saint, of the year A.D. 780, told Pope Zacharius—who demanded his excommunication for the "impious" statement—that the old Irish (the oldest split-off from the original Keltic race-stock) habitually communicated with a transatlantic world! Brazil, also spelt Bracie, Berzil, or Brasil, appears in maps of the Middle Ages as an island west of Corvo, in the Azores. The famous Medicean *portuolano* of A.D. 1351, and the charts of Picignano (A.D. 1367) and Andrea Bianco and Fra Mauro record it. There is, too, a *Brazil* rock, some degrees west of the southern extremity of Ireland, and this brings us to an experience of the author of this book.

A few years before the World War No. 2, I was in a southern county of Eire, of Ireland of the former Irish Free State, when I heard the story of the old Irish myth of *O Breasal*, or *Hy-Brazil*—the paradise of the Gael, the land far in the direction of the sunset, over the Western Ocean from the Arran Isles. That legend dates back to the days of the roamings of the old Irish, who, I repeat, are the

* It is an amazing fact, one not known to archaeologists or the conventional South American historians of British or American, or European nationality, that, in a remote mountain valley lying in the Southern Andean cordilleras, somewhere west of Miraflores and San Rosario, in North-Western Argentina, is a tribe of "Indians" speaking pure Gaelic or Erse! They are emphatically not emigrants from modern Ireland or Scotland, for their ancestors were in that region ages before the arrival of Spanish conquistadores. I met a colleague in a Civil Defence wardens' post, in 1943, whose Irish uncle, while on the pampas of Argentina, in 1910, met and talked with these Indians who are called *Patanian Indians* (Indiós Patanios), or Patanian Irish. The uncle spoke Erse well, and for some time lived and worked on the *Pampas Enthral*, near Miraflores. Some members of this tribe of Patanian Indians have the blue eyes and reddish hair of the Irish Kelt. Others are nigrescent. It is known that Indians in the region of modern Maryland had traditions of a strange people, living in their territories, who spoke the old Irish tongue, and worked metals. Pity that the Irish cleric—he was Fergil, or Ferghil, or Vergile, Bishop of Salzburg—did not indicate the source of his information about the far voyages of the old Irish, or sketch in the details of a picture which must now remain forever a rare and fascinating glimpse of a world of very ancient date from which a small corner of the veil has thus been lifted—and dropped. —AUTHOR

earliest branch to separate from the Keltic root stock, in Europe. On a forbidding mountain called Callan—noted for its "hideous moory height"—used to stand what is known as the Ogham stones, cut with old Irish, or ancient British letters. The peasants in the cabins and bogs, round about Callan mountain, have a legend about a tomb, in the mountain, containing the bones of an Irish king, Conane. Find the tomb, say the bog-trotters, and you will discover in it a key which will cause to rise out of the Atlantic Ocean a great city, sunken there. The city was named *Hy-Brazil*, or the Royal Island. I found, too, that the Arranmore islanders, off the coast of Galway Bay, have a legend that, on a clear day, this island Paradise of the ancient Irish can be seen afar on the horizon, glittering on the Atlantic waters. . . . Says one of the Irish bards:

> "it is the meadow of the Dead, the land of happiness and peace which you must pass the sea to reach . . . a beautiful land where a happy race, free from care and sickness and death, bask in eternal sunshine".

About 1,500 years ago, the old Irish Saint Brendan set out from the Abbey of Clonfert to find Hy-Brazil, in a ship with fifty monks, sailing over the western ocean. They found it, after a seven-years' voyage,

> "the fairest country a man might see, clear and bright, neither hot by day, nor cold by night, the trees laden with fruit, the herbage glorious with blooms and gay flowers. . . ."

And still the search went on for this happy land of Hy-Brazil, which figured on the early English charts. Even as late as A.D. 1650, General Ludlow, one of the regicides of Charles I., and Cromwell's general in Ireland, heard about this paradise of Hy-Brazil, and actually chartered a ship to look for it! The ship was chartered at Limerick, not far from the very place where the legendary vision was seen. Columbus had heard of it, under the name of the Isles of the Blessed, and it started him off on his voyage to the West Indies.

Who knows whether the old Irish Kelts came into contact with the people of Brazil, in South America, at a time when the jungle city found by the *bandeiristas* was in its prime—or far gone in old age and decline?

Colonel Fawcett's theory seems to have been that old Brazil was probably the cradle of our world's culture and civilisation; but it must remain, for the present, a moot point whether the torch was not, indeed, taken from the drowned island-continent of old Atlantis to her continental colony of Brazil. (On the basis of our present dim knowledge, the truth cannot yet be known.) Assuredly, the name

Brazil is far older than Cabral and the finding of the dye-wood, called *brasileiro*.

The naturalist Buffon believed that Ireland, the Azores and America were once part of the great lost island-continent of Plato, a belief, as to America, shared by the famous Brasseur-de-Bourbourg, and it is curious that the old Irish myth of *Hy-Brazil*—the royal land, or island—enshrines a story of a Paradise of the Gael, far across the western ocean.

How came it, too, that Fawcett found the mysterious writing incised in a rock in Ceylon's jungles?

Had some vanished race in that strange and beautiful island a contact with old Brazil or Atlantis, or some other drowned or vanished continent, and is this stone, in the Sinhalese jungle, a record of lost history, and not a mere cypher-script of a vanished Oriental priesthood? It may be so; for the ancient Egyptian priests can hardly have been alone in inscribing pillars, or rocks, with records of lost history. There is, indeed, an ancient tradition that Ceylon, or the Taprobane of Ptolemy, the geographer, is a fragment of a drowned continent. Pliny said that ancient Taprobane "is considered as the commencement of another world". There is also a forgotten Byzantine historian who said:

> "Taprobane is the island nearest located to the continent where was the former terrestrial paradise."

Possibly, these strange Brazilian ancients had carried the torch of civilisation and culture westwards across the Pacific, when there may have existed a land-bridge* with Ceylon. However the orthodox archaeologist may frown or smile at these theories, I should ask him or her to explain how such forms, obviously similar to Greco-Phoenician letters, could have been found by these rude Brazilian *bandeiristas* of A.D. 1750. They were hardly classic scholars. Indeed, as the old canon of Bahia noted, they did not seem to have had the ghost of an idea of the significance of these strange letters.

Ben Jowett, with his mid-Victorian dogmatism and positiveness, slandered Plato by talking of the "noble lie of Plato", about this lost world; but the more scientific attitude—one nearer the modern spirit, which, in our day, does not scoff at old traditions and deride them as total and childish legends—is that of Alexander von Humboldt, who wrote, more than a century ago:

---

* Was that long-lost land-bridge the *Rutas* of the Brahminical traditions of old Hindostan? This *goparam* tradition says that, hundreds of thousands of years ago, an immense continent in the Pacific was destroyed by volcanic upheaval, and that the displacement of the ocean-waters converted the then great islands of Hindostan adjacent to a central Asian divide, into the modern peninsular, sub-continent of India. *Rutas*, the lost continent, was the home of a highly civilised race who gave their alphabet to the old Hindus. *Rutas* is distinguished, in this very ancient tradition, from Atlantis, existing, as the tradition says, in the northern portion of the tropics in the Atlantic.

"Des mythes de l'ancienne limite occidentale du monde connu peuvent, donc, avoir eu quelque fondement historique. Une migration de peuples de l'ouest a l'est, dont le souvenir, conservé en Egypte, à été reporté à Athènes, et celebré par des fêtes religieuses, peut appartenir à des temps bien antérieur à l'invasion des Perses en Mauritanie, dont Salluste a reconnu les traces . . . et que, également pour nous, est enveloppée des tenèbres."

("Some of the myths of the ancient bounds of the known world of the west may, then, have had some foundation in history. A migration of peoples from the west to the east, whose memory, preserved in Egypt, has been transmitted to Athens, and celebrated there by religious festivals, may belong to a time much anterior to the invasion by the Persians of Mauritania (Morocco), of which Sallust recognised the traces . . . and which, also for us, is shrouded in darkness." *Translation.*)

In 1839, when these words were written, the world knew nothing about this lost MS. in the royal and imperial archives of Portuguese Rio de Janeiro!

I have left to the last my comments on one very eerie feature about these dead jungle cities in the highlands of Brazil. Just before Colonel Fawcett left Cuyabá, the frontier town of the Matto Grosso, an Indian approached him, and told him that the churches in that town were nothing in comparison with the far bigger and better buildings he, the Indian, had seen, with his own eyes, in the dead cities of his remote forest-home.

Said he:

"These buildings in my forests are of great age, *Señor.* They are loftier by far than these" (nodding at the town), "and they have doors and windows of stone. Their interior is lit up by a great square crystal on a pillar. So brightly does it shine, *Señor* Fawcett, that it makes the eyes blink and dazzle. It is a light that never goes out. My forefathers knew it of old. Always it has burnt undimmed."

Fawcett proposed to turn a little off his trail in order to visit such a light-pillar: "It is a tower-like building, says the Indian, which has partly fallen down, from the doors and windows of which always shines a light."

Now, light-pillars, as in the famous Pillars of Heracles, at the ancient bounds of the known sea-world, are a mark of sun-worshipping race. I have seen such a pillar, inscribed with Phoenician and other more mysterious characters, standing on a bleak down in the Cotswold Hills, close to Bisley, Glostershire, where, down below, in a lovely wooded combe, anciently stood a sun-temple, known to the Romans, but built by the Silurian-Basques. One Brutus, the Pauch, or Phoenician—Pauch, being the Hindu for Phoenician, the latter being not a Semitic, but an *Aryan* race—came there and stamped out devil-worshipping which had sway in the Stroud Valley around 2000 B.C.* Of course, the ancient pillar bore no light when I saw it; nor is anything left of the sun-temple save a red finial, I have handled, and ruins built into a farmhouse wall. But that it did bear such a light, night and day, thousands of years back on those Glostershire uplands, there can be little doubt. Similar lights, guides to wayfarers by day, and sea marks for mariners at night, anciently burnt on the lofty Furetana pillars of the Macares (Carians, with Melcarth for a god of the sun and fire), which stood, some thousand or more years ago, in the Colombia Highlands of South America. This ancient Brazilian white race of sun-worshippers may have known some way of eternalising a "cold" form of light. Whatever it is, or was, the method is unknown to modern science. It is believed by some people that the ancient Egyptians knew of such a form of physical energy and applied it to light their pyramid interiors. Whether or not Ezekiel had this in mind when he spoke of that "terrible crystal" of the Nile and old Egypt, who shall say?

Occult testimony, derived both from psychometric means and from traditions still current among certain mysterious brotherhoods in the East and in Egypt, is that the great central temple-cathedral of the capital of Atlantis—called, by some, Sardegon—which was engirdled by seven great mountain ranges, was built of a *white, shining stone* common in Atlantis. We may, therefore, surmise that the same stone was used by her imperial pioneers, or that its repute had so impressed men in her colonial outposts that the ancestors of the old Quichés, who may have had personal contact with the Atlantean pioneer-civiliser, Quetzalcoatl, the man in black, in Central America, associated the motherland, and, perhaps, her great imperial colony, Hy- (or Royal) Brazil, known to the old Irish Kelts, with great cities and imperial palaces and majestic temples shining in the sun, as its rays poured down on the glistening façades and colonnades. May be, or may be not—*quien sabe?*—we may have a chance to verify the truth of these traditions of extreme and shadowy antiquity, when, or if, as certain mystics say, Atlantis will emerge from the bed of the Atlantic, after 10–12,000 years of submersion, in the coming one hundred years, an event which, it is forecast, will

* This statement is, in part, based on the curious fact that the site of this ancient temple of the sun-worshippers of ancient Britain—Silurian and perhaps pre-Silurian—is close to a very pretty hamlet called *Customs* Scrubs. Now, the word *Customs* has nothing to do with manorial affairs of Anglo-Saxon or Norman times; for, some miles away, is a place called *Customs* Mede, near Standish, Glos. In each case, the first element in the name relates to an ancient custom, or rite, related to burning fire on sun-pillars, or the ancient *bealtine*.—AUTHOR.

coincide with the final war named Armageddon. Certainly, if the Second World War be not this Armageddon, it is a very close approach to its horrors!

It is significant that Quetzalcoatl—a man in black, *not* a god nor a nephilem, exactly as was the man Osiris deified later as an ancient Egyptian saviour-god—who came from the east, the land of Hy-Brazil, or perhaps Atlantis, the motherland, to give laws and the elements of civilisation to the savages and barbarians of pre-cataclysmic Central South America, is said, in a very ancient Quiché MS. and in the *Popul Vuh*—the Mayan bible—to have come from the other side of the sea from the place called "Camuhibal". Camuhibal, says the ancient MS., is the place of the *white* or *shining lights or life*. (*Quiché:* zak gazlem: zak = a white thing). It was also the place of the *shadow of colonnades*, or, in Low Latin, the *obumbraculum*, or a colonnade, or covered stone way with adjacent buildings, suitable for a promenade in the heat of the day.

There is no need to smile at Colonel Fawcett and call this story a mystical fantasy of his. The Brazilian forest Indians are not really accustomed to flights of imagination of this sort. If one of them told Fawcett he had seen such a fixed, strange light burning in a ruined building in the deep jungle, why, he probably *did*! Besides, if we are to believe St. Augustine and Cedrenus, the old Byzantine chronicler, "perpetual lamps", or lights, were by no means unknown to the ancient Egyptians, Romans and Greeks. St. Augustine says that such a lamp was in a fane of Venus in Africa. Old Memphis had many of these perpetual lamps, burning in the mausolea of the mighty dead. It was a symbol of the immortal soul, and ancient Egyptians are said to have believed that the astral soul of a mummy, hovering round a sepulchre for 2–3,000 years, might, at the sight of such a lamp, be induced to break the magnetic chain binding it to the dead body, and unite with the spirit. Plutarch says he saw a lamp of the sort in a temple of Jupiter Ammon, where, said the priests, it burnt, in all winds and rain, for years and could not be extinguished. In the time of Pope Paul III, of Rome, it was said that a tomb, opened in the Appian Way, was found to have in it the body of a beautiful girl swimming in a bright

> "liquor that preserved the lovely limbs and face, life-like. As the tomb opened, there was seen a lamp, which at once extinguished itself. It was said to be the body of Tulliola, daughter of Cicero."

I leave modern physicists to make their own comments about the theory of the old alchemists that such lamps could be created by reducing gold to an oily fluid, whereon in a properly made lamp, the gold re-absorbed its oily fluid and gave it out again. Of course, the word "perpetual" must not be taken *too* literally, and interpreted as conflicting with the law of conservation of energy. Allah and the prophet forbid that any scientific gentleman, whose eyes should scan these lines, perchance, should charge me with such scientific impiety! Yet, in a day when radio has become a commonplace, and the ends of the earth speak war and blood and foolishness, B.B.C. "humour", bawdiness and propaganda to each other, would a shining light, like this in the Brazilian jungle, be more wonderful than the unknown life-ray, which, in 1930, I saw functioning in a lonely house close to Doorn, Holland, and whereby meat, eggs, cut flowers, milk could be kept fresh and the bacteria of putrefaction eradicated, for months on end—so long as the ray was emitted from the transformer?

God is great. The world hath in it many wonders, which are not *all* known to scientists—or even the archaeologists. The day may come, sooner than one may now suppose, when some English-speaking explorer will come across one of these strange, fixed lights in an ancient Brazilian dead city of the jungle, and doubtless be reminded, for his pains when he reports home, of the life and trials of Baron von Munchausen and poor Louis de Rougemont.

It seems clear that the catastrophe that overtook these dead but once shining cities of ancient Brazil was of such an appalling nature that it drove everyone forth from them. Everything was left behind. Bars of silver and gold were thrown to the ground, in panic haste, by men thinking only of how to save their lives. It may be that the catastrophe was accompanied by terrific tidal waves, and vulcanism of a frightful character, general not local, such as might be caused by the approach to the earth of a body from outer space. Indeed, a lost book of Varro (referred to in Chapter I) confirms the strange tradition of the Aztecan "legends" that the planet Venus was seen to be changing her colour, shape and course hourly. This really indicates that some violent change in the orbit of the earth had taken place—such a change that, whereas, before, all rain fell in the night, and so rainbows were never seen, *after* it, the rainbow was taken as a new symbol of the intervention of gods and goddesses appalled by the horrors that had been brought on the earth, by their master, the *Demi-ourgos*. (Of course, as I have already said, were the men, before the Deluge, saints or devils, and the ancient myths hint that they had become degenerate, that would not have halted the catastrophe of natural forces by an ell or an inch. What would be would be!)

Was this cosmic body, adrift in space, our *Moon*? It may be; because a tribe of Indians met in Guiana, by Humboldt about 1820, said their ancestors existed before *the Moon*—like the Arcadians—and this may mean what it imported in ancient Arcadia, and not a too ingenious interpretation of an old Greek text alleged to confuse

Selene (the Moon) with the Greek word meaning pre-Hellenes. (*Vide* page 29, *supra*). It is also significant that Diodorus Siculus, the first-century B.C. historian who drew on archives in the old temples of Carthage, which probably recorded traditions and prehistory derived by the Phoenician and their close kinsmen the Carthaginian mariners voyaging the Atlantic, after the destruction of Atlantis, tells us of Basilea, sister of Atlas, one of the Atlantean kings—a man not a god, as she was a woman and not a goddess—who married her brother Hyperion, the sun or Lucifer, in the fashion of the later ancient Egyptian Pharoahs, and bore him Helio (the sun) and Selene (the moon). Basilea's brothers of Atlas slew Hyperion and drowned the child Helio (the sun), lest Hyperion might take the throne of Atlantis. Maddened by these murders, Selene cast herself from the top of a mountain and perished, while Basilea lost her reason, and when her Atlantean subjects tried to restrain her, a frightful hurricane, with lightning and thunder, arose and she vanished.

If we euhemerise these myths, we might say that what they import is that some cosmic body, whether or no Selene, the Moon, approached our own planet, the Earth, after the Sun (Helio) had vanished behind vast clouds into a night of blackness, and brought on an appalling cataclysm—the Great Deluge of the Old World myths and *Genesis*—in which Queen Basilea, symbolising the great island-continent of Atlantis, was seen no more of men.

In the imperial continental colony of Hy-Brazil, of the pre-cataclysmic Brazilian highlands, it is probable that many of the people of the dead cities were swallowed up in the frightful crevasses of the ground produced by violent quakes—such as the *bandeiristas* of A.D. 1743 saw. May be, too, many were asphyxiated by poisonous gases arising from eruptions and smoking craters. Some of these ancient cities must now lie below the level of the Marañon-Amazon basin. If no or few artifacts have been found in the ancient houses, or palaces, Time may long ago have rotted them away. Who knows, too, what later roamers plundered these dead cities and left memories of what they saw in ancient petroglyphs and rock-pictures found in wild *cañons* and cliff-faces from Oregon to old Perú?

In any case, these dead cities of old Brazil must be of incredible age, and destructive of theories that South America, in the era before the Christian, had no civilisation. Many of the riddles of their emptiness and utter desolation cannot be solved until we know far more about them than the 1750 story tells. After all, the *Relatorio* deals with only one dead city, while there are known to exist others. Fawcett kept what he knew to himself; but Time, that reveals many things and destroys others, may yet roll up the veil from the mysteries of a wonderful civilisation that cannot have been far behind our own—not that *we* have much to boast of when we have to record the glories of two World Wars in less than half a normal healthy man's or woman's lifetime! And it is a disturbing coincidence that ancient "myths" stress that the catastrophes of thousands of years ago were preceded by gigantic wars, and that men wandered forth warning of the wrath to come, of which these wars were the premonitions. But for the World War No. 2 it is likely that far more attention would have been devoted by scientists, now obsessed with and pre-occupied by war work and research, to the world-wide quakes, year after year since 1939, stretching from the Mediterranean to Perú and Los Angeles. It is already suspected that German submarines, caught on the bed of the South Atlantic in one of these volcanic convulsions, failed to make any port in 1940–41. Let us hope that the law of averages will fail to rule in this present year 1944–5.

Mr. Lewis Spence tells us that Colonel Fawcett wrote him: "I have good reason to know that these original (white Atlantean) people still remain in a degenerate state. . . . They use script and also llamas, an animal associated with Andean heights above 10,000 feet, but in origin a low country, hybrid animal. Their still existing remains show the use of different coloured stones in the steps leading to temple buildings and a great deal of sculpture in demi-relief."

It is exceedingly curious, one may say in passing, that the Amazon white women of South America, of whom I shall speak at large in a subsequent book to be published by Messrs. Rider and Company, are, in unpublished sixteenth and seventeenth century Spanish MSS. I shall there cite, also associated with similar architectural remains, and with a mysterious animal, not found elsewhere, reminding us of the llama, which Colonel Fawcett says the degenerate descendants of this ancient white and highly civilised South American still use today!*

Mr. Richard Oglesby Marsh, a distinguished engineer and scientist, former U.S. Secretary of Legation and chargé d'affaires at Panama, who has made scientific explorations from Bolivia and over the Andes into the headwaters territory of the Brazilian Amazon, has arrived at conclusions similar to my own about this very ancient Matto Grosso civilisation. He thinks that it was from this ancient Atlantean type of Brazilian civilisation of bearded men and beautiful women that the Mayans, and, later, the Incas, derived their cultures. He has found that this ancient Hy-Brazilian race used the same names for the zodiacal constellations that are used today. There are South American geologists, too, who point out that the Roosevelt tableland, on which this ancient civilisation founded their dead cities, has been above sea-level probably long before the Glacial periods.

Mr. Marsh believes that this ancient race, traditions of which and their mighty empire ranged from the Atlantic to the Pacific

---

* We owe to this great race the *cultivated* banana, which has no seeds, but is propagated from suckers. It is *alone* found *wild, with seeds,* in Brazil, and is called the *pacoba*. The Atlantean Brazilians introduced it into old Atlantis and what are now the Canaries.

shores, are today crystallised in the folk-lore of Brazilian Indian tribes. When the cosmic convulsion rendered these great stone cities uninhabitable—and its mephitic nature is clearly indicated by the bottomless crevasses found in the plazas and among the ruins of the shivered dead city found by the *bandeiristas*, in A.D. 1750—the climatic conditions were such that great reptiles, extinct elsewhere on the earth, moved in, making the places as Isaiah's home for the "hairy dragon". Before long, the green forest covered all of the old Brazilian highlands.

In fact, if the modern Indians be believed, this great plateau, more than 1,500,000 square miles in area, one of the largest and most dangerous unexplored regions of the globe, has rivers and great swamps where dinosaur types still wallow and leap on their gargantuan prey, much as is depicted in the late Sir Arthur Conan Doyle's novel, *Lost World*—referred to in a later chapter of this book. The same Indians, between the Rio Araguaya and the Rio Roosevelt, and Amazonas and the Goyaz plateau, an extension of the Roosevelt tableland, even assert that the forests of this unknown region are the home of other giant mammals, of monsters of fearsome character! All of which, of course, suggests that in this very ancient Atlantean-Brazilian world giants and monsters of the slime wallowed on its tropical fringes!

It is certainly not without significance that the *sertão*, or hinterland of the Brazilian state of Bahia, wherein, as I have said, the *bandeiristas* of the year A.D. 1750 found one of these Atlantean dead cities is, in parts, covered with the remains of monstrous, extinct animals overtaken by some great catastrophe. And the duration, too, of the great civilisation represented and connoted by these extremely ancient and splendid ruins, which, as Fawcett himself said, are something very much more than merely megalithic structures of some Pelasgian race of Ogyges, is suggested in the significant fact that in the same region will be found, either apart or in combination, both ideographic or hieroglyphic scripts and alphabetical signs. The history of ancient Egypt herself proves how long a span of years must bridge the gap between the hieroglyph or the ideograph and the alphabetical letter. Time's ever rolling stream bore much away ere this amazing race of Atlantis Brazil had created the first alphabet. Some of us may remember how the late Mr. Reid Moir was greeted with ridicule and scepticism when he said that man existed in the Pliocene Age tens of thousands of years earlier than science supposed. Yet, in 1936, the same Mr. Moir was elected a Fellow of that august and high and dry Olympian society, the Royal Society of England. It may seem that the like chronological correction may later have to be made in relation to the age of culture and civilisation. For, as the famous hymn says, so much, like the sons of Time, "flies forgotten as a dream dies at the opening day".

(1) High priest of Tiahuanacu with stairway, or "evolution" sign on sides of mitre. *Note* enlarged ear-lobe of Easter Island type. (*Vide* also No. 15, page 132.) (2) Tiahuanacu warrior with Egyptian slant of eyes, on ancient metamorphic slate under palace ruins. Note "Earth" sign on chest found (2*a*) today among Indians in Koaty and Sampaya Islands, Lago de Titicaca, Perú. (3) Native Peruvian *adoratorio* (wayside altar) at Carangas, the stairway evolution sign of

One might even wonder whether the walls of cyclopean cities of this ancient race were built as a protection against what monstrous serpents or marine lizards might swim out of the deeps against them? *Quien sabe?* Such negro autochthones as existed behind the ancient civilised regions would hardly have been regarded as serious adversaries, any more than a Zulu or Maori, in their tribal panoplies, would be a match for, say, a modern "tank-busting" gun, or low-diving bomber! As their civilisation had been extended by Quetzalcoatl to Central America, some significance *may* also attach to that queer clay dish which was dug up in San Salvador, a few years ago, and on which is a picture of men flying above a group of palms in curious machines, leaving a trail of smoke behind them, and which look remarkably like *flying-machines*!

Monsieur Lecointe, former French consul-general at Para, has made independent discoveries of his own in the *inferno verde* of modern Brazilian Amazonas. They include enormous stone discs divided into sections and covered with hieroglyphs. He has photographed some of these stones, which he calls "*solar disks*" of an ancient sun-worshipping race. Was it this ancient race that left the remarkable prehistoric obelisk, covered with drawings in many colours, found by Señor Julio Tello, near Trujillo, North Perú, in 1933? Was it they who left that *simbolo escalonado* (sign of the staircase), denoting evolution towards some sort of god-head, which is found in ancient, pre-Inca Perú, on remarkable ceramics in the island of Marajó (mouth of the lower Amazon), Brazil, and in Alaska and Patagonia, and is evidently of great age? The sign is also found, to-day, embodied in the wayside altars, or native *adoratorios* of the Quechua Indians, descendants of the old Incas, in the Peruvian Andes. Was it they who built the ancient forts and aqueducts in the Andes east of Cuzco, and left, with gold objects and ceramics, the small tubes of a material like glass, but not glass, and of unknown chemical composition, which have recently been found in ancient graves (*huacas*) at ancient, ruined Intihuantan, about ninety

---

Tiahuanacu. (4) Image of giraffe head found under Tiahuanacu ruins. (5) Image of fossilized human bone found under deluge-alluvium, Tiahuanacu. It bears on chest the *Earth* sign of the warrior and civilian castes of Tiahuanacu. (*Vide* also No. 14, p. 132.) (6) Volute of stairway-evolution sign of Arouwak Indians —possible descendants of the Tiahuanacu ancients. (*Vide* also Nos. 3 and 19 (latter on page 132.) (7) Unknown extinct animal (glyph) found in hidden catacomb, Easter Island, and on ancient pottery, Trujillo, Perú. (8) and (9) "Rayed" head-dress petroglyphs found, 1933, by Marshall Field Expedition, in the Sierra de Santa Marta, Colombia. (*Vide* also page 140.) (10), (11), (12) Petroglyphs in Sierra de Santa Marta, Colombia. (10) Has affinity with signs of Marajóense (prehistoric Brazilian–Lower Amazon) symbols on funerary ceramics, and with Egyptian sign of the goddess Neith, mother of sun-god Ra, *Raymi* (Peru), and Vi-*Ra* in Atlantean Brazil. (11) and (12) Stylized petroglyph heads recalling the *psenth*, or royal coiffure of ancient Egypt, and the nimbi of Christian saints.

miles from Cuzco? (The Incas and their predecessors knew not glass, or how to make it.)

We do not yet know. It will be the task of future British and American scientific explorers to clear up these mysteries of ages so remote that they "crowd on the soul", as visions of dead glories of incredibly ancient worlds that the modern evolutionist is reluctant, or refuses to suppose may have been antecedent to the glacial epochs.

The reader may recall the remarkable statement of the old *bandeirista* that the statue of the colossus he saw in the dead city had his hand outstretched towards the *north*! When this MS. first saw the light in the archives of a historical society in Rio de Janeiro, in 1840, this reference to the north led a Copenhagen professor to suggest that the strange letters were runes, and that the Scandinavians had reached ancient South America. So impressed was the King of Denmark that he even detailed a warship to go to Rio and land a lieutenant who had orders to go up-country and find these statues and the dead city of "Hyperborean" suggestion.

Here, one may recall that the Jew prophets Ezekiel and Isaiah located the ancient Paradise and Garden of Eden in the *north*; but if the reader glances at a map he will see that north of Brazil corresponds to that very *Amenti*-land of the dead, paradise of the ancient Egyptian—and the Kelt, under another name of Royal (or Hy-) Atlantean Brazil!—which the people of the Pharaohs said lay to the west of the Nile. Moreover, there was a *Men*, who was twelfth king in the calendar of the Mayas, in whose country—Guatemala—was a *Nile*, who corresponds closely with the *Menes* of ancient Egypt who built the temple of Memphis and turned the course of the Nile of Egypt!

Brazil, the old and mysterious, seems to be the ancient land which was, perhaps, the cradle of the world's oldest civilisation, may be 60,000 *years ago*, in a day when our own European ancestors were living in caves in the (then) far warmer regions of what is now Pyrenean France, Cantabrian Spain, or lacustrine Switzerland. It, too, is the Mecca of the treasure hunter, prepared to risk death in very unpleasant forms in order to trail the whereabouts of ancient gold mines, or lost mines of platinum, which latter appear on cryptic charts and *derroteros* made by wandering Jesuit *misioneros* of the late sixteenth and seventeenth centuries, and deposited in the old viceregal, Lusitanian archives, now found in the Biblioteca Nacional in Rio de Janeiro. Many of these lost mines, or caches, lie deep in the virgin forests of Brazil. Some of them were the quest of those hardy and valiant land-pirates, the *bandeiristas* of São Paulo, who waged war on Jesuit *misiones* and *reducciones*, where mining was done by the Fathers, with Indian aid, in the seventeenth and eighteenth centuries.

When I was in Rio, in 1938, I heard about a French engineer,

Apollinaire Frot, who had gone into the unknown region, west of the Goyaz plateau, to search for some very ancient gold mines. For half a century, Frot had hunted these ancient mines, and, in the course of his wanderings, had stumbled on ancient rock inscriptions in Amazonas and the Matto Grosso woods which, to his amazement, revealed the amazing fact that the *ancestors* of the ancient Egyptians were of South American origin, and had left these petroglyphs as *portolanos* to the location of the ancient gold mines they worked, and which are now shrouded in dense bush and lianas, haunted by poisonous snakes, loathsome insects whose bite is pathogenic, and dangerous animals. In some cases, swamps of vast size border the ancient mines, and, here again, if Indian stories are not entirely mythical, tracks, "huge and recognised", left in the slime of the marshy beaches by monsters of mesozoic type, leave no doubt as to what sort of lost world lies behind. (I shall refer to this aspect of mysterious South America in a subsequent book.)

Other inscribed stones, almost obliterated after thousands of years, have been found in these unknown jungles of Brazil, and purport that Phoenicians and their kinsmen, the Carthaginians, also wandered this way, thousands of years ago, trading and hunting valuable mineral lodes. Before my reader scouts the idea of these revelations of antique civilisations in South America, he or she must remember that more than 2,000 photographs of these ancient petroglyphs have been made by Frot and native pre-historians in Brazilian wilds, and that the inscriptions range from hieroglyphic (demotic or hieratic forms) to cuneiform or proto-Phoenician forms, such as have been found cut in caves in the Canary Islands, or are codified in Gesenius's *Scripturae Linguaeque Phoeniciae monumenta*.

Frot had been exploring these wild woods of Brazil since he was a youth. It was in the province of Amazonas that he came on an ancient carved rock hidden by dense jungle close to a river, which recorded the journey of a proto-Egyptian priest to what is now Bolivia. The ancient inscription went on to speak of Proto-Egyptian silver mines, located in what is now the basin of the Rio Madeira (south of the Madeira falls). These *portolanos* in stone must be the oldest treasure charts known. One of them reads as follows:

> "Look out with care for a high hill on whose summit are six palm trees. Close by the foot of this hill, thou wilt find yet another carved rock telling thee of what lies ahead on the road to the mines of gold we worked."

Stage by stage, these *portolanos* in ancient stone ran across Central Brazil, from some very ancient, proto-Egyptian port which must have been located between Bahia and Rio de Janeiro. In the plateau of Goyaz, on the edge of the mysterious wilderness which has never at any time been under sea or ice, and which, today, is known as the Roosevelt tableland, Frot found one of these stones, while he was running down an old Carthaginian trail. The clue of the hieroglyphics led him to a very ancient gold mine, in the middle of a virgin forest too thick for him to penetrate. Indeed, many of these ancient Brazilian-Bolivian gold mines, today, are buried in the middle of ancient woods. Frot* says his inscriptions prove that the ancestors of the Egyptians, long before they passed to Africa and the Nile, had established an ancient South American empire, ranging from what is now Bolivia to Bahia. So, while the treasure hunter is deeply engaged in trailing down caches of proto-Egyptian gold bars and ingots in South America's jungles and foothills, he may, by chance, blunder on some enigmatical obelisk of unknown age, carved with hieroglyphs and covered with multi-coloured drawings in imperishable pigments, such as Señor Julio Tello found near Trujillo, Perú, in 1933. Or, he may drop on a *huaca* (ancient treasure tomb) wherein he may find, as did Berliner archaeologists, eighty miles east of Cuzco, towards a Bolivian border and *terra incognitaa*, peculiar ceramics or tubes made of some material like glass, but not glass, being of unknown chemical composition.

One of the native Indian races of Brazil are the people of the Tapuya. It is possible that these Tapuyos are the descendants of a white helot race, serving the ancient Hy-Brazilian master-race, and sharing with them the exodus following on the Great Catastrophe, when Atlantis was engulfed. Southey in his *History of Brazil* tells of a Jesuit who, administering extreme unction to a very old Indian crone, asked if he could get her anything to eat. Said the old crone: "Father, my stomach rebels against food, but if you could only get me the tender hand of a little Tapuyo boy, I think I could pick the little bones; but woe is me, there is nobody to go out and shoot one for me."

Thus, while the descendants of the master-race of Hy-Brazilians lived to be exterminated (in Lake Titicaca, Perú), by savage Colloans of Carian descent, their helots became the food of cannibal Indians, and their children delicatessen for queasy old Brazilian Indian harridans sanctified for the Heaven of the Jesuits. Fawcett, as Mr. Lewis Spence says—and I trust he will forgive me for again quoting from one of his excellent books on Atlantean pre-history—spoke of these Tapuyos, in the east of Brazil, as refugees from an older civilisation—that civilisation I here style Hy-Brazilian. He said: "These Tapuyos are fair as the English. They have small feet

* It is to be feared that Monsieur Frot has left his bones in the unknown Matto Grosso where (I heard in Rio in 1938) he was on the trail of dead cities and ancient monuments. These lands are no substitutes for academicians' padded chairs in great libraries and museums, salons and offices. H.M. Ambassador in Rio de Janeiro informs me, June 1944, that Monsieur Frot is deceased.—AUTHOR.

and hands, delicate features of great beauty, and white, golden and auburn hair. They were skilful workers in precious stones and wore diamonds and jade ornaments."

Mr. Spence and other readers may, in this connection, compare Fawcett's story with what I myself relate about the remarkable adventure of the man of Medellin, among a similar white helot race, somewhere on the confines of unknown North-Eastern Brazil. (*Vide* pages 49–53 *supra.*)

One last very curious fact shows that a corner of the mantle of the culture of these ancient and highly civilised Hy-Brazilians has fallen on a tribe of modern Indians who, today, dwell in a creek and peninsula of Lake Titicaca. These Indians are Colloan or Aymara Indians, whose ancestors—as Cieza de Leon significantly recorded in the year A.D. 1535—exterminated some very *old*, *bearded*, white-skinned people who had taken refuge on an island in that lake, many centuries before the Spaniards irrupted their banditti-soldiers on old Incaic Perú. The old Spanish missioners found that these Indians of the borders and shores of Lake Titicaca possessed a very ancient form of ideographic writing inscribed with the juice of a plant, called *Solanum aureifolium*—the native name of which is "Nuñamayu"—on animals' skins, and, later, on paper. The old missioners turned a breviary of the Catholic faith into this script, and, among the ideograms of these Koaty Island (Moon Island in Lake Titicaca) and Sampaya Indians, one notes the signs following:

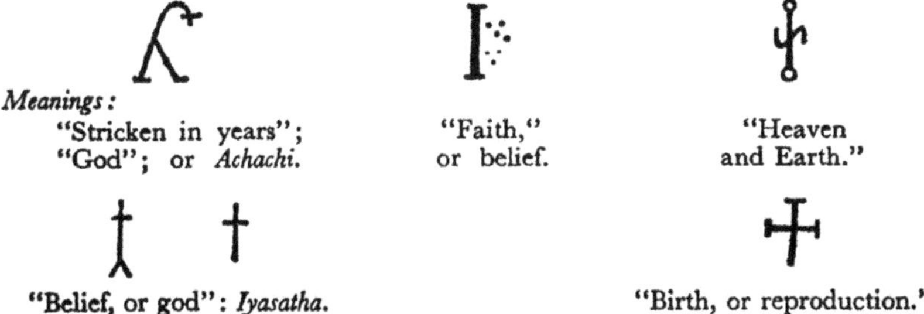

Meanings:
"Stricken in years"; "God"; or *Achachi.* — "Faith," or belief. — "Heaven and Earth."

"Belief, or god": *Iyasatha.* — "Birth, or reproduction."

The reader can compare the above signs with those found on the walls and monuments of the dead city of the Portuguese *bandeiristas.* (*See* pages 43, 45, 46, *supra.*) He or she may also note the significant fact that others of these ideograms of the Aymara Indians of Lake Titicaca and borders exactly correspond to unknown and very ancient rock signs found at Ferro (Canaries); among the Touaregs in the North African Sahara; to letters in the Ethiopian alphabet; rupestrian inscriptions at Thugga, part of the old empire of Carthage, in North Africa; and to one letter *Kaph*, in the Sidonian alphabet used in the cities of old Phoenicia of Tyre. In particular, the curious *dots*, above, *also* appear in rock inscriptions at Thugga, Sahara, in the deserts of the strange race of the veiled men of the Touaregs, and old Numidia. These forms have gone half-way round the world from the land of old Brazil, lively evidence of travels and unknown travellers of a very ancient world whose existence is hardly suspected even by our modern world and encyclopaedic historians.

CHAPTER IV

MISSIONARY MEN IN BLACK: FORERUNNERS OF THE GREAT CATASTROPHE

TRADITIONS ranging right round the world, from China to Colombia and old Perú, from the jungle and forest lands of Central America to old Burma, speak of mysterious men in black, from some far-distant highly civilised land, who suddenly appeared in the streets and highways warning the people of the eastern and western world of wrath to come, and the destruction of the rich, powerful and decadent cities of the plain. Both in Asia and old South America, they seem to have made their apocalyptic advent in a day when neither the mighty Himalayas nor the Andes had reached the cloud-topping heights at which they have been standing since the days of modern and written history. Chronology, even approximately correct, is, at this time, impossible to establish. All we can say is these men in black vanished, apparently as suddenly as they had appeared in America and Southern Asia, prior to 11,000 B.C., when Atlantis was submerged and the cities of Hy-Brazil, her royal and imperial colony, became, as the Hebrew poet said of other ages and peoples, annihilated in:

> " . . . The day of the Lord's vengeance . . . the streams shall be turned into pitch and the dust into brimstone, and the land shall become burning pitch. It shall not be quenched by night or day. The smoke shall go up for ever and ever. . . . The cormorant and the bittern shall possess it . . . and he shall stretch out upon it the line of confusion and the stones (or plummets) of emptiness. They shall call the nobles thereof to the kingdom, but none shall be there. Her princes shall be nothing. Thorns shall come up in her palaces, nettles and brambles in her fortresses; and it shall be a habitation of dragons . . ."

Had such a poet and prophet a vision of men, of a far distant day, sounding with plummets some bottomless well in just such a stone city of the unknown dead, as did the old *bandeiristas* of Lusitanian Brazil in the year A.D. 1750?

As other traditions, current in the mystic East, say of these lands of the morning of our world:

> "These great centres and cities of the plain became so degraded and corrupt, that it was impossible to purify them, and they were swept away by the besom of the wrath of the Great Central Sun of the Cosmos."

But it seems probable that when the men in black were preaching and civilising in Central America, on the western side of America, and in South-Eastern Asia, the giant disaster that wrecked the cities of Atlantean Brazil and the motherland of Atlantis was still an age away. May be, the general feeling of insecurity after a minor, but still terrifying volcanic upheaval of the earth's crust in Hy-Brazil, and ranging along an earthquake belt to the motherland of Atlantis, had sent them forth on the orders of their rulers. One can hardly conceive that the lands had sunk to the decadence pictured in the old myths, unless these men in black were merely the missioners of a decent minority of Atlantean folk. None can yet say. We know not.

Colonel P. H. Fawcett, who, with his son and son's friend, Mr. Rimell, may be presumed to have perished—there is no definite information either way, but only what amounts to a legal presumption, in the lapse of nearly twenty years—in the gallant effort to solve the mystery of the Atlantean Empire in old Brazil, points out an amazing fact about the tremendous age of this high civilisation of Hy-Brazil, Royal Brazil (or Imperial Atlantis), as the old Irish Keltic wanderers called it. He says that the ancient native Brazilian name for the Rio Amazonas, the Amazon, which is *Marañon*, was originally borne by the Mexican Gulf, in a day when *an arm of that gulf must have extended to the Amazon*. It is significant, too, that another old native name for the Mexican Gulf was *Orinoco*, the name borne by the great river of Guiana-Venezuela. The remote day when the Mexican Gulf reached to the Amazon was during the heyday of Atlantean Brazil, or Hy-Brazil, the royal colony of the great motherland.

The pioneer Quetzalcoatl, who, probably, came from Atlantean Brazil on a civilising mission to barbarian and savage Central America, was, it may be necessary to repeat, as the myths of ancient Mexico make clear, a man, *not a god*. One may call him a *divine* man, later deified as was Osiris, and the other gods and goddesses of the Egyptian Nile, who, as Manetho showed, were merely men and women who had achieved great pioneering and cultural works. The ancient Mexicans said Quetzalcoatl came to them from a land to the *south-east*, and that his symbol was the feathered serpent. It will be remembered that the serpent was found carved in stone in some parts of the dead Atlantean city in Bahia province. Slightly varying accounts are given of Quetzalcoatl.

Father Bernardino Sahagun, the famous missioner and historian among the Mexicans, after the days of the conquistadores, was told:

"Quetzalcoatl had a dark countenance, all his body was clothed in a shirt wrought like a surplice, that did not reach to the girdle of the waist. From the knee to the leg was covered with buskins of tiger-skin, ornamented with sea-shells. He wore sandals."

Fray Juan Torquemada, the Franciscan missioner, who collected traditions about Quetzalcoatl from the natives of old Mexico, among whom he worked in the years after the Spanish conquest, says:

"Quetzalcoatl, it is held for certain, was a man of upright character, elegant carriage and was white and blonde (*blanco*), with a ruddy face (*rubio*) and bearded. His beard was long. He was of benevolent disposition and learned, and a great personnage. His hair was long and black. . . ."

Torquemada, however, in the same rare book, *Monarquia Indiana*, says:

"Quetzalcoatl had *blonde* hair, and wore a black robe sewn with little crosses of red colour."

The Mexican *Codex Chimalpopoca*, written in the native Nahua tongue (and already mentioned in Chapter I), seems to suggest that there had been several (three) attempts from some land across the eastern sea to civilise the savages and barbarians of Central America; but that all had failed before Quetzalcoatl came on the scene. This seems to be borne out by the discovery, in A.D. 1927, by the American Indian Foundation Fund diggers, of remains of a great temple, beautifully coloured pottery, stone monuments and idols, or statues of men, all lying under many feet of volcanic ash, and far more ancient than Mayan or Aztec civilisations. These remains must be at least 12,000 years old. They were found in the Cocle province of Panama state.

According to Torquemada, twenty chiefs, led by a great man, Quetzalcoatl, arrived "out of the blue", one day, from the *north-west.* (?) They landed at Panuco, now a village about twenty-five miles south-west of Tampico, in Vera Cruz. . . .

"They were men of good appearance, well-clothed, in long garments of black cloth like the cassocks of priests, open in front, but without the cowls, the neck cut in crescent shape, short sleeves, but wide, with nothing at the elbows. This dress the natives use, today (in seventeenth century), in their dances and ballets, in imitation of these ancient folk. These latter went forward from Panuco, showing good manners, giving no occasion for war or fighting, stage by stage, till they reached Tullan, where the natives of this province received and lodged and entertained them."

The country from which they came, according to the *Popul Vuh*, or Bible of the Quichés of Western Guatemala, was in the *east*, "where red and white men lived in joy: their aspect gentle and sweet, their language pleasant, and their minds very intelligent".

Torquemada says the men were Toltecs, and that their leader, Quetzalcoatl, had come from a land not submerged, but one which the ruling class considered so unstable, owing to occasional cataclysms, that they looked out for a settlement elsewhere. On this point, it will be recalled that Colonel Fawcett pointed out that all the dead cities of Brazil had been overthrown by violent earthquakes.

Clavigero, another colonial Spanish historian of Mexico, describes Quetzalcoatl as high priest of Tula, capital of Tulteca. . . .

"He was white in complexion, tall and corpulent, broad in forehead, with large eyes, long, black hair, thick beard: a man of austere and exemplary life, clothed in long garments, gentle and prudent. He was expert in the art of melting metals and polishing precious stones which he taught the Tultecans."

Quetzalcoatl established contact with the powerful Central American race of the Toltecs, or Nagualecas; and, says Torquemada in a chapter headed, "De la Poblaçon de Tulla y su Señorio":

"They were men great in stature, excellent gold-and-silver smiths. When they landed at Panuco, Quetzalcoatl was at their head and they marched inland, under his direction. They built the splendid city of Tullan, with fine and beautiful houses, temples and palaces, all of the greatest magnificence."

The Toltecs intermarried with the natives of the country, and by command of Quetzalcoatl, colonised other parts of Central America. Tollan, says the native historian Ixtlilxochitl, was a place of fine palaces and temples. The kings of the country—this might fit either the motherland of Atlantis, or the great colony of Hy-Brazil, and it is part of the Deluge Myth found all over the world—grew licentious, and the provinces revolted. The gods were wroth with king and people, and great frosts, followed by heat, visited the city. The crops perished, rocks melted, and plagues finished the ruin. (Frosts are seldom experienced in Mexico.)

Eight leagues north-east from Mexico City is the plain anciently called the "Path of the Dead" (Micoatl). In it are two lagoons dedicated to the sun (Tonatiuh), and the moon (Metzli). Hundreds of pyramids surround these lakes, forming streets in dead-straight lines, running east-west, north-south. On top of the Mexican *teocallis*—a truncated, or polled pyramid, with a temple atop—stood two colossal statues, one to the sun, the other to the moon. Plates of gold sheathed the stone and the statues fairly dazzled the eyes. Naturally, the gold-hungry Castilian soldiers of Cortes stripped off the gold, and the statues were destroyed by a fanatical Spanish Franciscan priest, bishop Zumaraga, who broke up every "idolo" he could see.

In Anahuac was found the great Teocallis of Choluhuan. It is described thus, in an unpublished Spanish MS., by Don Pedro de los Rios, written in A.D. 1556:

> "In the interior was a square house, built of stone, pillared with beams of cypress. It contained—in the beams—two human skeletons, and there were idols of basalt, and curiously painted and varnished vases. There was no outlet, and the step-work was of bricks. An altar at the top was dedicated to the white-bearded man Quetzalcoatl; but the Indians say the pyramid was not originally meant to serve for the adoration of Quetzalcoatl."

This MS. has a curious story to the effect that the Teocallis was a Tower of Babel, and that a hymn was sung, there, by the Cholulans at their festivals, which began with the words: *Tulanian hululaez*. These two words are of no dialect known to Mexico, and are strangely like the Jewish *Alleluia*. Lescarbot heard a song, with the words *Aylo* or *Alleluia*, sung in Central America, which is singularly like the *Ya-Laylu* of the modern Copts of Upper Egypt, and the Arabic *hallal* and Peruvian *quillal* (moon). *Liniac*, in Quichua, Peruvian dialect, means gods of lightning and thunder, so that some people have gone so far as to suggest that the ancestors of the Inca Peruvians came to America across the land-bridge from the African shores of the Atlantic. Altogether, it is hard to resist the conclusion that this Mexican Tower of Babel was built some time, probably long ages, after Quetzalcoatl went back to the south-eastern land from which he never returned.*

* It is curious that in one ancient Mexican myth, Quetzalcoatl, like certain mahatmas and elusive sages of modern Tibet and the Himalaya recesses, is said to have periodically repaired to a Fountain of Youth, in the land of Tlalpallan, where he drank and recovered from the ravages of old age. American legends call this mystic land: "Place of the Shining Sands". It was variously cited as the Bahamas island of Bimini; Florida (where Juan Ponce de León sought it); and other American regions. The Red Indians of North America placed it somewhere to the East, which might fit either Atlantis, the motherland, or one of her Central or South American colonies. Prester John, the monk of Far Cathay, is alleged to have written a letter to the Byzantine emperor Manuel, locating the fountain as about three days' journey from the Paradise whence Adam was expelled. Saturn, whom Diodorus speaks of as a god-king (or man) of Atlantis, was turned from a white-haired man to a boy, or a man in the prime of life, by drinking of the waters of this mystic fountain. It would be curious if this same legend of the "Fontana de la Juventud" should be found, today, among Brazilian Indian tribes. In any event, the myth dated back to a pre-cataclysmic age.

Quetzalcoatl, and other Atlanteans from either Hy-Brazil or the Atlantis motherland in the Atlantic Ocean, were in the ancient dead city of Palenque, Chiapas, the frontier state of modern Mexico, but that ancient town with its palaces, temples, waterways, bridges, and pyramids existed long ages before the Mayas came there. It is at the other famous Mayan town, or dead city of Chichen Itza, in Yucatan, well known to American archaeologists, that there is found a significant memorial to Quetzalcoatl: he is represented, in stone, as *Atlas* supporting the world. And, as is known, Atlas gave his name to the drowned Atlantean island-continent. Quetzalcoatl and the other men from Atlantean Hy-Brazil made the Central American country so rich and fertile that it was said, in an old Quiché chronicle: "a head of maize was a burden for a strong man to carry."

Then there came a change in the spirit of the scene. The time of the Great Catastrophe was drawing nearer. A deadly enemy of Quetzalcoatl, one Huemac, of the strong hand, landed at Panuco with a great army and marched on Quetzalcoatl's city of Tullan, or Tollan, not Cholullan, located on the shores of a great lake. Like a very modern totalitarian dictator in Europe, or like the grinning savages of modern Japan waging a war of pure aggression on peace-loving, civilised China, Huemac of the strong hand burnt and ravaged all before him and left the people with only their eyes to weep.

Wherever he passed, great cruelties were done, and great tyrannies set up, say the old Spanish chronicles, derived from the native traditions, which are, possibly, confused, or are have gone off the rails, with native traditionalists, in identifying the Toltecs, which were led by Huemac, with the men in black led by Quetzalcoatl. More likely, the men in black were Atlanteans, or "builders" from Hy-Brazil, or Atlantis, and *not* Toltecs, who are confused with them, as "builders", in the myths. Anyway, Huemac established the Toltec power in old Mexico, and it did not fade away till some 465 years before Cortes landed in Aztecan Mexico, and ruined the succeeding Aztec civilisation whose last emperor was the ill-fated Montezuma.

Fray Bernardino Sahagun takes up the story, at this point:

"The day came when Quetzalcoatl persuaded the Toltecs (?) to go out from the city of Tullan. They left it at his order, although they had been there a long time, and had built fine and beautiful houses, temples and palaces, all with the greatest magnificence, and even possessed great riches in all the places where they had spread. Departing out, they took their leave, abandoning houses, lands, cities, riches; for, not being able to take all away, they buried much riches and gold under the earth, whence one draws it out today, full of admiration for the excellence of their works. Obeying the orders of Quetzalcoatl they went, pushing before them, with infinite difficulties, their wives, and sick and old, none making resistance to his commands. All went on the road, immediately Quetzalcoatl came out of Tullan to go up to the region of Tlalpallan, whence he never returned. . . ."

Torquemada was told that Huemac reigned in Tullan for seventy years after Quetzalcoatl quitted it; but, he varies the story of Sahagun by saying that Quetzalcoatl left Tullan in a rage because of the evil end he foresaw to a place which had become licentious, and that it was from Cholullan, where he abode many years, that he finally went to the sea. From Cholullan, Quetzalcoatl had sent out men who colonised Yucatan, Tabasco and Campeache and Onohualco by the sea—and, as bas-reliefs and totem-poles show, what is now British Columbia. There, these colonisers "built most splendid and great Roman edifices as at Mixtlan (Hell, in the Mexican tongue), which show that these men were of great intellect and powers who constructed these fine buildings". Quetzalcoatl, as Torquemada suggests, may have become an old man weighed down by the burden of years and weary of exercising a wisdom and skill which seemed likely to become a vanity and vexation of spirit. . ."when he departed from Cholullan, he pretended that he was going to visit other provinces that he had sent men to settle". However that may be, Huemac of the strange land, in a rage that Quetzalcoatl had removed himself from his reach, slaughtered all he found, and such fear came on men that they . . .

"worshipped Huemac as a god, endeavouring by that to darken and destroy the form of ritual that Quetzalcoatl had already bequeathed to that city".

There was also an ancient Mexican tradition handed down by the far later Aztecs* or Nahuatls, that the first settlers in ancient Mexico and Central America were *white people*. They were subsequently conquered by invaders of a dark-skinned race who drove them out from the land, forced them into ships and saw them sail away for a far-off land to the east, in the direction of the rising sun, where they settled. The natives of Guatemala, at the time of the Spanish conquest, also had this tradition:

"When King Quetzalcoatl, of the very white race, was conquered by an invading race with dark skins, he refused to

* There is reason to suppose that some of these Aztec tribes used polished mirrors of quartz or obsidian as heliographs to flash messages about Cortes and the men of his expedition!

surrender. He said he could not live as a captive, nor submit to savagery. So, with as many of his white people as could crowd into his ships, he sailed to a *far distant country towards the rising sun.* He reached it, and with his people, settled down there. They prospered and became a great race. During the great battle (in old Central America) many escaped into the forests and were never again heard of; but the rest were taken prisoners, and enslaved by the dark-skinned men."

To this there was a curious Aztecan tail-piece about the ultimate coming of a saviour from the land to which Quetzalcoatl and his white people had gone in their ships in the path of the sunrise:

"In a time to come, this white people shall return and again master this land (of Central America and old Mexico)."

An echo of a time of cataclysm is also found today in another region of Guatemala's forests. The late Dr. Thomas Gann noted how natives at the village of Pichek, near Rabinal, refuse to handle ancient figurines, jade statuettes and antique ornaments and the like, which, they say, "were made by an ancient people, allied with powers of evil at a time before the sun shone in the sky, when people could find their way about the dark earth only with torches". The natives of today say these antique figurines are endowed with life. Indeed, these *idolos* are used by the modern witch-doctors, or *brujos.* An Indian at Rabinal told Gann that there are great numbers of these figurines and relics in the ancient ruins, but that they appear only on Mondays and Thursdays, and even then run back into the ruins and hide, unless the proper incantations are said.

It is possible, though it cannot be proved, at the moment, that this race, "allied with evil", may have been identical with the unknown people of extreme antiquity whose remains are found, today, up the Rio Grande in Southern British Honduras, and whom Dr. Gann believed had Mayan links. (I am inclined, myself, to fancy that this mysterious race—possibly either emigrants from old Atlantis, belonging to the races outside the ruling aristocratic castes of that island-continent, or migrants from old Atlantean, colonial Hy-Brazil of Quetzalcoatl—may have contacted the mysterious Mayans (who had Mongolian traits superimposed on a more Aryan or Caucasian ruling type), at a time when they (the Atlanteans) had lapsed into degeneracy. Dr. Gann calls them the "Columbia race".)

He says these mysterious people never had any close connection with the Mayans of the old or later empire. They built citadels on hill-tops, left no burial mounds, but innumerable figurines of men, women and children of all classes, in their costumes. They flattened the hill-tops and erected these citadels on terraced mounds, faced with stone. There are rectangular sunk courts lined with blocks of cut stone, in these ruins, and approached by stairways of stone. Similar structures are found in ancient ruins in *Ceylon* and Angkor Wat (Cambodia). (*Vide*: Colonel Fawcett's discovery of the ancient inscribed stone in Ceylonese jungles, page 61 *et seq. supra*). Many subterraneans exist in these Guatemalan ruins, of stone blocks dovetailed each into other with no cement bonding. There is, in one ruin, a fine amphitheatre with tiers of stone seats for 6,000 people. The best seats were on a stone pyramid reserved for the king, nobles and high priests. Among the figurines are images of fishes, birds, beasts and *dragons*. The women wore tight skirts, ankle-long, and heavily embroidered bodices cut low and exposing the breasts. Their arms are bare or short-sleeved to the elbows. The men and women wore round ear-plugs with tassels, and the women also wore jewelled collarettes, beads and pendants. Both sexes are shown dancing together in quite modern style. One figurine is that of a woman holding a drum between her legs and beating it. Another is of a woman apparently suckling, at her breast, a little animal. There are on stelae dominant figures, as of rulers and conquerors. No one can read the writing they used. Rows of hieroglyphs are on the statuettes, and they are quite different, says Dr. Gann, from any in America, though some seem Mayan. Their land was about 3,000 square miles in area. Their society ruled by caste, and their religion was as unique as their writing, and certainly *not* Mayan. Not even a tradition of their existence remains, and the land they once occupied is under dense forest.

Are they, again, some of the people whom Quetzalcoatl tried to humanise, and in despair of whom he went back across the "Red Sea", to the land—Hy-Brazil, or Atlantis of the ocean, from which he came?

Much research will alone settle this point, if it can be established after all these ages. One gropes in the dark with only a fugitive ray occasionally penetrating the gloom.

Then, again, what unknown and mysterious race built the very ancient Central American city of which my friend, Mr. William S. Taylor, retired constructional engineer, of Seattle, Washington, tells me?

I believe the ruins of which he spoke to me are still to this day—1945—unknown to modern Mexican archaeologists.

Says Mr. Taylor: "About the year 1902, when I was manager of an engineering project in Georgia, I had a master mechanic working for me. To get relief from the arduous grind of the daily job, I used to have talks with this old roamer about a subject in which I grew mightily interested: the ancient things of old Mexico. He told me about a vast prehistoric city in ruins some way south-west of Mexico

City. No one has ever been able to visit it, after repeated attempts, and I'll tell you why. It was destroyed by tremendous earthquakes ages ago, and all the people in it perished. The quakes threw up a circle round the ancient city, of some miles in circumference. This circle consists of high, precipitous mountains completely girdling the city. All the buildings therein have long ago been destroyed as by some cataclysm. But the landscape otherwise remains unchanged. It is extremely difficult to get near these ancient ruins; for a man can pack in only enough grub to carry him half-way across the *known* area of the sierra. Several expeditions setting out from Mexico City to explore these ancient ruins have failed even to sight them.

"My old roamer said to me:

> " 'I went there with an expedition which planned to reach the high cliffs of the mountains overlooking the place. I took a job as extra carrier. We managed to reach these cliffs, and from a height right over the ruins, looking down on the floor on which they lay, I watched, as I lay down and rested. In every direction I saw nothing but a jumble of cut stone building blocks. I quit the expedition, and never heard what luck they had, or any more about them.' "

So many modern writers on the antiquities of Mexico have repeated, parrot-fashion, the conflicting statements of these old Spanish and Mexican historians, that it is easy to see why even authorities, such as Lewis Spence, have confused Votan with Quetzalcoatl, called Huemac of the strong hand only another name for Quetzalcoatl, and have wrongly identified Tullan with Cholullan, a city which was a considerable distance from Tullan, the town to which Quetzalcoatl came when he marched inland from Panuco on the Gulf of Mexico.

The (Aztec) *Codex Vaticanus* makes Quetzalcoatl the *son of a virgin*, thus exactly paralleling the Mediterranean myths of the dark-white race of Southern Europe who invariably bestowed this "supernatural distinction" on great men whom they subsequently deified.

> "Proceeding on his journey (from Cholullan), Quetzalcoatl came to the Red Sea, which is painted in this codex, and which they named Tlalpallan, and they say that, on entering it, they saw no more of him, nor knew what became of him. They say it was he who effected the reformation of the world by penance: since, according to his account, his father had created the world, and men had given themselves up to vice, on which account it had been frequently destroyed. It was Citinatonali

who sent his son into the world to reform it. . . . They celebrated a great festival on this sign, as we shall see on the sign of the four earthquakes: because they feared that the world would be destroyed on that sign (or date), as he had foretold them when he disappeared in the Red Sea, which event occurred on the same sign (or date)."

The *Popul Vuh*, the Bible of the Quichés of Central America, has also another Atlantean tradition, which may be cited here. This remarkable book is associated with Votan and the Votanes, who, I beg to repeat, must not be confused with Quetzalcoatl, with whom Lewis Spence and others have identified him. Votan, or Odin, or Woden, a man deified as a god, probably hailed from the Old World of Mediterranean Europe, or Punic Africa, and he probably furnishes a clue to the fact that puzzled Colonel Fawcett and others: the existence of tribes in old Brazil who worship the Scandinavian god *Odin*! His cult had clearly travelled far south beyond the land-bridge of Darien and old Panama.

In this tradition, the *Popul Vuh* tells of three "god-men", Balam-Agab, Mahucutch and Iqi-Balam, who came to ancient Central America from "the other side of the sea where the sun rises". . . . "They had been there a long time, when they died, and already they were very old men (or men who were venerated) called the high priests. . . . Afterwards, the princes of the Quichés bethought themselves of going to the East, conformably to the wishes of their fathers, which they had never forgotten."

The *Popul Vuh* goes on to say that these princes took wives long after their fathers were dead . . . "and later said: Let us go east, whence our fathers came, and they took their road". Their names are given as Qocaib, Qoacutec and Qoahau, sons of the god-men above. Brasseur-de-Bourbourg theorises that these ancient princes took the road towards the gulf of Honduras, perhaps a little above Livingstone.

Says the *Popul Vuh*: "They went by design and wisdom and took leave of all their brothers and relations, and parted full of sadness, saying: 'We shall not die; for we shall return.' And when they arrived in the East—for without doubt they passed over the sea—they received royalty. Now, here is the name of this Lord, the King of the Easterns: he is called Lord Nacxit of Ranaual, the sole judge, whose power is without bounds and to whom they conceded the insignia of royalty, and all it represents."

Brasseur-de-Bourbourg says that Nacxit was Quetzalcoatl, whose kingdom extended afar and was known as the "Empire of the East". This is a vivid glance at old Atlantis and her great colonial American empire! The insignia mentioned were "tents or baldaquins, worked in gold and studded with gems or ornamented with precious feathers;

flutes, and other instruments; powders of various colours*, perfumes, the tiger chief, the bird, the stag, the shells, pine-knots, trumpets, the royal emblems of the herons' plumes, the art of painting of Tulan, and its writing, they said; for that had been preserved in their history."

Therefore, it was after the Hy-Brazilian, Atlantean Quetzalcoatl went back to the dead cities—then still in their threatened glory—and crossed the "Red Sea" to Tlalpallan that the Great Catastrophe came on this planet Earth. It does not seem the first time he had gone back to Hy-Brazil from Central America; for a Quiché tradition, in Guatemala, tells us that "on returning to Palenque, he found other colonists of his own race there".

When Cortes came to Aztec Mexico, in A.D. 1519, the last Mexican emperor, Montezuma, told the men of the white-bearded race of Castilians that they were the men of whom his ancestors had been foretold that their coming would be one day from the east to deliver Mexico. Thus, the luckless emperor contributed to ruin his own country in the shadow of a mystic prophecy many thousands of years older than the beginning of the Aztec civilisation of a paranoiac New Stone age!

Cortes was so struck with Montezuma's strange story that he sent it over the ocean to the Holy Roman emperor and Spanish king, Charles V in old Spain. It is in his first letter, dated October 30, 1520:

> "It is now many days since our historians have informed us," said Montezuma, "that neither my ancestors, nor myself, nor any of my people, who now inhabit this country, are natives of it. We are strangers and came hither from very distant parts. They also tell us that a Lord, to whom all were vassals, brought our race to this land, and returned to his native place. That, after a long time, he came here again and found that those he had left were married to the women of the country, had large families, and built towns in which they dwelt. He wished to take them away, but they would not consent to accompany him, nor permit him to remain as their chief. Therefore, he went away. We have always been assured that his descendants would return to conquer our country, and reduce us again to obedience. You say you come from the part where the sun rises." (See *Francisco Lorenzanos' Documentos Mexicanos.*)

* In a subsequent book, I shall draw attention to some unpublished Spanish MSS., which I shall translate, which show the existence of these Atlantean insignia, in the seventeenth century A.D., in the strange land of Gran Paytite, and among Indians in the unknown region of eastern Andean Perú and modern Bolivia. The perfumes, the powders, the colours, the painting, the tiger-chief, the writing—all were found, or reported to far-ranging Spanish dons, by remote Indian tribes.

Torquemada has another curious, but significant version of what Montezuma told Cortes:

> "He told Cortes that Quetzalcoatl was a great magician and necromancer, and reigned king of that land, and that, on leaving that country, he betook himself towards the sea, feigning that the sun-god had called him to the other part of the sea on the eastern border; but he promised to return afterwards, with great power, and avenge his wrongs and redeem his town from injuries, and tyrannies; for they say of him he was a very merciful and humane man."

As we know, the luckless Aztecs did not find the sadistic, gold-crazed Castilian conquistadores—more bandits than soldiers—merciful; but it is remarkable that these good Catholic Spaniards, hearing that Quetzalcoatl was the Jesus of old Mexico and Central America, said he must have been the apostle, Saint Thomas. Of course, that could hardly be; since the apostle was born only nine or more thousand years after the passing of Quetzalcoatl! And, of course, that benevolent apostle of Hy-Brazilian culture, Quetzalcoatl, lived long before the ancient day of Votan, whose day in Yucatan, Guatemala and what was then proto-Mayaland is, in an ancient MS. copied by Don Ramon de Ordonez y Aguiar very soon after the Spanish Conquest of Mexico, made contemporary with the erection of a great temple at Rome, by the Consul Publius Cornelius Rufus, in 290 B.C. (The same ancient MS. of Votan, by the way, also says that Votan, identified with men of a Phoenician, Canaanite or Carthaginian race, went, in his travels from ancient Central America to old Europe and Asia, to Babylon from the great temple of Jerusalem, and saw the ruins of the Tower of Babel. *Vide:* Ordonez "Probanzo de Votan".)

Ages had passed before Votan set out on his travels from what is now Guatemala or Yucatan, and the Great Deluge and Cosmic Disaster that for centuries on centuries made the Atlantic Ocean impassable to the keels of the galleys and triremes of the ancient world had left the memories of great Atlantis and her South American empire, with their splendid cities overthrown by vulcanism and seismic disturbances, hardly even a dim legend among wandering tribes of Central and South America. Far and wide, as we see, were the Hy-Brazilians dispersed over South America; albeit, their posterity still, as I have said, survives today in remote and unexplored regions of modern Brazil, Venezuela of the Western provinces, and the Perú of the Andean Oriente—a posterity known as the "White Indians".

Somewhere about the time that Quetzalcoatl landed in Panuco, on the Gulf of Mexico, another old and bearded man of great wisdom and knowledge and benignity, dressed in black, like a Phoenician merchant in the old port of Gades, Spain, of 3,000 years ago, went out from Hy-Brazil and came among a country of high *savanas* in the mountains of what is now Colombia, South America. He found himself among the (then) savage race of the Muyscas, or Chibchas, a naked, repulsive and ferocious people, without laws, the elements of agriculture, or any sort of religion. They called him Bochicha or Zuhe, said he suddenly appeared from a *land to the east* of the cordilleras of Chingasa, and was agèd and bearded, and unlike a man of any race known to them. He carried a golden sceptre.

Their traditions—as told to the Spaniards at the Conquest—were that his name was also *Nemteresqueteba*, and that he wore long garments, and was also called *Chinzopoqua* ("sent from God"), but was a human person with a long and bushy beard, who came from the east of the Andes to Paxa and vanished at Sogamuso. With him came civilisation and laws. Bochicha built towers and introduced the worship of the sun, and taught the savages how to clothe themselves and form towns. It was in the "remote days before the Moon accompanied the earth"! Then, like Quetzalcoatl, his contemporary in Central America, Bochicha organised the government of the country. He nominated two chiefs, one of whom was to have civil, the other, ecclesiastical jurisdiction. Then he withdrew himself, says the tradition, into the holy valley of Idacanzas, near Tunja, where he lived in the exercise of the *most austere penitence for the space of 2,000 years!*

As this legend says that Bochicha came among the savage Muyscas at a remote time before the moon accompanied the earth, it suggests that those 2,000 years were, perhaps, not our present years of 365 days each. There was, as one noted above, a race of shepherds, musicians and soldiers, dwelling in Arcadia, in the Peloponnesus, in Southern Greece, in ancient times, which also boasted that their race was *older than the moon.*

When the Conquistadorian Spaniards overran the country in the sixteenth century A.D. they found the Muyscas still surviving: and they were greatly struck by the fact that the Muyscas, or Moscas, and two other Indian nations on the high savanas of Bogotá, lived in settled communities, tilled the land, and wore clothes, while, on the plains below, the other tribes were naked, brutal and barbarous to a degree. An old Spanish monk's MS. of the days of the Conquest of Nueva Grenada, or modern Colombia, gives curious details about Bochicha. He appointed a *zague*, or king, to stop the war that threatened among the people disputing authority. He also set up a council of four chiefs to choose a high priest, after his (Bochicha's) death. The Muyscas called Bochicha *sua*, or sun, and when the bearded Spaniards arrived, they called them "children of the sun", which, of course, implies that Bochicha, from Hy-Brazil, was a *white* bearded man. The name Muyscas means *men*, Chibcha being the name for their language.

It is significant that after Bochica, or Bochicha, came to the high savana of Bogotá, there appeared as money, small *circular plates of gold*. It will be remembered that João Antonio, the Portuguese *bandeirista*, in A.D. 1750, picked up in the dead city of Hy-Brazil, behind the sierra in the *sertão* of Bahia province, "a piece of gold money of *spherical* shape, "greater than our Brazilian gold coin of 6,400 reis. On one side of the coin was the figure of a kneeling youth; on the other, a bow, crown and arrow." (*Vide* page 46 *supra.*) In one part of the cordillera of the Colombian Andes (deep in the Sierra Santa Marta), there has been found remains of a splendid stone city, with paved roads, fissured and upheaved by tremendous earthquakes. It has even yet the remains of a square arch tiled with enormous slabs of granite. (It *may* have been a colony of the far earlier (?) empire of Lemuria, or Mu.) A great highway, paved with granite, leads no one know where, today, and in valleys adjoining there are ruins of great buildings, and tombs cut in the living rock—the sort of *huacas* whence modern treasure hunters take out emeralds, crystal collars of black and red gems and fine gold. In fact, it was a story, told by the Indians, of gold plating ancient palace ruins, of cyclopean type, and idols of the same solid metal that, when followed up by the same avaricious investigators, gave a very unpleasant time to the hungry conquistadorian soldiers, under Don Jiminez de Quesada, who led an army of hauberked and morioned men—Europe's finest *infanteria*—on the hunt for El Dorado.

No. 3 emissary from the ancient land of Hy-Brazil was he whom the Incas called the Ayar Manco Capac. He is also called Viracocha, which, again, means sun-worshipper. He, too, said the Inca Peruvians, was a "white man, with a full beard, who came over the Andean Cordilleras from a land to the east". Another Peruvian tradition is that the white, bearded man suddenly "appeared, from nowhere", in an island in Lake Titicaca, in the old Collao.

Don Antonio de Herrera, *Coronista major de su Majestad de las Indias y su Coronista de Castella* (Crown officer of the King of the Indies and Castile, in Perú) was told, by the Peruvians, the story following, about the year A.D. 1600:

> . . ."There presently appeared in the middle of the day, when the sun came out on Lake Titicaca, in the Andes, a white man, of a great body and venerable presence, who was so powerful that he lowered the hills, increased the size of the valleys and drew fountains from the rocks. They called him, for his great power, ... lord of all created things, and father of the sun: for he gave life to man and animals and by him notable

benefits came to them. And, working these marvels, he went a long way towards the north, giving, on the road, an order of life to the nations, speaking with much loving benevolence, correcting them that they might be good and upright (*buenos*), and joining them, one with another (*y se amassen*), who, until the last days of the Incas, they called *Ticeuro-cocha*, and in the Collao, Tupaco, and in other parts, Arrauâ. And they built many temples." (*N.B.* The Collao corresponds to the western region of modern Bolivia.)

Montesinos, who wrote a very rare book which he copied from a lost and very valuable MS. of the Jesuit Blas Valera, on the history of old Perú, says the high priest of the sun told the thirty-sixth Inca emperor, Huira Cocha Capac, that the ruin of the Peruvian Inca Empire would be brought about when there arrived "white bearded and very severe people, hitherto unseen". This prediction was made in A.D. 1320, and realised with the arrival of the bearded Castilian bandit, Francisco Pizarro, 200 years later. As we have seen, a similar prediction in Aztec Mexico, associated with Quetzalcoatl, promised deliverance, but also actually resulted in the ruin of the Aztec Empire, which immediately followed.

So Quetzalcoatl, Bochicha and Viracocha, the wise, black- or bushy-bearded men, clad in austere black garments, or robes, departed by sea or land to their home country of Atlantean Hy-Brazil, and the gods of culture, knowledge, wisdom, civilisation and enlightenment began to prepare for a long sojourn in the twilight. The wandering planet streamed into our earth's skies, and must have been noted in awe and amazement by the astronomers peering from their high towers in the white cities of Hy-Brazil, and the fatherland of older Atlantis. Warlike races from old Atlantis had, as the priests of Sais and Heliopolis told Solon, invaded Western Europe and the Mediterranean, and reached almost as far east along the North African shores as the land of Egypt on the Nile. As the world-dominators stood, confronting the pre-Hellenic races of old Attica, who alone opposed their overwhelming power and menace, tremendous earthquakes shook the ground. The blazing sky turned to night—a night rent with terrific lightning-flashes and a rain of vast meteorites upon the stricken earth. Men flew to the mountain-tops, only to be stricken with fear and madness, at what the skies disclosed. Aloft, the planet Venus seemed hourly changing her colour, course and size. Our earth was receding into space backwards from her old orbit, nearer the sun. The stars and planets receded fast, the great glowing ball of fire in the night sky shone like a sphere of sultry copper, while, in the day, only less black than the night of terrors, rising above the ball of fire the orange globe of the sun shot out an ochre penumbra of flame from its periphery, as, of course, seen above the swirling of the dense clouds of smoke and gases arising from the earth. On the sea coast, terrific tidal waves rolled in —higher than the highest hills, they crashed on to the beaches, and the immense force and momentum of colossal league-long rollers, coming on behind, drove them far inland, overwhelming cities, drowning whole country-sides, swirling up the sides of high mountains, driving the current of rivers backward towards their sources, even as the Earth was being impelled "backward" into space. Man called on the gods to save him. The gods were silent and powerless on high Atlantis-Olympus, looking down on the reeling globe.*

Out seaward, borne on the turgid and ever-rising waters of the obliterated rivers, floated thousands of bodies—human beings and animals; women, their hair clotted, or floating on the swirling, surging waters, swept by, clutching babies to their breasts, or clasping the arms of drowned lovers, or husbands, their eyes glazed in madness and terror as they gazed unseeingly at the sky where dwelt the impotent gods. Old men clutching coffers of gold and jewels, in hoary arms pressed to their chests, jostled with the dead bodies of priests, warriors or robed rulers whose utmost skill or might had not been able to avert by one spark the rain of fire and gases that had overwhelmed the world, or by one drop the appalling deluge that was drowning the world, nor by so much as one spark the rain of fire and gases yet to come! . . . Yea, woe unto them that gave suck in those days! . . .

> "There came a rain of fire following the sun of rain. All that existed burned. . . . Then there fell a rain of rocks, and sand-stone . . . the sky drew near the waters and the earth. *The planet Venus had changed her course.* There was darkness over the whole face of the earth . . . men flew to caves and the rocks fell on them and shut them in for ever. . . . They climbed trees and the trees bent and shook them off. . . . The sun went out and for five whole days no light pierced the black darkness. . . . Great and terrible earthquakes shook the land. . . . Flames belched out from the ground, and there came a rain of flaming bodies from the heavens. . . . Men came and went beside themselves. . . ." (*From an Aztec codex*).

So reported contemporary observers, in places as far apart as the mountains of old Pelasgian Greece, the land of Egypt, the highlands and burnt places of Central America, South America, Polynesia, Micronesia, Melanesia, and Africa. . . . For the great catastrophe that sunk Atlantis, the island-continent, into the depths of the ocean was accompanied by simultaneous volcanic outbursts in

* This reconstruction of the Catastrophe is actually based on traditions current among certain Brazilian tribes, ages before the Spaniards or Portuguese came to the country.

Cuneiform (Gilgamesh-Nineveh) version of Deluge Story. (British Museum.)

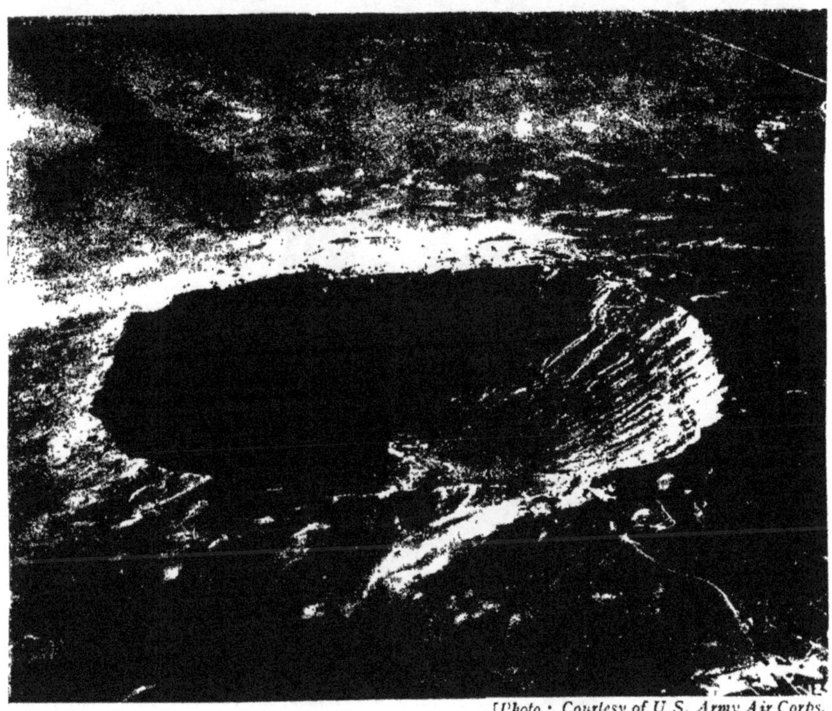

[*Photo : Courtesy of U S. Army Air Corps.*

Meteor (or Platinum) Crater, Arizona. Work of aerolite, 10,000,000 tons weight and 400 feet wide, some 10,000 years ago.

[Courtesy of S. Peruvian Railways.

Sachahuaman, ruins of megalithic pre-Inca unknown race, Cuzco Hill, Peru.

[Courtesy S. Peruvian Rwys.

Old Inca wall in Cuzco.

America, Africa, and the chain of mountains of Central Asia, and far out in the Pacific. What followed were great ice ages, all over the greater part of the northern hemisphere.

In the land of Hy-Brazil and the dead cities into which the *bandeiristas* were to blunder, 10,000 years later, no day could be told from night. The skies were darkened. Up from the ground swirled dense clouds of thick ash and vapours, choking and mephitic, poisoning all round. Terrific electric flashes rent the endless blackness, making it the more unearthly and darker. The maddened sea, in the mightier Marañon-Amazon gulf, rising like a thing demented, surged and roared in over the Amazon basin, dashing on the walled cities, with their massive breakwaters of stone.

In the highlands of this great Atlantis colony—the new Atlantis of old America—it was the fire from heaven and the earth below that ruined them. When the earth shook, and day turned to night, in these dead cities of the unexplored Matto Grosso, of today, there came from great and bottomless crevasses in the ground, in the paved roads, by the side of their splendid temples and palaces, volumes of deadly gases. Blinded, asphyxiated, maddened beyond human endurance, rendered insane by the appalling suddenness of the cosmic catastrophe, men and women, white-skinned, beautiful, some red-haired like Berenice the Golden, others fair and blonde as the Greek goddess Aphrodite, fled out of the cities, leaving all behind them. Parts of the cities sank into the ground, swallowed up by terrific earthquakes. May be, great fires swept through some of the buildings; for the old *bandeiristas* were puzzled by the absence of the least vestige of furniture and utensils. The great palaces and temples were shaken to their foundations. Those people of Atlantis-Brazil who did not manage to escape into the surrounding mountains, along the splendidly paved roads, now cracked and fissured and overwhelmed by great boulders and rocks which the appalling earthquakes and torrential deluge had toppled from the peaks into the gorges, were either burnt and calcined, or engulfed in the yawning earth. What was not incinerated was destroyed by the wild beasts and birds of prey who, for many thousands of years to come, would inhabit alone these cities of old Hy-Brazil, swept by the besom of destruction. The Andes had risen in a night and a day, and, far out at sea on the edge of another lost continent, *flames three miles wide or high* shot from a crater in what is now Hawaii.*

It was a scene that would have caused the fire of the Lord and the spirit of poetic prophecy to come on the old Hebrew poet Isaiah, contemplating the mournful remains of what had once been a wonderful civilisation. With fire in his eyes, he would have declaimed:

---

* So says an old Hawaiian tradition.

> ". . . And all the host of heaven shall be dissolved and the heavens rolled together as a scroll . . . it shall not be quenched night nor day, the smoke shall go up for ever and ever."

Yes, we have on the Earth no sure or eternal abiding-place!

If this sound to you, reader, like a new, flesh-creeping apocalyptic vision of a fanatic "world-ender", be pleased to note that this appalling catastrophe of around the year 11,000 B.C. had a "faint" reflection in something that befell modern Brazil, on August 30, 1931 (A.D.), when three giant aerolites roared down from the sky and depopulated hundreds of miles of forests. A lonely padre, Fidelio, reported the amazing event to the Vatican in Rome. . . .

> "They fell in a forest bordering the Rio Curaca. The heat engendered was terrific. their size was immense. Great flames sprang up from the mass of compressed air—incandescent and glowing white-hot—that is borne in front of the aerolites. The forest was set afire, and the conflagration lasted many months, when a whole wide region was denuded of people. The fall was preceded by remarkable atmospheric disturbances. At eight o'clock, in the morning, the sun became blood-red and a penumbra spread all over the sky till it darkened the air, as in time of solar eclipse. Then an immense cloud of reddish powder filled the air and it looked as if the whole world was going to blaze up. The powder was followed by a rain of fine cinders which covered trees and blanketed the vegetation with white. There followed a whistling sound that pierced the air with ear-shattering intensity—then another and another. Three tremendous explosions were heard. The earth trembled. Natives in the forest were thrown to the ground, or into the water, as they worked or fished. Indians, fishing, say they saw three enormous globes of fire fall from the sky and vanish earthwards."

Nor has this been the only cosmic visitation from outer space in South America of modern days. There was the huge aerolite that fell on a mill in the Argentina, crashed with an explosion heard for miles round, and reduced the mill to a smoking ruin (Dec., 1932). There was the amazing meteor that crashed to the earth, in the jungle, only ten miles from the camp of Dr. Wm. Holden, leader of the American Natural History Museum's expedition to Guiana, on November 18, 1937. He said (or saw) it cut a swathe *thirty miles long* in a forest fringing the wild mountain-side about 300 miles from Georgetown, British Guiana.

Up to date, as in the case of the appalling Siberian disaster in the icy, barren tundras, in A.D. 1908, when hundreds of miles of forest were burnt up and whole nations of Samoyeds wiped out, these "lawless", wandering bodies from outer space have managed to fall in lonely parts of the earth hundreds or thousands of miles from any large centres of civilisation. May it always be so; though Nature regards man and his Earth no more than anything else in the Great Unknown Cosmos!

The world was driven insane by that appalling disaster, of around 11,000 or 12,000 years ago. When the survivors, ages after, again congregated in communities, in Central America, and the Mediterranean, as also on the uplands of far-away Britain, of the New Stone (Neolithic) age, a very definite lunatic twist was imparted to their culture. They became obsessed with a desire to ward off any future catastrophe, and the desire became also queerly linked with a doctrine of propitiating the gods presiding over harvest. So, all over the northern hemisphere, from the great stone cities of civilised Maya and Aztec Mexico, to the high savanas of Bogotá, in Colombia, across the ocean to the summit of Bredon Hill, on the borders of Worcestershire, in England, and eerie Stonehenge on lonely Salisbury Plain, Wiltshire, you saw, before dawn of midsummer day, each year, a procession of skin-clad priests, followed by bearded chieftains, long-haired warriors, and staring women and children processing behind a fair youth and maiden along an avenue, between monolithon pillars, to a great stone circle of tri-lithons. Here the victim, bound with thongs of leather, was laid prone on a long block of stone: the slaughter-stone. At the moment of the nascent dawn when the sun cast his beams right along the stone avenue, till the level rays fell on the head of the victim bound to the slaughter-stone, priests, with knives of stone, killed the victim, in prehistoric Britain just as they did in old Mexico, as late as the days of Cortes—when looting Castilian soldiers actually met this fate in certain Aztecan temples of the sun-god. The Aztec priests, as is well known, tore the heart of the victim out of the writhing body, with knives of obsidian—volcanic "glass"—and actually ate it, as it smoked, in the sight of the worshipping multitude. . . . . To that state of lunacy and a horrible doctrine of atonement had the great planetary collision brought our Earth's pre-Diluvian civilisation!

The ancestors of the ancient Muyscas of Bogotá, in strangely incongruous memory of Bochicha, their humane and gentle civiliser from Hy-Brazil, and also to ward off the catastrophic perils of the skies, chose a victim at the end of every cycle of twenty years. He was called the *Guesa quichica,* which means "houseless" or "wandering" and "door", because his death was supposed to open a new cycle of 185 moons. This *guesa,* as on Bredon Hill and at Stonehenge, England, was a boy, or youth. He was taken from a village in the plain of the llanos de San Juan, the eastern slopes of which had seen Bochicha, the white saviour, enter the Muysca land from the unknown east of the cordillera. The *guesa* was carefully educated in a temple at Sogamoso, Colombia. At the age of ten, the boy was made to walk in the paths trodden by Bochicha, when he was instructing the people, and working miracles. Then, at the age of fifteen, he was led in procession to a circular place, in the middle of which was a lofty column, marking, as the gnomon of a sun-dial, the length of the shadow thrown by the sun. The priests, called *xeques*, wore masks, very like those of the priests of Pharaoh's Egypt, and, having followed the youth, they killed him as a sacrifice.

It is, again, queer that one of these masks represented the *Moon*, the "evil planet", first seen in the skies of the cataclysmal world. When the *guesa* reached the end of the road, or *suna* (Sun), he was tied to the column, a cloud of arrows shot at him, his heart torn out and offered to Bochicha, as a sacrifice, and his blood drained into vases. Once again, it is ironical that a civiliser such as this old, bearded white man, as gentle as he was wise, should have had, long after his disappearance, such a hideous ceremony attached to his memory. The post-Diluvian world in South America had, also, turned to a form of *paranoiac religion.*

In the western world, Quetzalcoatl's memory is mirrored in a strange but significant sign on a very old map, done by Bianco, in A.D. 1436, and showing the Atlantic Ocean, fifty-seven years before Columbus *re*-discovered America. This sign is that of a great red hand on an island in the middle of the Atlantic Ocean. It is titled "Yd lamon Satanaxio" (the hand of Satan). The legend is that a great hand rose from the sea and snatched men into the ocean deeps. Great Hand, or Iron Hand, was, as we know, the name of the barbarian conqueror who drove Quetzalcoatl out of Central America, and had himself worshipped as a god. By a curious and ironical transposition, *his* name was given to Quetzalcoatl by the men who were first civilised by that old and wise man of the spade-beard. *Huemac*, or Great Hand, became a god among Toltecs and Mayas, who (a second, later wave) are believed to have reached Yucatan around 220 B.C. when the last part of the old Atlantean continent of Antillia—leaving above water the modern Antilles—submerged.

The survivors of Hy-Brazil are heard of, from time to time, down the ages, since their splendid cities were made desolate. Some of them wandered across the wilds of Brazil and climbed the cordilleras into Perú, which had been "shot higher into the sky" since the cataclysm. A colony of the white-bearded men are heard of in an island in Lake Titicaca, in the Andes (as we have already noted), ages before the Inca empire began. Here, they were attacked by a race called the Colloas, who, my old friend, U.S. Senator Miles Poindexter, one time U.S. Minister in Perú, and an authority on South American pre-history and archaeology, suggests were a branch of the Toltec race—kinsmen of the same militarist Huemac, of the Iron Hand—who had wandered there from old Mexico's highlands.

The old priest and Spanish soldier, Pedro Cieza de Leon, heard about the fate of these lost Atlantean white men, when he was travelling the Andes, around A.D. 1550:

> "Before the Incas conquered the country, many of the Indians declare there were two great lords in the Colloa, one called Sapani, the other Cari. They conquered many of the fortresses called *pucaras*. They say that one of these chiefs, Cari, entered the large island where it is swampy, in la Laguna de Titicaca, and found there a white people, who had beards. They fought with them in such a manner that all were killed." (*La Crónica del Perú*).

So, once again Toltec Huemac, of the Great or Iron Hand, had sown the dragon's teeth of war and extermination among the luckless posterity of Quetzalcoatl of Hy-Brazil.

These white-bearded men came from the valley of Coquimbo, and lived in the Isle of Chiquito, says old Antonia Herrera, *Coronista major* of the king of Spain and Castile, in Perú, in A.D. 1610. The next people recorded to have seen them, but only at distance, up an inland rushy creek, nine days' journey from the dead city behind the mountains of Bahia, were the old Portuguese *bandeiristas* of A.D. 1750. Jesuit missioners have left MSS. stories of encounters with these white and bearded Indians, but those stories have long been lost to sight in the dust of South American libraries and archive-rooms. In 1932, as I may be pardoned for repeating, a German missioner sighted them in a wild and wooded part of the Oriente of Perú, but these shy, furtive and gentle men flee like the wind in the forest from the sight of strangers. They are the oldest race now alive in—at least—our western world!

CHAPTER V

THE SIGN OF THE SUN: WORLD'S OLDEST ALPHABET

In Chapter III, I told the romantic story of the discovery by the young gunner-lieutenant, P. H. Fawcett, in the jungle of Ceylon, in 1893, of a strange creeper-covered stone of ancient and unknown date, which bore hieroglyphs (or letters?) of peculiar and bizarre form, identical, so Mrs. Nina Fawcett tells me, with certain inscriptions found cut on a great slab over a vault (?) in one of the unknown cities of Atlantean Brazil. (The reader will remember that a copy of these strange letters was taken by the old Portuguese *bandeirista*, in or about A.D. 1750.)

I have myself discovered some queer links between these strange letters of old Brazil, and characters found in Tibet and Vedic Hindostan. One of the ancient letters is almost identical with a sign in *Sansar*—the ancient form of Sanscrit, which Hindu pagoda traditions said was derived by the ancestors of the Sanscritian Hindus from the drowned land of *Rutas*, which may be identical with the Atlantis of the Pacific Ocean, known as Lemuria or Mu. It is said to have been found on one of the leaves of the mystic *Kounboum*, or *Kounboun* tree discovered at the lamasery of Sinfau, or Sifau, by the famous Abbé Huc, who was subsequently unfrocked by his superiors for his candour and courage in declaring the identity of the ritual of the Roman Catholic church with that of Buddhism and Brahmanism.

The Kounboum tree, it may be stated, is the (white sandal) (?) tree of 10,000 images, found, it is said, in a great brick-walled courtyard of a Buddhist temple at the foot of a mountain. Each leaf of the tree is said to bear one of the characters of Sansar, or *ancient* Sanscrit, the language of the sun in the drowned land of sun-worshippers of the Pacific Atlantis, called Rutas. Huc said the sweat mounted to his forehead in his effort to detect any lamaic fraud about the tree, which, he added, "is very old, about eight feet high, with brilliant scarlet flowers, and nowhere else exists, and cannot be propagated from seeds or cuttings".*

* It is curious that while Huc says he saw these lettered Kounboum leaves, about the year 1845, in this lamasery, on the western frontiers of China, the Prussian *leutnant*, Kreitner, who visited the lamasery about 1880, saw neither Buddha pictures nor archaic letters on the leaves of the tree. He says he noted the ironic smile at the corner of the mouth of the old lama guide and suspected trickery with acids. Rockhill was at Kounboum in 1890 and saw only broken leaves with no visible images and none on the tree. Waddell was there in 1895 and had no better luck. It reminds one of the "testimony leaves", about Mohammed the prophet and Allah, which Ibn Batutah saw, on a tree in the courtyard of a mosque on the Malabar coast. Rockhill, indeed, asks the pertinent question why there has been a change from alphabet leaves to Buddha images on the tree. I myself am reminded of the magic money which the wily jadoo-wallah in the N.W. provinces of India makes, and which vanishes a short time after he has paid it over for good money received. But the mystery is further deepened for me. In winter 1942, a friend in Canada sent me a cutting, from the *Vancouver Sun*, of a feature by the well-known Ripley wherein pictures of the Kounboum alphabet leaves appear. From Dr. Randle of the India Office Library, I learn that a Dr. Gordon Stables supplied information, from Singapore, about these leaves, in 1940, when he wrote to a well-known London Sunday newspaper. Whether or not these characters appear on the leaves of the tree in the Kounboum lamasery, they certainly seem genuine and extremely ancient. In fact, no Orientalist has, to my knowledge, any acquaintance with the alphabet or tongue of which this inscribed letter forms a part. Other letters on these leaves are as follows:

AUTHOR.

Let my reader glance at the comparative table, below:

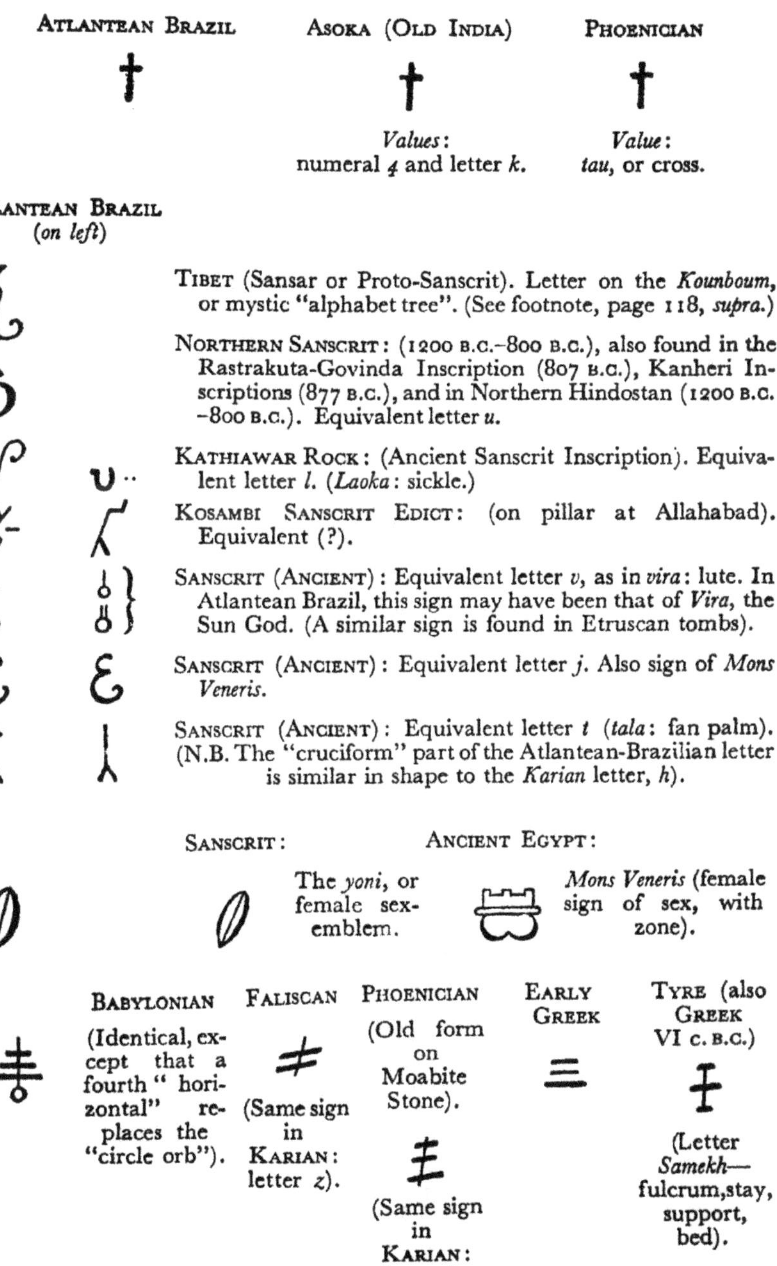

ATLANTEAN BRAZIL	ASOKA (OLD INDIA)	PHOENICIAN
	Values: numeral 4 and letter *k*.	*Value*: *tau*, or cross.

ATLANTEAN BRAZIL (*on left*)

TIBET (Sansar or Proto-Sanscrit). Letter on the *Kounboum*, or mystic "alphabet tree". (See footnote, page 118, *supra*.)

NORTHERN SANSCRIT: (1200 B.C.–800 B.C.), also found in the Rastrakuta-Govinda Inscription (807 B.C.), Kanheri Inscriptions (877 B.C.), and in Northern Hindostan (1200 B.C. –800 B.C.). Equivalent letter *u*.

KATHIAWAR ROCK: (Ancient Sanscrit Inscription). Equivalent letter *l*. (*Laoka*: sickle.)

KOSAMBI SANSCRIT EDICT: (on pillar at Allahabad). Equivalent (?).

SANSCRIT (ANCIENT): Equivalent letter *v*, as in *vira*: lute. In Atlantean Brazil, this sign may have been that of *Vira*, the Sun God. (A similar sign is found in Etruscan tombs).

SANSCRIT (ANCIENT): Equivalent letter *j*. Also sign of *Mons Veneris*.

SANSCRIT (ANCIENT): Equivalent letter *t* (*tala*: fan palm). (N.B. The "cruciform" part of the Atlantean-Brazilian letter is similar in shape to the *Karian* letter, *h*).

SANSCRIT: The *yoni*, or female sex-emblem.

ANCIENT EGYPT: *Mons Veneris* (female sign of sex, with zone).

BABYLONIAN (Identical, except that a fourth "horizontal" replaces the "circle orb").

FALISCAN (Same sign in KARIAN: letter *z*).

PHOENICIAN (Old form on Moabite Stone). (Same sign in KARIAN: letter *x*).

EARLY GREEK

TYRE (also GREEK VI C. B.C.) (Letter *Samekh*—fulcrum, stay, support, bed).

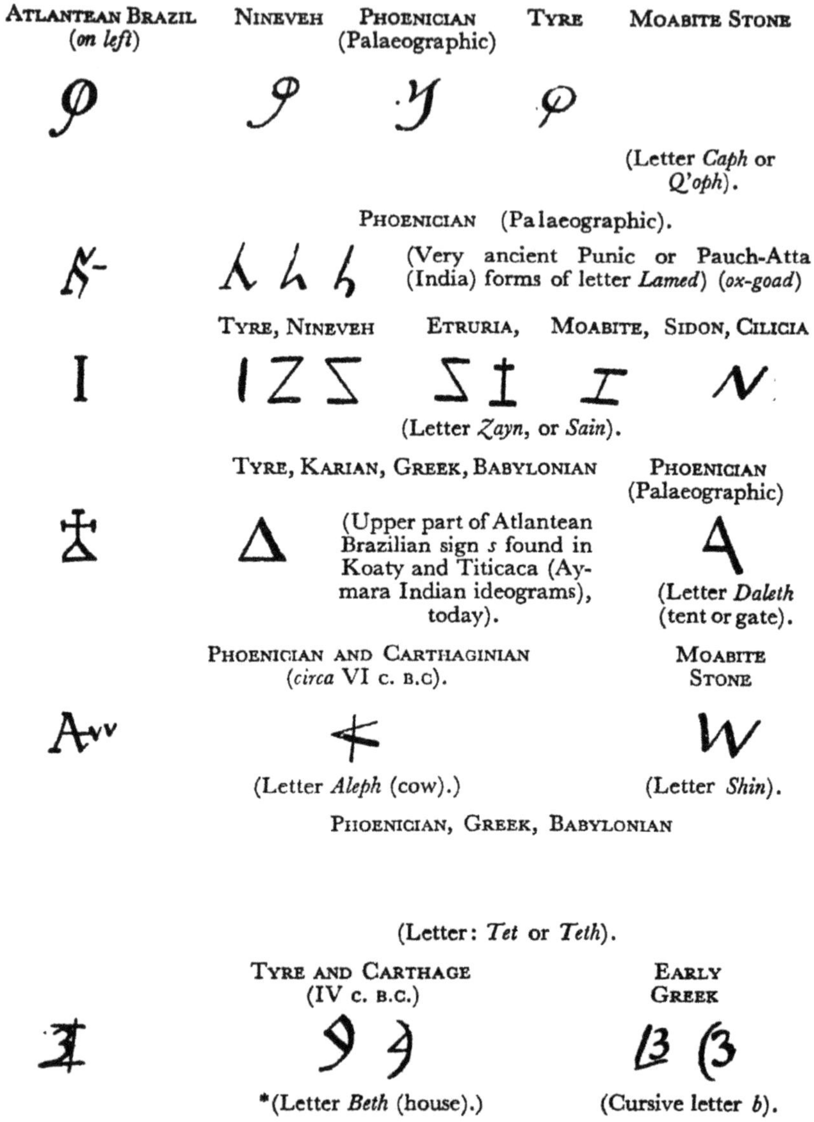

ATLANTEAN BRAZIL (*on left*)	NINEVEH	PHOENICIAN (Palaeographic)	TYRE	MOABITE STONE

(Letter *Caph* or *Q'oph*).

PHOENICIAN (Palaeographic).

(Very ancient Punic or Pauch-Atta (India) forms of letter *Lamed*) (*ox-goad*)

TYRE, NINEVEH ETRURIA, MOABITE, SIDON, CILICIA

I

(Letter *Zayn*, or *Sain*).

TYRE, KARIAN, GREEK, BABYLONIAN

(Upper part of Atlantean Brazilian sign *s* found in Koaty and Titicaca (Aymara Indian ideograms), today).

PHOENICIAN (Palaeographic)

(Letter *Daleth* (tent or gate).

PHOENICIAN AND CARTHAGINIAN (*circa* VI c. B.C).

(Letter *Aleph* (cow).)

MOABITE STONE

(Letter *Shin*).

PHOENICIAN, GREEK, BABYLONIAN

(Letter: *Tet* or *Teth*).

TYRE AND CARTHAGE (IV c. B.C.)

*(Letter *Beth* (house).)

EARLY GREEK

(Cursive letter *b*).

(* It is doubtful if there is any relation with the *Hy-Brazilian* character).

Even more remarkable similarities and identities in respect of these ancient Atlantean-Brazilian signs have been found in the islands of the Sun and the Moon (Titicaca and Koaty), in Lago de Titicaca, of Perú. It was in this very lake that the last-known living colony of bearded white men and women of old Atlantean, post-cataclysmic Brazil was annihilated by bloodthirsty and savage Colloans, whose descendants, today, may be the Aymara Indians of modern Bolivia. (See chapters II and IV, pages 48, 117 *supra*). It is exceedingly probable that the elements of culture and the syllabary, or alphabet, or hieroglyphs of the old white race of Atlantean Brazil survived for ages afterwards among the primitive races of later Brazil. The Atlantean civilisation lasted for thousands of years, and evidence exists to suggest that Diodorus was right in asserting that the ancient Egyptians derived their hieroglyphs from old Atlantis, and that the Phoenician seamen traders took their alphabet from the same civilisation, but in a far later day, when decadence had overtaken the Atlanteans of old South America and the Great Catastrophe was near at hand. By the side of South America one suspects the civilisations and cultures of the so-called old Worlds of Asia and Europe may be mere parvenus and inheritors. Nor, one must repeat, is the white race of old Atlantis, as found in old South America, extinct today.

It is, again, one of the ironies of history that the lost colony of these old Atlanteans exterminated in Lake Titicaca—as reported to old Cieza de Leon by the Inca priests and chronologists—should have fallen under the sword of a chief, Cari, who, as his name attests, was a descendant of those very Carians, Europe's oldest navigators, whose female relatives, the Amazons, were first driven across the Atlantic Ocean after battles with the militarist elements of Atlantis, fought on the confines of Southern Europe and in North-West Africa—*and* after the war of Troy!

Here follow a few of the ancient ideograms, of Atlantean Hy-Brazilian origin, found by the old Spanish missioners to be in use among Indians, in old Perú, on the borders and shores of el Lago de Titicaca (Lake Titicaca). These Indians, it may be surmised, were akin to the other Indians in Uycali, Perú, near the source of the mighty Amazon, whose remarkable books of paintings and hieroglyphs were seen by the Franciscan missioner, Narcissus Gilbar, in the early nineteenth century.

Swastika, denoting movement, creation, conception, rotation. (*Luratha, Camatha, Indkatha, Hakkutta*). (*Koaty* and *Titicaca*).

Denoting eye, first, before. *Nayra, Nayran, Nayrakatahana*). (*Koaty* and *Titicaca*).

"A very old woman" (*Apachi*) (*Koaty* and *Tititaca*).

"A very old man," stricken in years", (*God, Father* (*Achachi, Auki, Achachela*). (*Koaty* and *Titicaca*).

Hy-Brazilian-Atlantean character.

ϛ ɛ ξ

Signs at end of a period.
First two characters appear in Hy-Brazilian-Atlantean dead city).
(*Koaty, Titicaca* and *Hy-Brazil*).

Koaty and *Titicaca* (Perú) signs similar to characters in African Touraeg (Sahara) and Ferro (rupestrian, v. ancient) in Canaries.

"Earth, universe, earth and heaven". (*Koaty* and *Titicaca*) "Hell" (sign on right) (*Koaty, Titicaca* and *Tiahuanacu*).

God, Uru (*Cf. Vira,* Atlantean-Brazilian for Sun (*Dyaus,* the Unknown God"). (*Koaty* and *Titicaca*).

Two Gods (*Koaty* and *Titicaca*).

"To create" (*Luratha*) (*Koaty* and *Titicaca*). *Cf.* with similar Babylonian sign (Greek *xi*).

Six (*Sojta*). (*Koaty* and *Titicaca*).

Besides the characters above, there are also three Koaty and Titicaca ideograms identical in form with three of the Atlantean-Brazilian characters, reproduced *supra*, in Chapter V. In the *Koaty* and *T.* ideograms their meanings are "Sky and Earth"; "I create"; "I believe". Moreover, as remarkable evidence of ancient world-wide diffusion of culture in the heliolithic age of 15,000 20,000 years ago, a system of "dots", occurring in the *K.* and *T.* Aymarâ Indian (Bolivian Perú) ideograms, is also found in ancient rock inscriptions at Thugga (Tunisia); in Numidia and among the Touaregs ("Veiled Men" of the Sahara). Another *K.* and *T.* ideogram is identical in form with Karian (Asia Minor) letter *ss.*

It is likely that American—and other prehistorians and archaeologists —may be forced, sooner or later, to revise their ideas on the antiquity of civilisation in North and South America. The discoveries of really revolutionary character are on the increase. For example, in the one year of 1940, there was found, by American archaeologists, a colossal head in stone of a man of a clearly highly civilised race of unknown age or origin. It was carved, with great art and sense of character, in basalt, and was found deep in the jungle at Tabasco, Mexico, which is twenty miles from the modern Mexican coast, and more than 100 miles from the nearest source of this volcanic stone. It is obvious that a system of good roads must have linked what is now deep and almost impenetrable jungle and forest with the distant quarries. The head—one of five—is of a man of *white*, civilised race, of masterful character, a sense of humour—judging by the expression—and clearly one of a master-race. The features are as majestic as the heads of the Pharaohs at Karnak and Thebes and the great Rameses. The experts of the Smithsonian cannot tell what race sculpted these colossal and majestic features. I may note, however, that Tabasco is the place to which the Atlantean civiliser, the humane Quetzalcoatl, man in black of peace and culture, brought the torch of civilisation from Hy-Brazil, the great imperial colony, of the motherland of Atlantis. In or about 15,000 or 12,000 B.C. Quetzalcoatl—man *not* god—sent to Tabasco colonies from his capital, Central American city of Tollan, or Cholullan (?).

The other strange discovery is of a bowl, or olla, found, also in 1940, by Dr. Ousdal, the palaeontologist, in the mountains of Southern California, in the top of a sandstone boulder which erosion has thrown on to its side. The bowl bears round its rim the writing of a highly civilised race; for the signs are geometric and phonetic. They were made with great care and not merely scratched on the surface. For how many thousands of years the bowl has lain in the hollow of this rock none yet know. But a clue to the advanced civilisation of this great unknown race of North-Central America I give in the two signs—among others carved on the bowl-rim—with their probable signification:

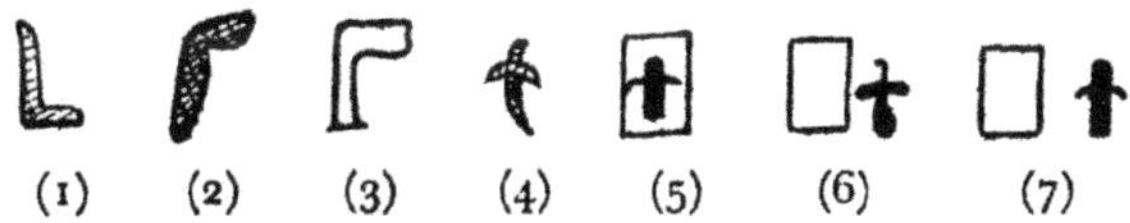

(1) Letter on bowl (or *olla*) of unknown, very ancient race inhabiting what is now a mountain range in S. California, U.S.A. (2) Similar ancient Brazilian sign on ceramics and funerary urns at Marajó Island, Lower Amazon. Both probably equivalent in meaning to (3): Ancient Egyptian symbol *Toré* or *Teri*: God. (4) Another symbol on *olla* ((1) above). Compare with ancient signs: (5) at Marajó, Brazil; (6) China and (7) ancient Egypt. *Meaning:* river spanned by bridge.

Nor is the above the only amazing example of diffusion of culture in an incredibly ancient world of civilisation—preceding even the dynastic Egypt of the priests of Thais and Thebes and the ancient Egyptian temple-archivists of Solon's day. This same Amazon basin confronts us with identical signs and symbols stretching hands across a very ancient world of wise men, from China and old India to South and Central America of a far, pre-Columbian age. How old these symbols may be none yet can say. They may take us back to the days of the heliolithic culture of 15,000 years ago, before the onrushing waters of the outer Atlantic drowned the black-white-red civilisations of the ancient Mediterranean basin. They were found about seventy years ago in the large island of Marajó, at the mouth of the lower Amazon, which is separated from the port of Belem, North Brazil, by the Rio Para. In this island there is inset a lake wherein is a small island, called Pacoval. Here have been found many highly artistic ceramics, idols, ornaments, funerary urns, buried in mound-dwellings.

Nothing is known about the long vanished race who made them; but one strange fact about the craftsmen emerges, when one examines the relics: they depict an extraordinary variety of human faces,* so that it seems as if this ancient and unknown people of the old Amazon basin had studied every race in the world! Some of the figures on the vases and ceramics are strikingly similar in their characteristics to figures found on ancient Mexican monuments.†

These ceramics are often very highly finished and artistic; but what is odd is that no two funeral urns have the same devices, and on only one of them is found a decoration of part of a plant. Their colouring is vermilion or dark black, and in this all primitive races are alike, even to the days of the Palaeolithic man of the famous Altamira caves of the Basque mountains. Red, black, or yellow is the limit of their colour-apprehension; and, in fact, even the Greeks of the heroic, epic time of Homer, and the much later Aristotle, recognised no more than three colours. Blue or violet was not recognised as such, until the days of modern Europeans, proof of which is Homer's frequent epithet of the wine-bright, or wine-dark Mediterranean sea, and not purple or blue. Primitive and even classic art was morphologically developed, but the apprehension of colour rays of the spectrum and the sense of perspective are remarkably modern developments of human consciousness.

This unknown race of Marajó Island had some queer ideas—non-Egyptian—about interment and the future life, beyond the grave. Their funerary urns were used to house desiccated skeletons of corpses previously buried elsewhere. The skull was placed on top of the skeleton, and the earthenware cover over the urn. Holes were left for the worms to enter and eat the rotting flesh! All the cooking-pots and utensils of the dead were smashed by this unknown race, and not placed, even in miniature model form, with the remains of the deceased, as was, of course, the case in the tombs of the Pharaoh's Egypt. The ancient "Marajans" seem to have come to old Brazil from three or four directions: over the flanks of the eastern equatorial cordilleras of the Andes; along tributaries on the northern bank of the Amazon, or Marañon; and by sea. There are also traces of an ancient sea-faring race (the Carians?), who wandered to the Marañon basin southwards from what is now Florida and Louisiana, and the waters of the West Indies. They seem to have reached Brazil from the lands of Central America, by way of Venezuela and the Guianas.

One of these unknown races, settling in Marajó Island, practised phallic-worship. The human generative organs are found realistically depicted in terra-cotta, and the *yoni* and *lingam* appear exactly

* Compare with the submarine relics brought up off the coast of Ecuador by diver of Señor Muñoz, the *haciendado*. (*Vide* pages 20 and 183).

† Along the Rio Counay in the Brazilian Guiana, are other ancient tombs, in caves nine feet deep, covered with heavy granite slabs, and containing glazed ceramics of art even superior to Marajó.

as they did in ancient Babylon, or old (or modern) India, in the cult of Shiva. This unknown Marajan race had exactly the same notions of the generative force of the universe symbolised in the dualism of the sexes. This ancient form of worship they seem to have shared with other vanished races, traces of whom have been found at Chillicothe (Ohio), in California, in the ancient ceramics of Perú, and in the ancient temples of old Yucatan. Here is a terra-cotta phallus found in a mound at Marajó. Side by side with it is a phallomorphic representation of the "sexo feminino", or *yoni*—both being depicted on the ceramics, or in conspicuous places on the vases, between a special type of arabesque, and painted either in vermilion, or black:

PHALLI (ancient Brazil): *lingam* (male); *yoni* (female).

But the amazing feature of these ceramics of old Marajó's unknown race of unknown date consists in the queer resemblances and exact identity of forms found here, in old Brazil, and in ancient Egypt, India, China and Aztec, or pre-Aztec Mexico. No one can yet say what chronological relation they bear to the higher and vanished white, Atlantean civilisation of the dead cities of Hy-Brazil; but it may be surmised that Marajó's ceramics and mounds belong to a much later age than the former incredibly ancient and vanished civilisation.

The reader will find these comparative symbols (set out below) of great interest, if he or she is interested in ancient South America, probably the cradle of the world's earliest civilisation:

THE SHADOW OF ATLANTEAN WHITE BRAZIL PROJECTED INTO MARAJAN BRAZIL, PHARAOH'S EGYPT, OLD INDIA, ANCIENT CHINA, AND PRE-AZTEC AND AZTEC MEXICO

A comparative Table of Symbols found on Ancient Pots, Funerary Urns and Ceramics in the Mounds of Marajó Island, in the Lower Amazon-Marañon, Modern Brazil

(All symbols in first column, below, are found on Marajó Island Funerary Urns and Pots).

It should be here observed that, sixty years ago, Dr. Ladislão Netto, of the Archivos do Museu Nacional of Rio de Janeiro made a fine and careful comparative study of these remarkable inscriptions on the ceramics and funerary inscriptions of Marajó, to which one has been able to add little, except a comparison with the strange letters found in 1940 on the rim of the *olla*, sunk in an ancient rock on a mountain-top in California. (*Vide* chap. V, p. 123, *supra*).

BRAZIL (MARAJÓ)	MEXICO	CHINA	EGYPT	INDIA
	(Identical symbol found in the other four ancient lands).			

In Marajó Island, it is found engraved, and also painted in ceramics; but seems to have undefined meaning, except as bearing some affinity to an act of phallic worship. In India, of the Hindus, it appears to have had the same inner significance as the *Delta* of the Greeks. In ancient Mexico, it symbolised the action of pricking, or breaking into parts, or the noun *thorn*; also the idea of union. Some exegetists translate it as *Ui-Hui-Uh*; and others see in it a resemblance, or likeness to the Egyptian sound *Hou*, having for symbol the same figure.

Brazil Mexico China Egypt India

Sign sometimes found painted, or represented in front of a mound, or tumulus. When upside-down, it is an ancient Mexican character, meaning *cup*, or *vessel*, translated by *Cax-Cax-Itl.*

Brazil and S. California (Unknown race). Egypt

Means God, or Toré, or Teri (Egypt).

Brazil Egypt

Means a mountainous region, a strand by the water wherein such a mountain is reflected. Hence, the symbol of plurality.

Brazil Mexico China

A house, or the verb, "to dwell".

Brazil China Egypt

A battlemented wall, or defensive barrier (found painted or engraved). Means also a palisade on the bank of a stream.

Brazil China Egypt

This is the only vegetal sign found on Marajó ceramics. In Egypt and China, the sign meant a place covered with woods; also, in Egypt, the syllable *AM*.

BRAZIL  CHINA  EGYPT

A river spanned by a bridge

BRAZIL  EGYPT  CHINA

The symbol for *night*, also suggests a form of lantern, or *pharos*. Means, also, division of day and night, in ancient Chinese.

BRAZIL  MEXICO 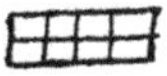 EGYPT

Means govern, or command. In Egyptian is equivalent to the phonetic symbol *ph* or *p*. In the Mexican is equivalent to *petlatl*.

BRAZIL  EGYPT  CHINA  INDIA

Umbrella, shelter, cover, calm.

BRAZIL  EGYPT  CHINA

Rock, or mountain.

BRAZIL EGYPT CHINA

Character not met alone, but in combination. Means *pyramid*, or *stela*.

BRAZIL  EGYPT

In Egypt, is equivalent to the phonetic symbol "N". Stands for goddess *Neith*.

The symbol of old Egypt's *Uraeus*, idea of cunning, or wisdom. Is also the symbol of Quezalcoatl, the wise man in black from Hy-Brazil, who civilised the barbarians and savages of Central America, perhaps about 12,000 B.C.

Brazil Mexico China Egypt India

Sign which sometimes represents two arched eyebrows united to the nose. Is identical with the *tau* of the Greek alphabet, and corresponds with the Egyptian cross, where it symbolised omnipotence, grandeur, eternal life. In phallic symbolism it means the act of coition between male and female. In the Aztecan Dresden Codex and No. C. Troano MS. it has same meaning. It was also the sign borne by the ancient Egyptian goddess of fire, Sekhet.

And from the Serapeum of Isis, Horus (the son), and Osiris, the Alexandrian Christians took it for the Christian ritual cross. It is, thus, *in origin*, as much a phallic symbol as the spire of the mediæval church, or the dome of the Moslem mosque, or the curious monolithon stones of the Stone Ages found today in various out-of-the-way parts of our English shires, or the abandoned old East India army cannon (of old John Company) to which, not so many years back, East Indian women of the Hindu religion were seen, in a jungle clearing, praying for male offspring.

Means divine light, or sight. Idea of seeing or knowing, or sagacity. Aztec TX—IX/LT.

This ancient Brazilian symbol is identical with the Mexican Aztec symbol, in which Landa says it means the 17th day, called *Ahau*, King, or, a period of 24 years. It also stands for demon, chief of the Legion, and invokes *Hun-Hau*, of the Quiché Bible *Popul Vuh*, and alludes also to *Hun-Camé*, associated with the wise old man, Quetzalcoatl of Hy-Brazil.

[Courtesy of South Peruvian Railways.

Colossal Head at Tiahuanacu.

[Courtesy of Grace S S. Line

"Ra-mac": colossus.

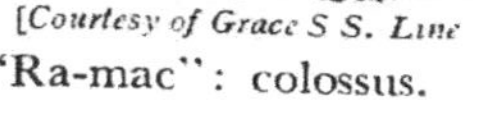

Evolution ign on Mayan Cap

[Courtesy of Museo Nacional, Mexico City.

Human sacrifice stone from Aztecan teocallis (pyramid), near Mexico City.

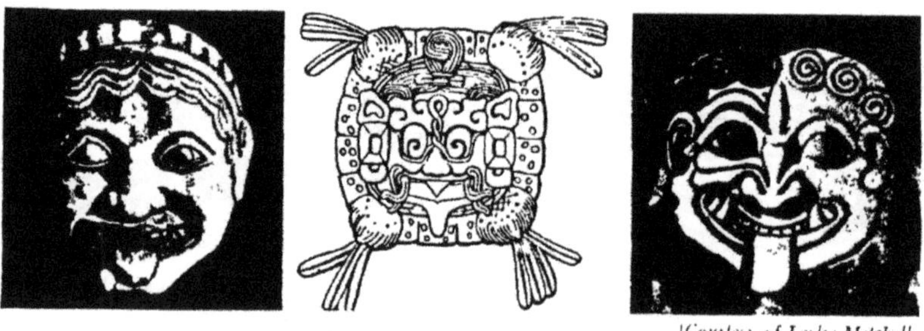

[Courtesy of Leslie Mitchell.

(1) (2) (3)

Nos. 1 and 3: Gordon-Medusa heads, old Greece and Syracuse. No. 2: Same motif at Palenque of Quetzalcoatl. World-wide heliolithic culture diffusion.

[Courtesy of M. le Marquis de Wavrin.

The evolution (stairway) symbol (as at Tiahuanacu) on backs of Boro Indians, Amazon headwaters, West Brazil.

BRAZIL EGYPT

Cut in rock, or stone, is a symbol sign representing a lizard, or reptile. In Egypt, it stood for the crocodile, and, as the *bent tail*, represented the West —which was the abode of the dead, or the land, or island-continent from which the ancestors of the Egyptians came to the Nile, *via* (perhaps), old Spain, from South America, or Rutas-Lemuria (?) of the proto-Egyptian.

BRAZIL CHINA EGYPT

A reptile, or residence, between or upon mountains. May be a royal city with two exits, and located between mountains. Or suggests a dead Brazilian city, or Atlantean city, moated, or surrounded by water, as many of them were and are (both in African ruins and in South American jungle cities of the dead).

BRAZIL MEXICO EGYPT

Means lagoon, basin of water, or water limited in area. Identical symbol in all three countries. In the DRESDEN Aztec Codex its value is *ATL-* and *Mauh.* May be a veiled reference to the drowned Atlantean island-continent.

BRAZIL CHINA

Meant a city, or the four cardinal points, or natural forces. In ancient Chinese, the sign meant royal residence, or palace.

BRAZIL EGYPT

Figurative sign of a *passaro,* or bird. Has same sense in Peruvian antiquities. May be compared with the sign of the Egyptian god *Horus,* and the Mexican *Toztli,* a kind of parrot with golden feathers. It is also, for this reason, the emblem of the *sun. Teotli,* or *Teotl.* In Mexican means *God. N.B.—Horus, the hawk-headed god of ancient Egypt, was the god of sunrise and the day.* It was said that only the falcon, or hawk, was able to gaze on the sun and not be blinded, or dazzled.

BRAZIL	EGYPT	CHINA	INDIA

A compound, or composite, symbol having the idea of a temple, surmounted by the "T", or *tau*, that thus appears a universal divinity. This primitive form of pyramid was given to the temples of all the early races of America and Africa. Presumably the idea of the pyramid came from the drowned continent of Atlantis to Africa (Tanis, in old Barbary) and the Nile, and to America, South and Central, across the then existing land-bridges. But the identity of these ancient Marajans, who thus adopted this very ancient sign, remains a riddle, sixty years after the discovery of their fine ceramics, funerary urns and statues.*

CHAPTER VI

SIGN-POSTS TO THE SHADOW OF ATLANTIS

"They fly, forgotten,
As a dream dies at the opening day."

"As above, so below. What has been, will be again."

These words, in the ancient mysteries, whispered into the ear of the neophyte, at low breath, mouth to ear, and in hushed voice, as the freemasonic ritual has it, arise to the surface of the conscious mind at every interval of a half century in the history of mysterious South (and Central and North) America, when the great god Chance, or the Zeit Geist, or the Central Sun of the Cosmos, or what you will, breaks a little cranny of light into the practically impenetrable veil shrouding the mystery of the ancient American world.†

Who are the mysterious mound-builders, whose remains are found in Ohio? What relation do they bear to the races migrating from old Atlantis? Had they any dim knowledge at all of that ancient world of Stone-Age culture, which yet knew how to work copper?

In 1927, one of the mounds of this mysterious race, or races, was

* This vast island of jungle and thick grass, today reaching five feet above the heads of the tallest men, is known to be inhabited by head-hunters. Two officers of the Atlantic group of the R.A.F. Transport Command crashed there when an engine failed in February 1944. Radio flashed out the S O S, followed by a carrier pigeon. American and R.A.F. 'planes located the wreck of the 'plane and the survivors, at the outlet of the Rio Arapixí. U.S. Army and Navy airmen in a motor-crash boat were directed to the scene from the air and forced a way through swamps where caymans and poisonous snakes abound. But they had to turn back. Eventually, the two Transport Command officers were rescued by a Navy blimp whose crew made a daring landing in the jungle and an equally risky take-off. I mention this story in order to indicate the nature of the terrain that field workers and archaeologists will have to face in this strange island of Marajó.

†*Vide* pages 122–23, *supra*.

examined by Dr. Wm. C. Mills, of Columbus, Ohio. There are thousands of these mounds scattered all over that state, and in the Mississippi Valley. As is well known, mounds in ancient Central America formed the basis of the pyramid-temples on which they were erected. Prominent men—chiefs or medicine men—were buried in them, often at ground level, as in the case of Stone-Age tumuli in Britain. The earth was then heaped over them. (In Britain, as we know, the earth was often heaped round and over a tri-lithon structure of stone, as in the dolmen, and a hidden tunnel-gateway provided for some purpose, which, it may be surmised, was not of the future tomb-robbers.)

The mound-builders of America were artists in the use of copper. They also had rich pearls, wove fine fabrics, and made artistics objects of bone, stone and shell. No iron has been found in these mounds.

Copper, again, was their precious metal.

The earlier culture built their mounds on terraces; the later used bluffs. In the graves have been found obsidian—volcanic glass—arrow-heads, though obsidian is not found nearer the Mississippi than the Yellowstone. There are also beads made from shells found along the Gulf of Mexico, which is evidence of trade and contact with members of the race who had migrated to Central America. It has been estimated that the earlier mound-builders migrated to America some 12,000 years ago, which is about the date given in the Solon-Plato-Sais account of the cataclysm that sunk Atlantis to a watery Hades.

The race do not appear to have known the potter's wheel; yet there have been found in the ancient mounds hand-fashioned bowls and pots of such beauty and symmetry that the unaided eye cannot detect the least defect. They cremated their dead, in some cases, and in one such mound in Ohio, there was found, in 1927, four "princes" lying in beds of pearls and covered with exquisitely woven fabrics decorated with artistic designs. Some of the skeletons show that the people were afflicted with tuberculosis and other "modern" diseases. Again, some of these ancient mounds are larger than the pyramids of old Egypt. Like the makers of the petroglyphs, to which we shall soon refer, the mound-builders wandered in groups down the Pacific coast southwards to Mexico, Central America and across the land-bridge to South America.

Arriving in the region of Mexico City, they founded a civilisation. Pottery was made and from a species of wild grass they developed corn. From this centre, their arts spread north and south, and they traded and inter-married and invaded, eventually importing their inventions and culture to the Illinois, Ohio and Mississippi valleys. In one county of Ohio—Fulton alone—are some 1,600 mounds. In the older terraced mounds, the skeletons are found flexed, the limbs

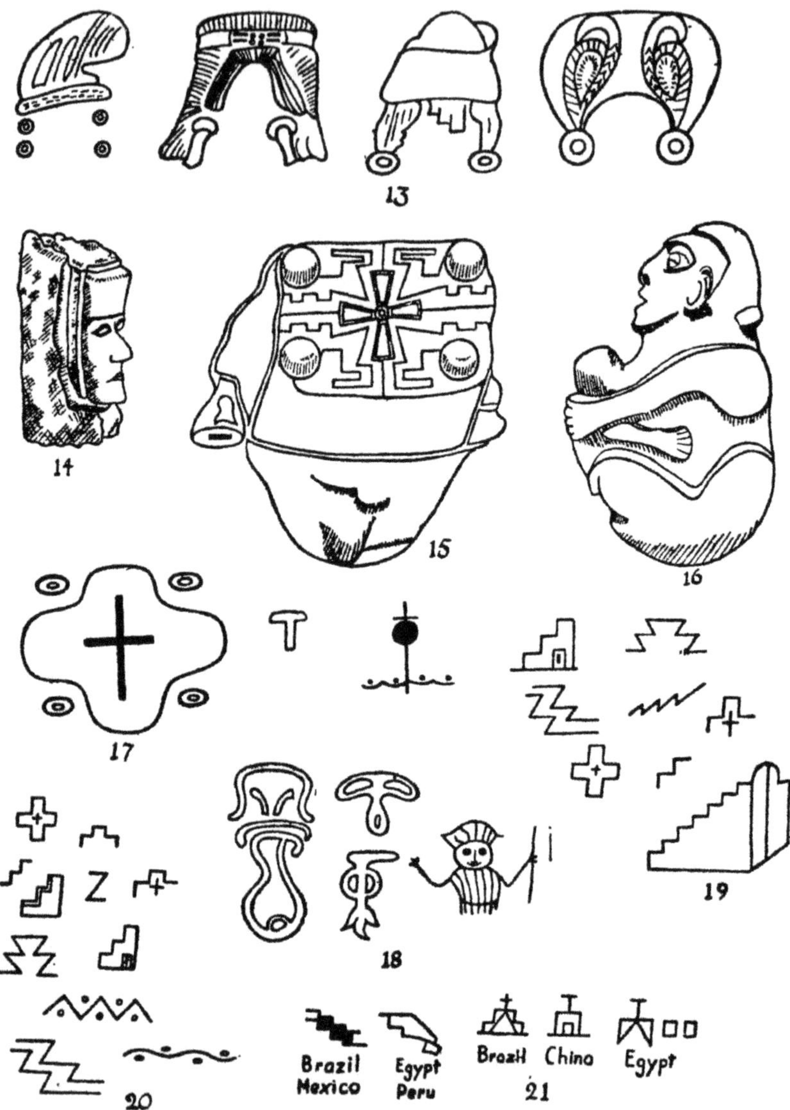

(13) Petroglyphs, Sierra de Santa Marta, Colombia, found 1933. Note the proto-Greek, *Carian*, and Phrygian type head-dresses. The Carians, defeated by the great Pharaoh Rameses, emigrated across the Atlantic to the Americas. They called their *aldeias* (villages in Brazil) *Tabas* (Thebes, of the Pharaohs?). (14) Splendid head of Tiahuanacu notable. (*Vide* (5), page 90.) (15) Stairway-evolution sign on "dome" of high priest, Tiahuanacu. Also central cross: ancient phallic symbol, identical with *Onkh* symbol of Egypt's Pharaohs ("to live"). (*Vide* also (1), page 90.) (16) Stone statue from ancient midden, British Columbia. Type of prehistoric head-dress found in old Atlantean Brazil and Columbia. (*Vide* page 90.) (17) (*Left*) Venus (phallic coition) sign on (Central American) Mayan glyph. (*Middle*) identical symbol of Egyptian *tau*, and Christian cross

being folded on the chest. Pottery of a different sort is found in these older mounds. In the mounds on the bluffs—later in origin, since the terraced mounds have been found buried under them—the skeletons are buried fully extended and a different type of pottery interred with them.

Below the level of the earlier terrace mounds skeletons of another race have been found with longer and lower skulls. Whether these are men of an entirely different and far earlier people, or whether the skulls of the later arrivals changed in shape has yet to be determined.

Thousands of years before the day of the North American Red Indian, this ancient race made splendidly shaped pipes—statuettes of human figures resembling other Caribbean culture statuettes found in Honduras and the Friends' Islands, in Rattan. Some of the skulls found in the mound-graves have artificial copper noses fitted, indicating that they had been operated on after death, though the why and the significances are mysteries. A copper claw of an eagle, exquisitely made, and a fine statuette of a handsome beardless man, or youth, come from other graves. The race, of course, was not nomadic, as were the Red Indians.

An even more apparently insoluble mystery of a race of whom not even an Indian tradition remains unexpectedly came to the light of modern day, when, in 1940, Dr. Asbjorn Ousdal, of Santa Barbara, California, found on a mountain-top in Southern California the queer primitive bowl sunk in the rim of a great sandstone boulder which had slipped on its side during ages of secular erosion. Cut into its surface was the mysterious inscription in letters, not hieroglyphs, on which one has essayed to throw a very dim light. (*Vide* page 123 *supra*).

The words of the famous hymn sounded, again, in summer 1940, when close to an American episcopal mission at Point Hope, Alaska, remains of a prehistoric city were found, with an unknown type of very high culture. Even the Eskimos, who usually have a tradition explaining such remains, could say nothing of these. It is quite unlike any other finds in Alaska, or the Far North. Unless, however,

---

of Serapeum. (*Right*) Venus sign, Tomb of the Bulls, Tarquinia of the mysterious Etruscans (Atlantean type race?). (*Vide* page 128.) (18) Petroglyphs, Sierra de Santa Marta, Colombia, also found Amazonas, Brazil. Top middle glyph like sign of *Toré*, or *Tere* (God), ancient Egypt and identical with one letter of strange alphabet on rim of ancient *olla*, found, 1940, on S. California mountain. The man in the "rayed" head-dress with staff suggests some ancient prophet or civilizer, like Quetzalcoatl. Figures this type found also on rocks of Orinoco headwaters. (19) (*Top*) Stairway-evolution signs, Tiahuanacu. (*Bottom*) Same sign on modern Quichua (native Peruvian) wayside altar, Andes. (20) and (21): (20) "Los simbolos escalonados" (stairway signs), and also Zodiacal (deluge) sign, *Aquarius*, Tiahuanacu, and all over S. and C. America, and S.W. of U.S.A.; (21) similar signs, ancient Brazil, China and old Egypt.

more finds of the sort are made, in later years, it will remain a riddle, exactly as that of the rocks of South and North America, whereon, written by a far-wandering race, is an Odyssey none may read, or interpret, as yet!

These petroglyphs have been traced to the Aleutian Islands, where the Jesuit missioner and archaeologist, Father Bernard R. Hubbard, in 1937, found in the islands Attu and Agattu, farthest eastward, an aboriginal people speaking a strange language which he thinks has some relationship to the speech of the hairy Ainu, the old Stone-Age inhabitants of Northern Japan. These rock signs run right through the Aleutians, though they really start, so far as at present traced, in Central Siberia. They mark the passage of an unknown race who had reached a fairly advanced stage of culture.

The trail is again picked up in the gorges of the River Columbia, in the state of Washington, west coast of U.S.A. They cross the Rockies, into the states of Nevada and Arizona, and bear away southwards, through the still mainly unexplored sierras of Mexico, to the cordilleras of Colombia, South America, and the gorges of the Orinoco and Marañon-Amazon. Yet, do these petroglyphs differ considerably in degree of artistic execution and subtlety of symbolism —as I hope to show here.

More than a century ago, Humboldt and Schomburghk (wandering in Guiana wildernesses and along the upper Orinoco), and, almost forty years later, Bates, in the cañons of the Rio Xingu of the Matto Grosso, of Brazil, came on fresh passages of these Odysseys of the rocks. It is significant that in the llanos of Venezuela and Eastern, and still mostly unexplored Colombia Humboldt found no rocks covered with inscriptions of the sun and animals, though, on the banks of the Rio Caicara, where the forest joins the plain, such rock-drawings are seen. This *may* mean that the unknown race travelled through the river gorges and valleys in a day when a vast morass, more than a million square miles in area, separated these gorges from the nascent Andes, from whose slopes the waters were draining into this terrible region of swamps, fevers, and, it is likely, fearsome prehistoric monsters, or feral saurians of gigantic size. (Queer stories of such monsters, leaving tracks unrecognized in the beaches of swampy lakes are, as I have said, still current in places on the foothills of the Eastern Andes, much about where Sir Arthur Conan Doyle probably placed his "Lost World".)

It was on rocks, in 7 degrees North latitude, and at a considerable height, that Humboldt saw those figures of animals, boa-constrictors, the sun and the moon, stars and strange hieroglyphic signs. The whole country, he says, was a savage desert in 1810–20. It is not more "civilised", even today, in 1942. The natives said that, in this country of the rock-pictures, and of the queerly Phoenician-looking signs, found carved in rows, in a cave, their ancestors, *in the time of the great waters*, came in canoes to the tops of these mountains, and that the rocks were so plastic that a man could trace marks on them with his bare fingers.

Humboldt remarked that the tribes of his day, in that wild region, knew nothing of the use of chisels, or metallic tools. From all of which it may seem that some of these inscriptions came *before*, and some after a great catastrophe, that wiped out the culture of the great civilised race of ancient Brazil and the mighty Marañon-Amazon basin and valley, far wider, then, than even today. As I have suggested in this book, it is probable that great aerolites from the sky, and vulcanism, with tidal waves below, brought the "sun" of fire and water, as ancient pre-Aztecan sacred books, traditions, or codices have it, on these dead civilisations. May be, then, I hazard, the more primitive petroglyphs, of the naïvely primitive sort, such as men with the intelligence of children might make, were done *with their fingers* in these rocks, as the Caribs told the baron, after the time of the great waters. The inscriptions that preceded the terrific South and Central American cataclysm, described luridly in the Mayan bibles, such as the *Popul Vuh*, are, probably, the work of *very* different peoples and cultures. Time may lift the veil.

Humboldt's words are worth quoting here. He said, in 1820:

> "In the interior of S. America, between 2° and 4° N. lat., there extends a great plain, bounded by four rivers: the Orinoco, Atabasco, Rio Negro, and Casiquiare. On them are found rocks of granite and syenite, equal to those of Caicara and Uruana, covered with symbolical representations. There are colossal figures of crocodiles, tigers, houses, and domestic utensils, and signs of the sun and moon. At this day, this unfrequented region is entirely without a population over a space of 500 square miles. The neighbouring tribes, exceedingly ignorant, lead a miserable vagrant life, and are not capable of drawing hieroglyphics. In S. America, a belt of these rocks, covered with these symbolic emblems, may be followed from Runupuri, the Essequibo, and the Pacariama mountains, to the banks of the Orinoco and the Yapura, over an extent of more than 8° of longitude. These marks, thus engraved in the rocks, may belong to several different epochs; for Sir Robert Schomburghk has seen on the Rio Negro a drawing of a Spanish ship which, of course, must be later in origin than the beginning of the sixteenth century, and this in a savage country where the indigenous stock was probably quite as uncultivated as the present inhabitants." (*Ansichten der Natur.* 3 *Ausgabe, Bde I.*, p. 240.)

These picture writings range north, from the gorge of the Xingu, on the eastern side of the Matto Grosso of Brazil, to the highlands of modern Colombia, and south through Maranhão, Ceara and Parahyba, in lands which, as I have shown, were within the actual zones of influence, if not always residence, of the great white race of the Atlantean Brazil, of the pre-cataclysmic age, at least 11,000 years ago. One feature marks them all: they are carved on high rocks, in gloomy cañons, impossible to climb. No more than in North America has one, at present, the key to these inscriptions, and it is still, palaeontologists contend, very much an open question whether man existed in ancient Brazil in the time of the giant mammals. (Until one hears the Indian rumours of what lies between the Goyaz and Roosevelt plateaux in Brazil!) His bones have certainly been found mixed with theirs in Brazil and other South American regions.

In the Rio Negro, of the Amazon, there are many of these rock-pictures. Two of them strike the imagination: rock-glyphs of tall men, of archaic type, in long robes, one with arms extended, the other grasping a long baton or staff; and they are depicted wearing remarkable head-dresses, like extended haloes. Similar figures are also found in the Upper Orinoco region. True, they are in a style such as a child, or man with a child's mind, would draw; but they suggest most graphically that the primitive artist was copying monuments of a dead civilisation, far higher than his own, or, perhaps, engraving memories in stone of the leaders of a great race to whom his forefathers had been helots of some sort. Schomburghk wrote to Humboldt that he had seen colossal human figures in the rock of Timeri (interior of Dutch Guiana), and close to the great cataracts on the upper waters of the Rio Corentyn, on the borders of Dutch and British Guiana. These figures were executed with much greater care than any discovered in Guiana (Venezuela). . . .

> "The size is about seventy feet, and the figures seem to represent the human body. The head-dress is extremely remarkable. It encompasses the head, spreading outwards considerably in breadth, and is not unlike the haloes in the paintings of the heads of saints. I have left my drawings of these figures in the colony (British Guiana), and I hope some day to be able to lay them before the public. . . . In the Cuyuwini (N. British Guiana), I saw ruder figures, and they extended over a space of 192,000 square geographical miles."

It is curious that head-dresses, somewhat of this type, are found in some of the monuments of what are probably the world's most ancient ruins: those at Tiahuanacu, and also close to mysterious hieroglyphics on rocks in the Santa Marta Mountains, Colombia. The late R. B. Cunninghame Graham, "El Gran Caballero", "Don Roberto", saw rock-pictures of this sort in Mexico—though he does not say if they depicted colossal men with curious head-dresses—at a great height; but, in the days "when I passed through the valley, the Mescalero Apaches made things unhealthy for archaeologists".

Who were the Homers of this Odyssey of the rock-pictures? May be, there were more races than one; for, as I have pointed out before, the pictures vary greatly in type and skill of execution. Some may be of far later date than others. R. B. Cunninghame Graham jestingly suggested that Don Gonzalez Jiminez de Quesada, the conquistador of Colombia, as a lawyer, might have thought that the writings, figures and pictures seen at a great height at a place known as La Peña Tejada, where the mountain stream had cut a passage through the living rock, were a "species of Indian conveyancing".

But were they a sort of *pateran* or route-map and trail, of wandering ancient South American "Romanies", showing to people coming on behind, years later, which route the pioneers had taken? Or, again, had the makers of the rock-glyphs chanced on some incredibly ancient grey stone American city riven by thunderbolts, or upheaved by earthquakes in a far-off day? Had their imagination been so impressed by what they saw there that they copied some of the hieroglyphs, or syllabary forms, or ancient alphabets, or some of the monumental representations of colossal human figures, and reproduced them as they journeyed on, ever on, into the great unknown? (Or, again, were the rock-carvers migrating refugees from some submerged land—Atlantis?)

So, on the forehead of rocks high in mountain gorges they had carved a sign to future, wondering men that, even of old, in the night of time, or the morning of the world, or the twilight of cosmic castrophe, men knew that they had no continuing city on this planet, and that, aeons after the destruction by cataclysm of their own incredibly ancient civilisation, the far day must dawn which the priests of old Hindostan called the "Night of Brahma", when life and motion cease, or, as the modern physicist would say, entropy increases and energy degenerates into a molecular degradation of heat, the solar system ceases to rotate round its blazing centre, and the universe falls asleep till the next dawn. . . .

However fantastic this may sound, and whether or no some of the far-spread American rock-pictures *are* mute memorials of some past Heliacal year of deluge, destruction and the passing away of great civilisations which have not left even a bone or a shred of pottery, as in the dead cities of the highlands of Brazil, it is true, generally speaking, that the petroglyphs and ancient rock-pictures of South America's mountain gorges and the cliffs along the affluents of the Marañon-Amazon, such as the Rio Negro, are more advanced or artistic than those of North America. Yet, in both, oddly Phoenician, Semitic, or Asiatic signs appear, and may *not* be their (ancient South America's nomads') direct reminiscences of those other wandering races of the ancient worlds of *Asia* and *Europe*, or as accidental as some American and Brazilian professors would have us believe.

At the moment, we know more of the tides of migration from North to South America than of the meaning, or meaninglessness or mere conventionality of some of these petroglyphs. One trail starts at Celilo, on the River Columbia, of Oregon, close to Big Eddy and Roosevelt, Washington. The petroglyphs cross the Rockies into what is now Nevada and New Mexico, and reach southwards to Perú, on whose rocks similar signs have been cut. May be, there were two distinct streams of migrants: those on the east, from the shores of the Mississippi; those on the west, wandering from the banks of the Columbia, Oregon, to the Rio Ucayli, of the Andes.

It must be remembered that, thousands of years before Menes, the ancient Egyptians cut perfect hieroglyphs on rocks and monuments, and designed canals. Just so, the ancient American races, lapidarian artists, built twelve miles of canals—so far traced—and irrigated 90,000 to 150,000 acres of land in Western North America. Some modern American archaeologists say they were men of the Shoshonean race, makers of baskets, far older than the cliff-dwellers, who reached the highlands of Central America from the Far West.

One's general impression, after a study of these petroglyphs, is that the sculptors may have had contacts with an ancient civilisation in America, probably long after its passing into the abyss of time. For among the meaningless scrawls on the rocks are significant pictures of serpents and animals, and forms suggesting the letters and hieroglyphs of old Phoenicia and Egypt. But those signs probably came neither from Egypt, nor the wandering Phoenicians, but from the sources whence those ancient races derived their letters and glyphs: *Rutas*, the great vanished continent of the Pacific, whence came the old Sanscrit forms, or the northern tropical sea-continent of the Atlantic, called by the Greeks of Plato's day *Atlantis*.

The different races and periods of these rock-painters and carvers are suggested in the comparative illustrations below:

Petroglyphs found in the Aleutians, in 1937, by Father Bernard Hubbard, S.J.

(These signs may, later on, be compared with the rupestrian inscriptions to be mentioned in a subsequent book, as found in the Canaries, the Sahara, and old Spain.)

Petroglyph from Cliff in Oregon.

Serpent, or earth, trailing gaseous fire-mist in the Azoic Age? (Possible Sanscritian conception derived from either Atlantis or Rutas-Lemuria.)

Ditto: similar idea.

Tadpole, symbol of generation. Frogs were worshipped in old Brazil as in ancient Egypt, as a symbol of generation. (Similar sign ends Phoenician (or Karian ?) rupestrian inscription at Graves Creek, Ohio Valley.)

Utah cliff-dweller's glyph.

Ancient Brazil: Marajó, Amazon mouth.

Mexico: sign of Quetzalcoatl, the pacifist pioneer, who, from Atlantean Brazil, or the mother-land of Atlantis, brought elements of civilization to savage North and Central America.

New Mexico: Petroglyphs on cañon walls.

Rio Negro Valley, *Amazonas*, Brazil: Men with rayed headdress suggestive of preachers or pioneers (?) from Atlantean South America (?). They are *not* the people depicted in the New Mexico petroglyphs at left. Another theory is that the head-dresses are feathers, which is not convincing.

Petroglyph on Arizona cliff.

More advanced feeling for pictorial art is shown in this Amazonian rock inscription in the valley of the Rio Negro, Brazil. (Animals may be the S. American aquatic rodents, the *capybaras*).

Along the Orinoco and the Amazon river-gorges and in Mexican sierras the signs are often found on inaccessible cliffs. In Siberia, near Krasnoyarski, and in old Tartary, the glyphs also take the form of rude figures of men, quadrupeds, reptiles and birds cut in the rocks at places where the rivers run close under the granite cliffs, which, in some regions, are smooth, steep and unscalable.

May it be that the rock-carvers are of different races of various dates; that they migrated, in some cases, from a common centre, not necessarily in Asia, as many scholars advance, but *in ancient America*, or even across some ancient land-bridge, long since disrupted in the Pacific, linking Lemuria with ancient America? In other cases, the evidence seems to point to a wandering, from Asia, across the Bering Strait, or the existing land-bridge of the Aleutians.

What do we know of the extent of the migrations from Atlantis, in the far ages preceding or after the various cataclysms presaging the final catastrophe of the Egyptian account handed down to us in the Solon-Plato dialogues? It may be that some of these Atlantean migrants went wandering in thousands of years eastwards, right across Europe into Asia, eventually reaching the American continent, which other Atlanteans had, in ancient South America, colonised in a westward approach.

My theories are equally as good as the more conventional and fashionable ones; for none of them are written on volcanic basalt as enduring as the petroglyphs on inaccessible cliff-walls in America or Northern or North-Eastern Asia!

Perú has a number of mysterious and ancient rock-inscriptions, and, in many cases, they are far anterior to the Inca's civilisation. One of them was found by the Peruvian historian, Dr. J. von Tschudi. It lies about a league from Huari, in a very ancient settlement of an unknown race:

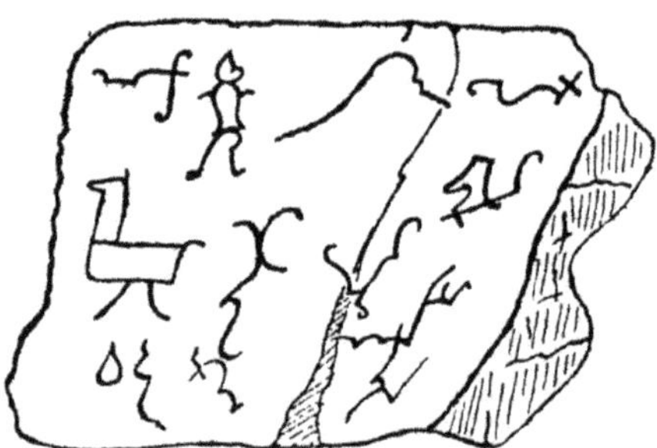

Inscription of unknown and ancient race, near Huari, Perú.

These inscriptions of Huari, Perú, resemble shorthand consonants; but three of the characters are remarkable. One appears to be a representation of a large running bird, such as an emu or ostrich. Neither exists in modern South America. Another is a bare-legged man in a short tunic, or one of those individuals who appear in Mr. H. G. Wells's novels of worlds in A.D. 2500, and shapes of things to come, or in Professor J. B. Haldane's lively scientific sketches of the future. The third appears to be the head of a horse—though the hippine species is supposed to have been unknown in North, Central or South America before the coming of the Spanish jennets of the conquistadores.

There are other quite different characteristics of some pre-Inca culture cut in a rock at Sahpuayacu, Perú, in a territory not known ever to have been conquered by the Incas, which lies about 190 miles east of Cuzco outside the bounds of the old Inca Peruvian empire. To the archaeologist, these inscriptions at Sahpuayacu are a standing puzzle. No one of them can make up his mind, though sorely tempted to say they are merely conventional inscriptions, or pictographs cut on the rock in the idle moments of some savage, or primitive gentleman, who, had he lived in the days of Sam Slick, the famous Yankee clockmaker, would probably have spoiled some blaspheming farmer's new five-barred gate to a cattle-fold, by carving his insignificant name, date, and initials of his sweetheart on the top bar, in oak, or hickory. It is unsafe to dismiss them as conventional, or ornamental, merely; *since one sign appears thrice and three others twice each in the two rows.**

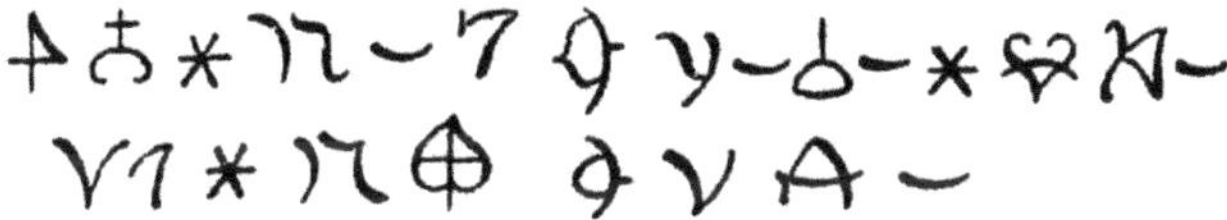

Unknown signs at Sahpuayacu, Perú.

The third discovery is the most remarkable of all. It was made, says Señor Mariano de Rivero y Ustariz, on a granite rock eight leagues from Arequipa. Many of the engravings are of animals and flowers and of a fort anterior to the age of the Incas. At one place, called Huayti, was found a ruined palace, of unknown age and origin, and certainly not Inca. Here, a mass of granite was engraved with these curious figures. The "hot cross bun" sign is exactly the same in form, and, perhaps, significance as that associated with the mysteries of the sun-god, Baal, or Bacchus, or the Phoenician letter *Teth* (Tyrian alphabet). As for the primitive gentleman standing on the back of a large bird, and with the rays issuing from the crown of his head and tips of his fingers, one might speculate whether or no he had some knowledge of aviation or electricity, or electro-magnetic healing.

Here is the place for one to ask how much longer American archaeologists or their British confrères mean to persist in the absurd and unhistorical assertion that Perú of the Incas had *never* devised a form of writing? That all they had invented were a crude system of knots, *quippus*, known to the conquistadores and early chroniclers and which remind one of the mediaeval system of

* Compare these unknown signs in old Perú, with pre-Phoenician, rupestrian inscriptions found in the Sahara, in parts of old Spain, and in the Canaries. (To be referred to in my subsequent book on S. American riddles). Berthelot suggested that unknown races all over the world, some 20,000 years ago, had a sort of *lingua franca* in these signs cut in stones.

One of the above signs appears in a writing of Indians, in an island in Lago de Titicaca. *Vide* Chap. V., p. 122 *supra*.)

tallies, made of wood, current among the secretaries and accountants of the royal scriptoriums, or primitive state offices of the English middle ages. These *quippus* were coloured knots used as a mnemonic aid; but the earlier Incas had actually devised a system of writing, far older in date than the *quippus*, known in Quichua as *quilcas*. The Incas lost this early system of writing when an insane and superstitious tyrant of an Inca emperor* forced the caste of *amautas*, or learned scribes, to adopt the *quippus*. Fernando Montesinos, whose authoritative "Memorias Antigas Historiales del Perú" was largely copied from the lost and most valuable MS. "Vocabulario Historico del Perú", of the learned Jesuit, Blas Valera, son of a Peruvian lady and a conquistadorian soldier, tells us how this came to pass.

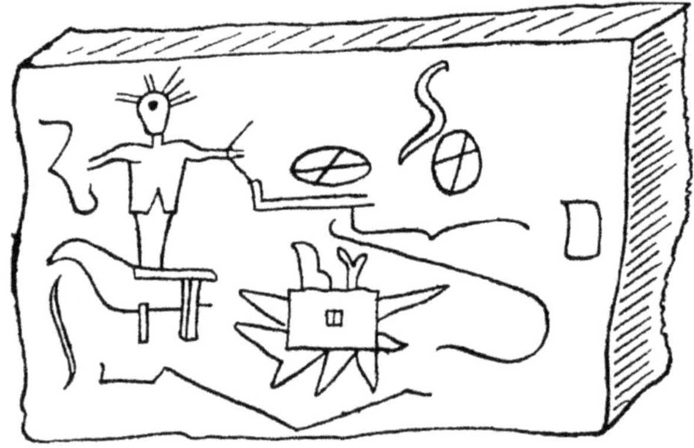

Rupestrian Inscription (unknown and ancient race near Arequipa, Perú).

(That MS. vanished from the Jesuit college of La Paz, Bolivia, in or after 1631, when the historian of the Society of Jesus, Padre Anello Olivia, saw it.)

Montesinos, repeating what Blas Valera had collected of oral traditions and history, from the mouths of Peruvian priests and nobles, in the days just after the Conquest, says that, in the reign of the Inca Huanacaui:

> "The *amautas*, or learned scribes, who knew the events of those times by very ancient traditions passed from hand to hand, say that the Inca had letters and also wise men, *amautas*, who taught reading and writing . . . as far as I am able to learn they wrote on the leaves of plantain trees, which they dried, and then wrote upon, whence the idea came to Juan Coctovito, in his

* Neither the word *quilca*, nor *vira*, is found in Quichua, or makes any sense in that tongue of the Incas. There are Brazilian Indian tribes, knowing nothing of the Incas, who sing each dawn to the sun. Their song is an invocation to *Vira-Vira*! In the language of the Nahuatls of old Mexico *quilca* means *write* or *paint*. Did this word, too, come from the civilisers from white Atlantean Brazil?—AUTHOR.

'Itinerario Hierosolimitano y Siriano' (*lib.* I, *c.* 14, *fol.* 92), that the ancients wrote upon these leaves, and that the lines which are used in parchments in Italy, today, owe their origin to this custom. And also in Chile, when paper for his 'Araucana' was lacking, to Don Alfonso de Arcila (Ercilla), an Indian filled his need with leaves of the plantain tree, and on them he wrote great portions of his poem, as the Padre Acosta says. Also they (the old Incas) wrote on stones. A Spaniard found among the buildings of the Quinoans, three leagues from Buamanga, a stone with some characters which none could read. And thinking that the memory of the *guaca* (burial place, or tomb, in Quichua) was inscribed there, he kept the stone for the sake of understanding better. These letters were lost to the Peruvians through an event which befell in the time of Inca Pachacuti the Sixth."

This king is said, in Montesinos, who is following the lost work of Blas Valera, to have been the seventy-eighth king of the Incas. He was the sixth Pachacuti. He made great sacrifices to appease the *Illatici* (Herodotos's *Alilat*, god of lightning and thunder), who was associated with Viracocha, the man in black from Atlantean Brazil, who performed the same civilising and cultural task in old Perú as Quetzalcoatl, his fellow-countryman, had in old Mexico. One of the priests told Inca Tupac Cauri Pachacuti—to give him his full name—that letters were the cause of the plague and none ought to use them or resuscitate them from that time forth, or great harm would come:

"So (about A.D. 300?) the Inca decreed pain of death to any trafficking in the *quilcas*, or writing-material, which were the parchment and leaves of the trees on which they used to write. Nor were any to use any sort of letters. And, because, in later times, a learned *amautas* invented some characters, they burnt him alive. So, from this time forth, they used threads of *quipos*."

However, the plagues, as well as earthquakes and floods, happened as frequently *after* this reactionary Inca had turned back the hands of the clock of Peruvian culture. These hieroglyphics, written or copied on the *quilcas*, were the royal mail of the Old Inca Empire. One Inca Inti Capac set up post-houses on the Andean roads, and *chasquis*, or runners, travelling on foot—*running* 12–14 (*long Castilian*) *leagues a day*, surely a record of speed and endurance hardly matched in any part of the world, at any time!—carried the letters until they handed the folded leaves to the runners at the next mail-house. So the post travelled till the letters reached the provincial governor. After the use of letters was stopped the post-runners were forced to commit the messages to memory.

It was, by the way, Blas Valera who compiled a list of kings of the Incas going back to 1220 B.C., "a date" which, says Mr. Philip Ainsworth Means, "is too early. In all probability South America, at that time, was an uninhabited wilderness."

In advancing this theory, Mr. Means has gone badly off the archaeological rails! As this book has shown—or it has failed dismally—old Brazil was a highly civilised country thousands of years before 1220 B.C. True, it may be that the Inca tribe of Cuzco did not rise to Imperial power till A.D. 1100, and that, as Bartolomé de la Casa (who was in Perú in A.D. 1532) says, other dynasties of chiefs ruled in the Andes before that date, of A.D. 1100. That does not alter the fact that Blas Valera's informants among the Peruvian priests and the descendants of the old class of *amautas*, living in the late sixteenth century of our era, were neither fools, liars nor romancers.

Let us consider the significance of what they told him: *Ayar*, *Manco*, and *Pirua*, names of Peruvian-Inca kings, *have no meaning in Quichua*, the language of old Perú. *Pirua*, the name of the first dynasty of the Incas, is a corruption of *Vira*, meaning *sun*, as it probably did in the Atlantean lands of old Brazil, of the dead cities. Blas Valera says it was an archaic term and meant "storehouse of creation". *Ayar* was the name applied to the four brethren of the Paccari-Tampu myth, who issued from a city of caves in the high Andes, and founded the old empire of Perú.

And what was the ancient forerunner of this late Empire of the Andean cordilleras? Again "chance", or adventure, gives the answer!

In 1929, a romantic adventure befell Mr. Lawrence Griswold, an American traveller, who brought the famous Komodo dragons from the Lost World Island of the Dutch East Indies to the Zoo in New York. It is graphically suggestive of the far past of ancient South America, and tears another small hole in the veil of mystery shrouding this most ancient land of the world. Mr. Griswold was captured by the Shuara Indians, a branch of the notorious Jivaro tribe of head-shrinkers. He was somewhere up the Rio Juara, a tributary of the Amazon, when he was captured, and the tribe took him eastwards to the foothills of the Andes. One day, he was chasing a peccary along the bed of a dried-up stream, when he stopped as he saw, jutting from a hill, the foundations of an ancient building. Digging away the soil, he came on some carefully jointed stones extending backwards and upwards into the overshadowing hill. There were two pyramidal structures and a horse-shoe amphitheatre, its open wings separated from the pyramids by a distance of thirty feet. Mr. Griswold thought it might "be Tiahuanacu work of 5000 B.C." The *Unta*, or old man of the tribe holding him captive, said the ancient builders were the "ancestors of the Shuaras". Many, many years ago, he said, the Shuaras were great bearded men, like gods, and *only since the Flood* had they taken a form like that of apes,

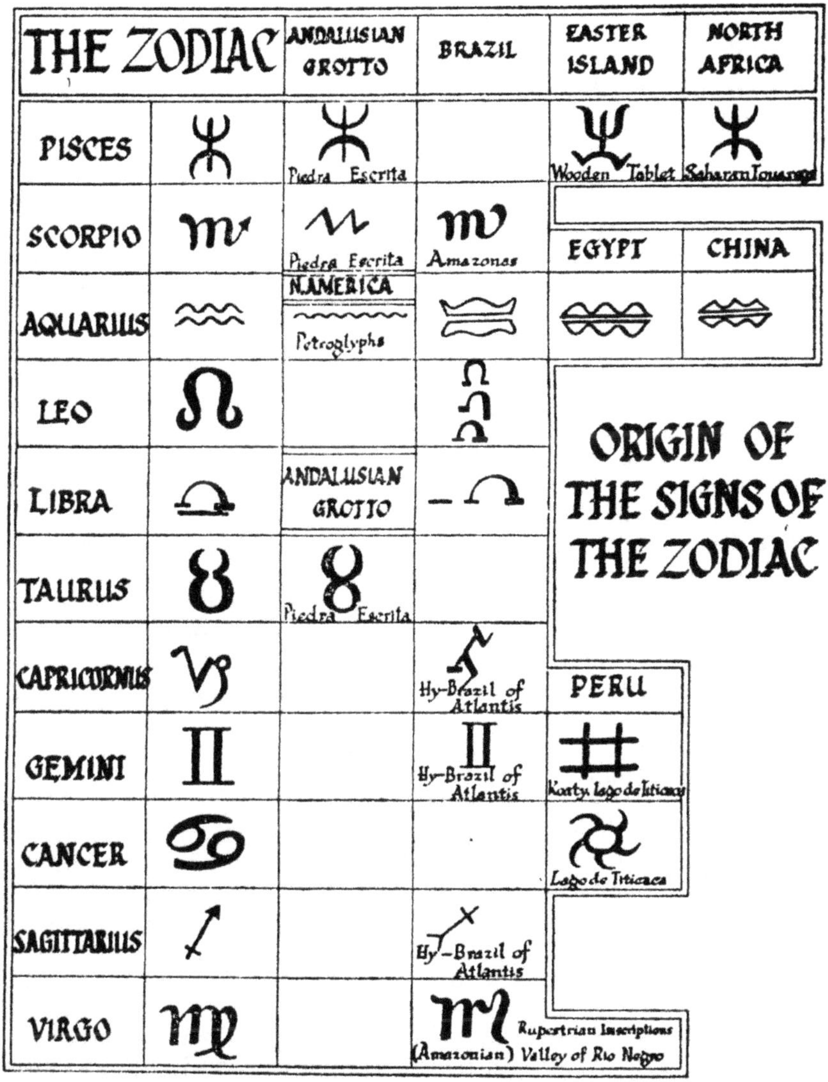

ORIGIN OF THE SIGNS OF THE ZODIAC

THE ZODIAC		ANDALUSIAN GROTTO	BRAZIL	EASTER ISLAND	NORTH AFRICA
PISCES		Piedra Escrita		Wooden Tablet	Saharan Touaregs
SCORPIO		Piedra Escrita	Amazonas	EGYPT	CHINA
AQUARIUS		N. AMERICA Petroglyphs			
LEO					
LIBRA		ANDALUSIAN GROTTO			
TAURUS		Piedra Escrita			
CAPRICORNUS			Hy-Brazil of Atlantis	PERU	
GEMINI			Hy-Brazil of Atlantis	Korty, lago de Titicaca	
CANCER				Lago de Titicaca	
SAGITTARIUS			Hy-Brazil of Atlantis		
VIRGO			Rupestrian Inscriptions (Amazonian) Valley of Rio Negro		

Grimaldi, in 1905, traced earliest Zodiacal inscription to Babylon (Tigris), *ca.* 1187 B.C.; but the priest-astronomers of Atlantean-Brazil may have originated them between 20,000 and 12,000 B.C.

and this was because of their antediluvian misdeeds. "These gods were as tall as you," said the old *Unta*, "and red-haired. And it was your red beard that saved *you* from death when we captured you. We thought you must be one of the old race who built that city, on the hill yonder." The *Unta* gladly gave Griswold an escort to the nearest post on the Amazon, the village of Caracaica, whence he returned to Manaos and took steamer for Rio and New York to persuade an American archaeologist to return and inspect these ruins. It is probable, though Mr. Griswold does not seem to have heard of the adventures of the *bandeiristas* of A.D. 1750, in the dead city, that *this* may also have been one of their outlying cities.

Fawcett said he had met a tribe—he does not say where, but it may have been in Brazil—who had a name for every planet barring Neptune; which suggests that the old civilised race of astronomers in prehistoric South America from whose elements of culture certain fragments had passed to the ancestors of these South American tribes, had not discovered this planet, and is evidence of their extreme and astounding antiquity. It is on the—at present—outermost elliptical ring of the solar system, and on account of its immense distance away, little is known of it by modern astronomers. Neither Babylon nor the even more ancient world knew Neptune. But, in 1836, Lieut. W. Smyth, in a trip from Lima to Para, encountered the tribe of the Sencis, living on the Rio Ucayli, a tributary of the Amazon in Northern Perú. These Indians actually had names for Jupiter and Mars and ten constellations. They are (or were) savages; so, here, again, there must be fragments surviving from the far-off day of some vanished white Atlantean civilisation of South America. It was among the Indians of the same Rio Ucayli that the Franciscan missioner, Fray Narcissus Gilbar, in the eighteenth century, found an old man reading, under trees on the pampas of the Rio Sacramento, MSS. on plantain-leaf paper, covered with orderly arranged bold characters, and single hieroglyphs and pictures of men and animals, the whole in colours. Earlier in the same century, another missioner among the Paños, in the valley of the Rio Huallagu—west and adjacent to the gorge of the Ucayli—found similar MSS. of plantain leaves among the Indians. Juan de Lucero says they told him these MSS. contained "a history of events in the days of their ancestors".

When the Franciscan friar, Fray Narcissus Gilbar, came back to Lima he got in touch with Baron Alexander von Humboldt, who, about 1820, was visiting Perú, on his travels of Central and South America. The friar told the baron his very curious story.

Says von Humboldt:

"When I was in Lima, an extremely curious fact came to my knowledge. The padre Narcissus Gilbar, well known for his courage and spirit of research among the independent Indians of the Paños, on the banks of the Ucayli, at a little to the north of the point where the Rio Sarayacu (on the pampas of eastern Perú) joins the Marañon (Amazon), found among them some MS. books of paintings, which, in their external appearance, perfectly resemble our own volumes in quarto. Each leaf was 11¾ inches long, by about 7¾ inches broad. The books were covered, or bound in leaves of a palm tree, with a very thick parenchyma (tissue from bark and pith of stems), and glued together. A piece of tolerably fine cotton formed the leaves, which were fastened by threads of agave. When Gilbar reached the dwellings of the Paños, he found an old man at the foot of a palm tree, seated and surrounded by several young people to whom he was explaining the contents of these books. The savages would not, at first, permit a white man to approach the teacher, and informed the friar, through the Indians of Manos, who, alone, understand the language of the Paños, that these paintings contained hidden things which no stranger ought to know. With great difficulty, Gilbar procured one of these collections, which he sent to Lima, for the inspection of P. Cisneros, the learned compiler of a periodical called *El Mercurio Peruano.*

"Several people, of my acquaintance, have seen this book of the Paños which is covered on every page with paintings. These were figures of men and animals, and a great number of isolated lines of characters, which were deemed to be hieroglyphs. They were arranged with admirable order and symmetry. The liveliness of the colours was particularly striking; but, as no one at Lima had seen a fragment of Aztec MS., it was impossible to judge of the identity of the style of paintings found at a distance from each other of 800 leagues. P. Cisneros wished to deposit this book in the convent of the missions of Ocupa; but whether the person to whom it was entrusted lost it on his passage over the cordilleras, or whether it was taken and sent clandestinely to Europe, it is certain it never reached the place of its destination. Every search for it has proved in vain . . . and the regrets of not having made a copy came too late. . . . The missioner, Narcissus Gilbar, with whom I was intimately acquainted at Lima, promised to get me another collection of these paintings of the Paños. He knows that several exist among them, and that they themselves say that these books were transmitted to them by their fathers. The explanation they give, of these paintings, seems founded on an ancient tradition which is perpetuated in some families.

"The Indians of Manos (or Manoa), whom Padre Gilbar commissioned to make researches into the meaning of these characters, imagined them to relate to travels and ancient wars with neighbouring tribes."

Manoa, of course, reminds one of Sir Walter Raleigh's Golden Manoa of El Dorado fame!

Humboldt adds that the Paños were savages dwelling in deep and sultry forests, and such recent inhabitants of the soil, that it was very unlikely they originated these paintings. Indeed, like the ancient glyphs on the granite rocks of the Orinoco, and the Guiana savanas, and the elevated plains of the cordilleras in the paramos of Guanca, these Paños paintings and MSS. must have been there long before the ancestors of modern tribes came into that region of the Peruvian pampas. The problem of their real origin, however, was not to be solved in the light of the knowledge available in A.D. 1820—or, it may be said, in A.D. 1920! But, with the evidence I have gathered in Brazil, and reinforced by my own arduous researches in English, Spanish and Portuguese source-material and MSS., I have no hesitation in saying that in these plantain MSS. we see the hand of the lost white imperial race of Hy-Brazil, of Atlantis the Great!

Pedro de Garcia, of the Order of Preaching Friars, noted a peculiar use to which Peruvians, at the time of the Spanish conquest, put "paintings in image-characters with which they confessed their sins, and painted each one of the ten commandments, in a certain manner, and use ciphers to indicate the offences against the commandments". The friar thought this meant that the Incas used symbolic paintings, ruder and more unpolished than the hieroglyphs of the Aztecs. He admitted that *quippus* were ordinarily used by them; but, oddly enough, for that age, refrained from suggesting that brethren from the Lost Ten Tribes had been sent by Mosheth to old Perú to convert the Peruvians to Jahveh, the hook-nosed demi-ourgos and vindictive old gentleman whose spirit, under other skies, had so often striven with other lesser men in fire, plague, slaughter and clouds of loud hosannahs.

Were these MSS. or *quilcas*, that had escaped the attention of the fanatic Inca Pachacuti the Sixth; or were they relics of a far earlier civilisation? Until a MS. of this sort reaches civilisation the question remains in suspense. We do not *yet know*, though, like the author of this book, one may have strong opinions.

Von Tschudi, in his *Antigüedades Peruanas* (Vienna, 1851), gives us the clue to the probable origin of these ancient letters, though he did not perceive its significance, when he wrote:

> "It was reputed, on investigation (among the Paños Indians of the pampas of the Sacramento, on the banks of the Rio Ucayli) that these MSS. referred to the history of a nation that arrived, from the *north or the east*, to the mountains of the Ucayli; and that they brought with them the knowledge of that writing; or that they are the remains of an ancient civilisation."

There is no *proof* that the Mayas' culture penetrated so far south and over the Andean cordilleras to old Perú. But as von Tschudi knew nothing of the existence of the inscriptions in the dead cities of Brazil—although transcripts of them already existed in the old Royal and Imperial Library at Rio de Janeiro, in his day—he naturally did not connect this ancient civilisation with Atlantean Brazil.

A slender clue to the range of some of these South American, vanished civilisations, though its end is and may ever remain lost in the night of time, may exist in the dense and dangerous forests and jungles of the interior of the republic of Haïti, and across the border in the sister republic of Dominica. It was in the latter, behind the mountains of Santiago, in a region far less known today than in the fifteenth century A.D., that Bartholomew Columbus found the strange, deep gold-mines spoken of by George Hornius, the (Dutch) Leyden professor, in his *De Originibus Americanis* (1652 edition):

> "In Haiti are found the wonderful mines (*fodinae*) out of which (Bartholomew) Columbus judged the fleet of Solomon sailed to fetch gold. Of these in his voyage he writes: 'Bartholomew Columbus found in Hispaniola a cave very high and very ancient, whence they say Solomon dug up his gold. This gold mine is 16,000 feet deep and very ancient. The proof is great that at one time men went to the island for metals, as in all times the Phoenicians and those of Spain did. For these mines were not made by the Haitians, who, of metals and mines are completely ignorant, and of veins in the bowels of the earth, as is certain. They get their gold out of rivers.'"

Bartholomew Columbus, who was then adelantado of San Domingo, took a trip to these ancient mines, with a troop of soldiers and miners. The natives told him the mines* lay sixty Spanish leagues from the town of Isabella. When he reached there, the obvious antiquity of the workings impressed the imagination of Bartholomew. He saw that the pits extended over an area of nearly six miles. The miners, riddling the earth of the workings, at several points, affirmed that they found such great amounts of gold, hidden in this soil, that a single miner might easily pick up "six drachmas of gold a day. This was on 5th day of the Ides of March, 1495," says Peter Martyr. (As those mines have long since vanished into the

---

* These prehistoric gold-mines of extraordinary depth may lie behind the still unexplored mountains of Cibao in modern Dominica's territory; but, as even maps of the late seventeenth century show, Peter Martyr, or Bartholomew Columbus, must have been greatly in error in stating that the region of the Montaña de Cibaos, where these mines may be presumed to,lie was sixty Castilian leagues' distant from the township of Isabella (Ysabella de Torres.) If that were the distance, then Bartholomew's soldiers must have gone a very roundabout way to their objective. However, in a coming day, startling archaeological and prehistoric discoveries are going to be made in this *terra incognita*.—THE AUTHOR.

jungle, lost to sight and memory, there must be a fortune waiting some prospector in the wilds of modern Dominica.)

My friend, Captain John Houston Craige, late chief of police, during the U.S. occupation of Haiti, says an American marine is the only man he has ever known to reach *near* these mysterious gold-mines.

Peter Martyr, or Peter Martyr de Anghiera, speaks of ancient works of art found in this old buccaneering island. He died at Granada, old Spain, in 1526.

Saint-Méry, in his *Description de la patrie française de St. Domingue*, speaks of a stone cut with strange and unknown letters, found in the mountains of Guanaminto, in Haiti. That find was made in 1787. "In these mountains, as in neighbouring isles, there exist great grottoes, worked by man, and ornamented with sculptures, analogous to those of the moon of *Caurau*, and preceded, usually, by two stelæ of the *chemis*, always found two by two, as in Asia," said Abbé Brasseur-de-Bourbourg, the *Américaniste*. E. Nau, who wrote an infernally dull book, titled *Histoire des Caciques d'Haïti*, adds that the Caribs of Haiti had no traditions about the ancient builders of these monuments and the workers of the ancient gold-mines, which were shrouded in their forests and jungles. . . .

> "There are vast crypts hollowed in the rocks, walls of great extent and length in drystone, or only *en terre* (earthworks). Another race, other men more polished in culture (*policés*) must have occupied this country in remote times, and the Indians of the last epoch must have succeeded to the civilisation of people extinguished by time or revolutions. Whence came these first occupants? Were they autochthones? The savants are divided over these questions. They are obscure and inextricable."

Queer caverns were also among the discoveries of the conquistadores in Hispaniola, or San Domingo. One of them, named "Jouanabaina", was on the land of the cacique of Machinech, and the object of the worship of the natives. It "was ornamented with various paintings. At the door stands two carved *zèmes*. Then, the original natives went on pilgrimage to these caverns." (*Zèmes*, or *chemis*, were idols of the old Antilles.) A later French traveller and naturalist, Michel-Etienne Descourtilz, author of *Voyages d'un naturaliste, en Haïti*, in 1799–1803, found similar Haïti-Domingan caverns at Dubeda, among the Gonaives; on the Selle mountain, at or near Port-au-Prince; and at Doubou, near Cap François. . . .

> "They are natural excavations lit from the top, so as to let pass the first rays of the rising sun. The interior of these grottoes is covered with idols, carved, engraved and inlaid in the rock,

in rude and bizarre forms; toads with heads at the ends of their feet, monstrous human figures with crooked body diminishing like a cone, terminated by a spherical knob; tortoises; and other animals, especially snakes."

My good friend, Dr. Price-Mars, sénateur de la République and President of the Society of History and Geography of Haïti, has kindly sent me a copy of a very interesting brochure titled *L'Art Précolombien d'Haïti*, which was published by the authorities of the republic at the time of the recent third congress of the Caribs. In this illuminating booklet are reproduced some striking photographs of discoveries, in that island, of remains, statues, *betyles* (statues of a god, or the shrine of a deity), and stelae. These remains are of a people of unknown race and date who knew not of iron. Like the race in Atlantean Brazil, they seem to have been heliolithic, and of very advanced culture. The statues show that *two* races existed there thousands of years ago: one white, the other black. One of the heads is a sculptured funerary face of a white man and another of a white woman of Atlantean type. There is also a remarkable head (*masque*) of a black woman, in polished but weathered granite—of prehistoric date—which bears a strange resemblance in shape and peculiar, coronal head-dress to a splendid terra-cotta head of a negro Venus, found in British Nigeria and now in the palace of the native ruler of Ife, where it is worshipped as a goddess. (As, doubtless, was this similar head in Atlantean old Haiti.) The Nigerian head—of great beauty—was carved by an artist of great skill belonging to a very ancient advanced, black civilisation in Africa.

Frobenius, who associated this ancient culture of West Africa with Atlantis, was probably right. Had he seen this similar head in Haïti, he would also have remembered that, in Atlantis, and her colonies, and empire, red, white, and black races commingled. Part of the old Empire of Atlantis extended from the far greater Gulf of Marañon—the Mexican Gulf of today—into the island-continent—as it was then—of the West Indies, not then shattered by cataclysm.

One may also infer from these pictures, in the *L'Art Précolombien d'Haïti*, that necromancy and black magic of the Voodoo type existed in this strange island long ages before ever the Spanish or French introduced negro slaves into old Hispaniola. Who can say whether such black cults came there from the motherland of Atlantis far gone in decay?

There are also extremely ancient petroglyphs of a curiously symbolical whorled type recalling similar rupestrian inscriptions in modern Colombia—both baffling to modern archaeologists and pre-historians.

Yes, on Haïti-Dominica, too, rests the shadow of great Atlantis!

CHAPTER VII

THE ATLANTEAN "SUBTERRANEANS" OF THE INCAS

"The topaz blazing like a lamp,
Among the mines beneath."

("Mad" *Kit Smart.*)
(*The Song of David* (A.D. 1760).

TRAVELLERS both in Mexico and on the bleak and lonely paramos of the high Andes, in Perú, and far down on the trail of the old conquistadores that led to Potosi and the Argentine, are pretty sure, at some stage of their journey, to meet, especially in the short twilight at those heights, a strange light, called *la luz del dinero* (money light). It is a phenomenon for which science and physics, at this time, has no explanation. Indeed, it is pretty safe to say that, in Europe, no physicist has ever heard of this phenomenon. You meet it about the time of the pale, lambent dusk along the solitary tracks that lead across the cordilleras and the bleak paramos from old Cuzco.

Of course, the European or American traveller departing from that old city of sad and depressing memories is likely to be in the mood and frame of mind to be receptive of this marvel of the trail. And yet it is certainly not a subjective illusion, existing only in the mind of one who has just left a melancholy place of ghosts, where the apparitions of ruffling, Spanish hidalgos, with fierce dark eyes and haughty, saturnine countenances, steal in the pale moonlight across the plaza and down shadowy streets, with carved doorways, still emblazoned with heraldic beasts, ramping on Castilian coats of arms. (Yet, despite all his mail and hauberks and his flaming matchlocks, the Castilian and Estremaduran soldier—even with the cold-hearted, sadistic monk, lurking in the background with *his* fiery faggots of the auto da fé—was never able to wrest from the gentle and solemn-eyed Incas the secrets of their lost caches!)

As you jog along on horse-back, or afoot along any of these old Spanish gold trails from the mines to the coast ports, in old Perú, or the old Spanish Argentine, you may meet, at a turn of the cold and stony ways, some Indian, or mestizo half-caste, or even a white man, hunting for buried gold. A man will swear to you that, in a lone cañon, just off the old, gold way, he saw one evening, as the sun had sunk into his ocean bed, far away to the west behind the walls of the valiant cordilleras, yonder, and the stars wheeled up the deep, blue sky, a strange whitish light, or queer, greenish luminosity, appear, hovering above the rocky ground.

"*Está la luz del dinero, señor,*" says he.

"It is the 'money light', and where that wavers on the trail, why, *Carajó*, there is a *tapada* (a treasure cache) . . . *un tesoro entierro!*"

The colonial Spanish trail from Potosi to Tucuman, in the Argentine, is pitted with holes showing where generations of seekers have dug for *tapadas*. Some of these *tapadas* may be caches of royalist, or ecclesiastical gold and jewels made when the monarchist armies were retreating from before the advancing legions of Simon Bolivar *el Liberador*. These mysterious lights often appear in the dusk, or darkness, when they may trail along the ground like slithering snakes, emitting a greenish luminosity, or a queer, whitish shine. At other times, the lights may stand upright like shafts of the columns in an old Inca temple of the sun: or take the form of tropic trees. The *tapada* hunter drives a stake in the ground, and retires to some resort of wine and warm and cheerful company, song and fandango, to await the coming of broad day. There are *demonios* abroad, as everyone knows, in the night hours, and not for all the lost treasures of the Incas will your *mestizo*, or your full-blooded Indian dig in the darkness for these treasures. His *piquete* serves the same purpose as a buoy to the salvor of silver wrecks. None will brave the evil spirits of buried treasures and darkness in the high *altiplanos* of the *tierra fria* to grub up his *piquete* and jump his claim. . . . "*Si, señor, hasta mañana*, when we will return and hunt for the gold where the 'money light' has shone!"

I have heard some say that it is caused by the emanations of gases, such as is probably the cause of the mysterious *Faro de Catatumba*, in the Gulf of Maracaibo, in the Venezuelan oil regions. May be, and may be not! I have heard others compare the light to the jack o' lanthorns, or will-o'-the-wisp lights, which used to be frequent, a century or less ago, in the neighbourhood of undrained English fens and marshes. An old, blind and crippled gold-bug bitten friend of mine, who died a few years ago, in his bed in a West of England infirmary, swore that the *luz del dinero* was a radio-active emanation from buried gold. Yes, but radio-activity is not usually associated with the breaking-up of *stable* atoms, such as we find in gold. Better say that the mystery remains still unsolved.

This old engineer friend of mine, who was the nephew of a former Bishop of Bath and Wells, Somerset, England, spent many years of his adventurous life in the Argentine and Mexico.

Said he to me: "I owned a gold-mine in South America, which I found by this small, bluish-white light coming from the ground. There, I dug up a very rich piece of quartz-ore. It was hardly an inch below the surface. I always found metal after digging where these lights were seen in the dusk. The *peónes* and the *Indiós* fear this apparition, and give it a wide berth. Were it not for this fear of the supernatural, many more treasures would have been discovered by its means. It always struck me, this *luz del dinero*, as resembling alcohol burning with blue tongues of flame. It can be seen for a long way, and the *Indiós* and Spanish-American 'greasers' have sworn to me that the light extends over a radius equal to that of the subterranean metal causing it. . . . I once hired an old *hacienda* in Mexico where an old Indian woman told me she'd seen this light. I searched walls and floor, but found nothing; yet a man who took the place after I left found a tin of gold doubloons in the roof."

Yet, no mystic, lambent flames of a money light will ever suggest the location of the amazing lost cache of ransom-treasure of the last, and murdered, Inca emperor, Atahualpha, a treasure which the Spanish chroniclers and historians say consisted of from 600–650 tons of gold and jewels, worth 384 millions gold *pesos de oro*. (If we suppose, conservatively, that there were 600 tons of gold in this vast treasure, then, taking the value of gold at the pre-Great War No. 2 rate of £7 10*s*. a troy ounce, the metal, at raw gold value, leaving out of account all antiquarian values, would have been worth, in 1938, about £147,000,000, or say, $835,000,000). . . . And yet, there is good reason to believe that, as an Inca nobleman told Benalcazar, the Conquistador of Quito, even this immense treasure is but a kernel of corn compared with a heap from the harvest-field, in relation to another very ancient subterranean treasure which I shall mention, later, in this chapter.

As Pedro Cieza de Leon virtually said, in A.D. 1545, the backs and bottoms of the stoutest galleons of that age would have been broken transporting these immense heaps to the bar of San Lucar and the stone houses of the Casa de Contratacion in old Seville, even had that mystery sprite of the sea, Davy Jones, consented, under old Father Neptune, to its passing overseas.

The *gente decente* of old Spanish descent, who govern, today, the administrations in Lima and La Paz would lend more aid than they do to the efforts of enterprising gringos from New York and London to find some of these immense, Inca caches, were it not for fear of the vigilance of millions of Quichua Indians, who still revere the memory of the murdered Inca Emperor of the Sun, and who would flame into revolt at the first bruiting of such an enterprise. The down-trodden Indians, who bear small resemblance to the pictures of the Incas which one can see, today, in the old church of Santa Ana, a little northwards of melancholy Cuzco, dream of the day when, led by their reincarnated ancestors, they will find the wheel again come full circle and the vanished glories of the old Inca empire of the sun once more dawn on a Western, South American world.

Where do whispered, native Quichua traditions say these lost Inca hoards lie?

They lie in forests, the bottoms of lone mountain tarns where the brooding shadows retreat into limbo only for the short space of time when the almost vertical, mid-day sun casts his beams on to the deep, tranquil, dreaming waters; in sealed caves to which mystic hieroglyphs, whose key is possessed only by one descendant of the Inca, at a time, in each generation, give the open sesame; and in strange "subterraneans", thousands of years old, which must have been made by a mysterious and highly civilised vanished race of South America in a day when the ancient Peruvians, themselves, were a mere wandering tribe of barbarians, if not savages, roaming the cordilleras and the high passes, or still living, perhaps, in some long-disrupted Pacific continent, from which they came in ships.

"If all the gold that is buried in Perú . . . were collected, it would be impossible to coin it, so great the quantity; and yet the Spaniards of the conquest got very little compared with what remains. The Indians said:

> " 'THE TREASURE IS SO CONCEALED THAT EVEN WE, OURSELVES, KNOW NOT THE HIDING-PLACE!' "

This was what the Peruvians told Cieza de Leon, the soldier-priest, about fifteen years after the conquest of Perú. They did not think fit to add that there were *some* among them who knew and closely guarded the tremendous secrets. Cieza de Leon adds:

> "Within the space of eight months, in the year 1598, 35,000,000 of gold and silver crossed the bar of San Lucar, on its way to old Seville, in three cargoes."

It is golden-tongued Lasso (Garcilasso de la Vega, *El Inca*) who tells how one of the world's greatest treasures came to vanish in such a way that the secret of the cache has baffled all the cunning and scoundrelism of gold-crazy adventurers of almost all nations under the sun, as well as the ingenuity of the cruellest, keenest wits and intellects, in the brains of men, who ever shipped themselves aboard galleons from Cadiz and the old port of Barrameda to fly poverty and the ever-enduring curse of old Spain, in all ages—*la hambre* (hunger)—and the plagues and miseries springing from the wars and European broils financed by this stolen gold of the Americas, in the late sixteenth, the seventeenth, and early eighteenth centuries. Verily, the gentle, lofty-browed Inca had, by his sun-god, been revenged on the avaricious and most religious sadists of old Castile and Estremadura and Aragon, upon whose own lands, in far-away Spain, there now descended the deadly plagues of unemployment and almost universal poverty. So scarce was food to become, that, if the caballero wished to give a present to the *señorita* who was queen of his heart, or the *doncella honrada*, his Nina of the scented *calle* of San Sebastian, he was reckoned a "verie parfait, gentle knyghte" if he gave her a gammon of ham, a large and savoury capon pie, or a sirloin of beef or haunch of venison, instead of a jewelled miniature, or a bouquet of flowers, which, after all, stayed the wamblings of no one's hungry belly. As for the lower orders of old Spain, after the mostly stolen riches of the older Americas had poured into old Seville and Madrid, what, after the conquest, befell them?

It happened to a *hungry picaro*, or famished knave of a boy-porter, once well off under the old Moors of the Alcazar, and Granada, that he accounted himself lucky could he be employed to carry great weights, or a heavy basket, as an *esportillero*, and thereby earn a *sueldo* to silence the call of hunger after the daily portion of soup had been handed out at the abbey. Surely was this a peculiarly ironic punishment on old Spain who, by her conquistadorian banditti, and fanatic black priests, had wrecked a civilisation of ancient date wherein no man or woman starved, or lacked clothing and shelter, albeit gold was deemed only a medium for ornamentation and not a medium of exchange. *La venganza* upon Spanish bandits who had committed the atrocities whose authors Las Casas forebore to name ! Now let us raise the curtain on this drama of history.

Today, at Caxamarca, you are shown a room which the Inca Atahualpha had to fill with treasure for his ransom. A heap of gold ornaments as tall as his upraised arms could reach, and as broad as the span of his arms outstretched. The conquistadores were not niggardly in their estimation of what his Inca majesty's liberty might be worth! The usual estimate is that this room could contain around $500,000,000, or, say, £100,000,000 of gold. The conquistadores did not welcome gems. They looked with disfavour on them, in fact; for had they not found so many splendid emeralds, pearls, turquoises and diamonds of fine water in the Peruvian empire that the bottom of the lapidarian market had been knocked clean out? Wedges of gold were preferred, till even they became so common that a Castilian soldier-man would liefer have a jennet or Castilian stallion, or a quart of wine or pair of shoes.

Don Francisco Pizzaro, *el gobernador y marqués del Perú*, drew a line in bright red round the walls of this cave-room of Aladdin or Ali Baba's forty thieves, which is seventeen feet wide and twenty feet long, and which the Inca said he could easily fill with gold. The red line was nine feet above the stone floor. The Spaniards stripped the gold-plating from the Cuzco royal temple's walls, and the yard-wide gold guttering which ran round the temple like a coronal frieze. They even took the gold pipes which fed with pure water, from the snows of the cordilleras, the five fountains rising and falling in iridescent displays in the lovely garden-close of the temple of the sun. The native goldsmiths were a whole month melting down this gold from Cuzco Temple into bars worth, today, some £5,000,000 or

$25,000,000. So exquisite was the jewellers' work of some of these antiques that even the rude bandit Pizarro was moved to preserve it to send to the Court, in old Spain.

But, like soldiers in all ages, the Castilians and Estremadurans might be trusted never to forget that they had a belly with two desires, and that, after the hard battle, the warrior wanted his recreation.

These hardy soldiers swore by Venus as ardently as by Midas's golden ass's ears. I have an engraving, of piquant character, taken from a very rare book published at Frankfurt on the Rhine, sixty-six years after the conquest of Perú. It is a Latin history of America, and tells the story—not to the approval of later, Spanish historians! —of what happened the morning after the amazing victory over the Inca's hosts, outside the walls of old Cuzco. The Spaniards ate and slept all night, as far as they were able; for they had fought like Israelites in David's famished armies, or like buccaneers in Darien who were so hungry they could have sacrificed "Sambolloe" Indians to their teeth. In the morning, they strolled into the country, a mile outside the camp at Caxamarca, and lit on many handsome, nude, Inca women bathing in the imperial, open air baths. The picture shows the bearded Castilians wading into the water and haling the reluctant women to the nearby groves. These, with others ravished in the Inca's camp, totalled, if we are to believe some old and not too discreet, Spanish chronicler of the *Indias Occidentales, no fewer than* 5,000 *women*! *Valde*, as the Latinist historian hints, Venus, Bacchus and St. Midas had a rare day out in that year of 1533, in the dying empire of old Perú!

When Atahualpha was brought prisoner into the presence of Pizarro, the Inca emperor was wearing a magnificent collar of emeralds of great size and extreme brilliancy. The gems blew such a flame of avarice alight in the brain (or soul) of the conquistadores, that, as Cieza de Leon writes:

> "If, when the Spaniards entered Cuzco they had not committed other tricks, and had not so soon executed their cruelty in putting Atahualpha to death, I know not how many great ships would have been required to bring such treasures to old Spain, as is now lost in the bowels of the earth and will remain so because those who buried it are now dead."

Pizarro at once sent emissaries hot foot to Cuzco, and three of the conquistadorian soldiers brought back gold to the Spanish camp, at Caxamarca. Each horse soldier got a share of 8,800 castellanos de oro (gold castellans), and 362 marks in silver, each mark weighing eight ounces. The *infanteria* got half as much each man. The share-out started a great gambling saloon going night and day which beats almost anything even in the great days of the Poker Flat saloon in the wild west of Bret Harte's prime.

As John Harris picturesquely put it, in his *Moral History of the Spanish West Indies* (London, 1705), written as if he had been on the scene as an eye-witness, rather than one writing nearly 200 years later: "Debts were paid in wedges of gold and no Spaniard troubled if a creditor got twice the amount of his debt. Nothing was so cheap, so common, so easy to be got as gold and silver . . . a sheet of paper went for ten Castilians of gold."

The three emissaries brought back, also, the rifled treasures from the sun temple of old Cuzco. They comprised an immense freight of gold and silver vessels loaded on the backs of 200 staggering, sweating Indians. It was almost more than twelve men could do to heave even one of the gold vessels; and when there entered the Spanish camp the great massy gold throne of the Inca, and a heavy gold funnel of a fountain, Pizarro felt as did Nadir Shah, in the middle of the eighteenth century, when he broke into the Dewan-i-Shah in the old throne-room of the Moguls in Delhi and bore off to Iran the great golden peacock throne.

The Inca's queen, says an old Quichua tradition, I heard in Perú, had, when her husband was made prisoner, offered for his liberation a room full of gold "from the floor up to the ceiling, as high as his conqueror could reach, and before the sun set on the third day". She kept her promise; but Pizarro broke his. For he said, struck with the marvellous exhibition of such treasures: "I will not release the Inca; but will murder him, unless you tell me whence all these treasures come." Pizarro had heard, goes on the native Peruvian tradition, that the Incas possessed a secret and inexhaustible mine, or enormous depository of mysterious character, which lay in a vast, *subterranean tunnel, or road, running many miles underground beneath his imperial dominions*. Here were kept the accumulated riches of the country.

The poor queen begged for delay, and, in the meantime, went to consult the oracles of the priests of the sun. In the course of the sacrifice, the high priest asked her to look into the *black mirror*.*

* This must have been the Inca equivalent of the *Unjun*, or *Anjan*, of which the famous Victorian traveller, Sir R. F. Burton, speaks. It is a lamp-blacked, magic mirror, prepared in a peculiar manner and then applied to the palms of the hands of a child, or other virginal person, who had to stare hard into it, and so produce a dilation of the normal consciousness. "This art for finding hidden treasure is practised by Yogis, Sanyasis, and other Hindu devotees," he says. From other sources, one learns that the *black mirror* was prepared in the province of Agra, and also in Tibet and China. Brasseur-de-Bourbourg, the famous savant and historian of Central America, where he was abbé in the frontier, Mexican province of Chiappas, cites a native historian who said the ancestors of the ancient Quichés of Yucatan brought the *black mirror* to Central America from *old Egypt*. The Peruvian sun-worshippers knew it, as we see. When the Spanish Conquistadores landed in Central America, the king of the Quichés ordered his priests to consult the mirror so as to learn the fate of his kingdom and "the demon reflected the present and the future as in a mirror". Of course, what happened is that the normal consciousness transcended the normal plane and had a fourth or fifth dimensional peep into that world where all space lies stretched out in time, and past, future and present are all one.

She looked, and, shuddering, saw a picture of the fate of her husband, inevitable whether or no the gold were delivered to the conquistadorian and most Spanish Catholic bandits. The horrified, grief-stricken queen ordered that the entrance to the great tunnel—a masoned door in the rocky wall of the cliff-gorge—be closed, and this was done under the direction of the high priest and the magicians. The chasm was hidden from sight and entirely closed by filling its depths with huge masses of rock. When the levelled-off surface was reached, it was hidden under green grass and bushes, and made to appear like a natural lawn covering a rock; so that not the slightest sign of any fissure was perceptible to the eye. Spanish avarice was foiled, and the secret was known only to pure-bred Indians of Quichua-Inca birth, and never to *mestizos*, or half-castes, who, it was thought, could never be trusted with any such knowledge.

(I have a remarkable sequel of this story, to tell, later.)

As the fatal day drew on, the Inca asked to be taken into the open air to see a large comet, green, black and nearly as big as a man, which streamed across the Peruvian skies. It was on a day in July or August 1533. Then, at the suggestion of the infamous and fanatic black monk, Valverde, a monk of that very order, the sadistic Dominican, which, in the "Most Holy Inquisition", drenched the white worlds of old Europe, and Asia, and the Americas in blood and tears, on the pretence of securing the salvation of burning souls, the luckless emperor of the more rational sun-cultus was strangled—for the good of his soul, after he had been baptised, so they said, that he might escape burning at the stake in the public plaza of old Cuzco. A mass was held, and a solemn funeral followed, when the dirges and the chants rose to the diabolical skies. Here, and in the chapel, Gonzalo and Francisco Pizarro attended in black mourning habits. Whether this was out of pure hypocrisy, or dictated by remorse, or twinges of conscience, only those can say who may penetrate into the dark depths of the souls of these ruthless, stern, and fearless men who built a great empire on the tarnished blades of men who were simultaneously zealous Christian Catholics, hardy pioneers and brigands who would stick at nothing to gain gold.

Theodore de Bry, writing in 1596, in Latin, shows the monk—the black Dominican Vincent de "Valle Verde"—approaching the Inca, in the middle of the tumult of the Indians, with cross and breviary in hand, or, "as some say, the Bible". An engraving shows Pizarro, the breaker of faith with the Inca, ordering his strangling "by blackamoors" and closing his ears against the advice of some of the Castilian captains that the Inca be sent home to the "Kaiser" Carlos V., in old Spain, and that the Spaniard should not pollute his hands with the blood of an inoffensive man, and a king at that! . . . "Also, for the dead emperor, Francisco Pizarro put on black mourning clothes and ordered a ceremonial funeral." The gold and silver brought into Caxamarca by the Indians were weighed. There were 26,000 lb. of pure silver; 3,600,500 castellanos' worth of gold, called pesos by the Spaniards, and reckoned each at a crown and a half (*tricies vicies sex milleni et quingenti Castiliani*). They gave Carlos V., in Spain, a fifth (400,000 pesos), which suggests that our Lord the King was unlucky in the division! Each knight in the conquistadorian army got 8,900 gold pesos, and 185 lb. of silver; ninety captains got 30–40,000 gold pesos; while Hernando Pizarro, the conquistador's brother, received a fifth of the treasure. Yet, sagely comments de Bry: "It is worthy of note that the barbarous murder of that Prince, the Inca, did not remain unpunished; for afterwards, they perished miserably who had conspired to cause the Inca's murder." It may be added, too, that, in the following century, the Spanish Council of the Indies, at Seville, allowed no man to ship from Seville, in any galleon bound to the "Indies", unless he attested in writing that he was *not* of the kin of Pizarro and Almagro. (I freely admit that Bartoloméo de las Casas, the noble Dominican monk and champion of the Indians, made what atonement he could.)

Certainly, no Spanish kings, or holy Roman emperors, would, or did, approve of the assassination of home or foreign kings and emperors, whose personages they would deem sacred, no matter whether, by divine right, they governed wrong or right. Anyhow, the brothers Pizarro followed the Inca's bier in deep mourning, and after bearing the royal corpse into the yard of the convent of San Francisco, they allowed the Peruvians to take the body over the Andes to royal Quito, where, as it was his birthplace, the soon dying Inca had said he wished to be buried. Perú, as England of the dark ages, had reason to say to her dark soul: "Woe unto thee, O land, when thy king is a monk, and not a soldier!"

When the news reached the queen she followed her husband into the land of the shades, committing suicide to escape a fate worse than death—no cant phrase, this, in that age!—which, later, befell the young Inca princes and nobles, whom the devilish-hearted, cold sadist, *el Virrey*, Don Francisco Toledo, a man after the heart of the butcher Alva, exiled to the fever-haunted frontiers of the Darien peninsula, or broke their hearts by deporting them to the snowy wastes of the southern Andean cordillera.

The story, usually told of one of the lost caches—that of the immense treasure that was whisked away from the clutching hands of Don Francisco Pizarro waiting for it in the camp near old Cuzco—is that 11,000 llamas, freighted with gold from Cuzco, and elsewhere in the old empire of Perú, were on their way to Pizarro's camp when the Quichua Indians heard of the assassination of their Inca. The Indians drove the llamas off the road, and buried the 100 lb. of gold with which each animal of the caravan was laden. Sir Clements

Markham, whose opinion as one with peculiarly intimate knowledge of Perú must carry weight, said that the 1,100,100 lb. of gold lies hidden in the mountains behind Azangaro. The Cordillera de Azangaro is a wild sierra little known to the Americans, or the British; but I may add, for the information of those interested, that the name *Azangaro*, in the Quichua tongue—the tongue of old Inca Perú—means "place farthest away". It is believed that it was the farthest eastern point in the Andean cordilleras, which the old Inca empire dominated. Yet, despite the fact that the early conquistadorians and Pizarro's other camp-fellows worked old Inca mines in the eastern *montaña* of this wild region, no inkling of the location of the wondrous cache ever reached their "hungry ears".

There is a tradition current in the mystic east, and, perhaps, derived from Atlanteans who quitted their great motherland before the time of the terrible cataclysm (which, we may recall, the Egyptian priests of Sais and Heliopolis told Solon happened about 9700 B.C. when a militarist section of the Atlantean peoples had overrun Western and South-Eastern Europe and North Africa), that the central cathedral temple of old Atlantis's capital, hill city, "Sardegon", had a dome-shaped ceiling from which flamed a magnificent *central sun of blazing gold.* The late inheritors of the remains of the civilisation of the Atlantean imperial colony of Hy-Brazil, of South America, the Incas of Perú—Perú, as one has stated, being derived from a word (*not* found in the *Quichua*, or native Peruvian tongue) *Vira*, meaning the god of the sun—had a glorious sun of purest gold which shone with truly dazzling refulgence from the walls of Cuzco's great temple of the Sun. It was there when the keels of Don Francisco Pizarro's caravels and galleons touched the shallows of the Peruvian coast in A.D. 1530. The very eye-balls of the beholder were pained by its scintillations.

But when Pizarro's conquistadores laid their bandits' hands on this ancient civilisation, as the Carian-Colloans had done before them in relation to what was left of the communities of the old, white, bearded Atlanteans of Hy-Brazil in the islands of Lake Titicaca, Perú, that glorious sun of gold vanished. For four centuries its whereabouts have remained a mystery, the close secret of one, or not more than two, of the Inca's posterity. Be sure, that there is living, today, in one of the valleys of the Peruvian cordilleras, some Peruvian, little suspected by his fellows, who knows where this sun went to ground!

In the neighbourhood of modern Cuzco, I have heard some of the traditions about this mystic lost sun. How well its shining wonder attests the old melancholy and vanished grandeur of a great race! The Quichuan *peónes* say it was fashioned as a human face of solid gold, radiating shafts of light as it blazed from the walls. It personified, to the people, the Sun, and, hieratically, to the priests, no doubt, the "Great Central Sun of the Cosmos"; the unknown God whom Paul of Tarsus proclaimed to the men of Athens, as he stood on Mar's Hill, or the Areopagus; or He whom the Brahmins of old called *Dyaus*, the sky, the *Deus* of the Romans.

This glorious face of refulgence was really, at Cuzco, a massive plate of purest gold, of enormous width, encrusted thickly with emeralds of superb size and quality, and other gems. At his rising, the rays of the Sun fell directly on to this face in the temple, where gold blazed back everywhere from walls and ceilings. The cornices were of gold and a broad frieze of gold, let into the stonework, surrounded the whole exterior of the temple.

Don Marcio Serra de Leguisamo, last of the conquistadores of old Perú, spoke of the "child" of this Sun, when he wrote the preamble of the will he made at Cuzco, on September 18, 1589:

> "I had a figure of the sun made of gold, that was placed by the Incas in the House of the Sun at Cuzco, which is now in the convento de San Domingo. I believe it is worth 2,000 pesos; and yet I die poor, with many children, and I beseech his Catholic and Royal Majesty, Don Felipe, our Lord, *el Rey*, to have pity on them, and may God have mercy on my soul."

Leguisamo gambled this smaller sun away the night after the day on which he had taken it. "He plays away the sun before the dawn," said Fray Acosta, the monk, of him. But this sun of Leguisamo was merely a plate of gold on which the image of the sun was carved, and which acted as a lid, or cover to a great, hollowed stone, in the outer wall of the temple, into which libations of *chicha* (fermented maize beer) were poured, by the people, in the festival of *Raymi*, which reminds one of *Ra*, the sun-god of old Egypt. On either side of the image of the great sun sat the embalmed bodies of thirteen Incas, in their chairs of gold, standing on gold slabs. In these chairs they had sat in life. The outraged Indians made haste to hide these sacred mummies, with the rest of the treasure, and only twenty-six years later did the hungry and never-resting Polo de Ondegardo, conquistador, accidentally light on the mummies of three kings, and two queens—the latter removed from the corresponding temple of the moon. All the corpses were, of course, stripped of their jewellery and broken in pieces by the sacrilegious hands of these insatiable treasure hunters.

Along with the royal mummies, in 1533, there also went to ground the great, gold, life-size statue of the Inca Huayna Capac, and only one man knew the secret of that cache, and he, again, no Spaniard, or half-bred *mestizo*.

"If the Christians have not found the Inca's treasure," said the prudent Peruvians to Pedro Cieza de Leon, in A.D. 1550, "it is because they are so concealed that even *we* know not the place." *Y, por la Santissima Virgen* had any one, at that time of day, admitted that he had so much a blind horse's wink of knowledge about *one* such cache, then *el Virrey* would have experienced such a good, Catholic, fervent desire to assoil his soul of the accursèd memory of hidden gold that he would have called on a holy Dominican Father of the Holiest Inquisition to shrive him with fire, anoint him with burning oil, and crown him with faggots in the open plaza of Cuzco or Lima, unless the secret were instantly divulged to the *Audiencia*! Nobody went about boasting of knowledge of that sort, in those picturesque days, or tried to lead hungry, official Castilians up old Inca fairy golden gardens, on false trails of ancient gold-bugs, unless he wished to save himself the trouble of committing suicide. If you wiere a Catholic *conquistador*—not of *hidalgo* rank—of the post-Pfzarro age, and did not need soul-saving of this sort, you yet found it best to keep your knowledge to yourself; for you were a long way from the justice and the alguazils of old Spain, did *el Virrey* or the *adelantado*, hearing how that you frequented *bodegas* and *posadas* in a way you were not accustomed to, of old, and oft sounded fellows about the locations of likely *haciendas* for sale, sent to *señor el Corregidor*—and had you cast into the *carcel* to explain your unwonted prosperity, and forever cut away from yourself the root of all evil.

In the archives at Cuzco, I have seen an old, yellowed parchment, insect-bitten, as is the way in these countries, written by one, Felipe de Pomares. He tells a romantic story about a Inca hoard of Arabian Nights' splendour and variety, sealed up somewhere in, or under the ancient fortress of Cuzco, on the Sachsahuaman Hill. Carlos Inca, a descendant of an Inca emperor, had married a Spanish lady, Doña Maria Esquivel, who did not think he was ambitious enough on getting on as he ought, and did not keep her in the style she deemed befitting her rank, or his descent from kings.

"You may call yourself Inca—a lord, or *hidalgo*—but you are only a poor Indian," she one day twitted him.

Carlos, who did not rule his poultry run in the way advised by old Spanish *hidalgos*, or, yesterday, by ex-Wilhelm II, *Rex et Imperator* of Prussia and the German Reich, that is, as cock of the walk, was content to keep *oviedos* (sheep) and alpacas, and not worry about gold of any origin. She somehow found out that he knew where great treasures were hidden. The poor Carlos was plagued, night and day, until, to gain a night's peace, he consented to blindfold his wife, and, late at night, lead her out into the patio of the old *hacienda*. Under the cold light of the stars, when all around were asleep, and no unseen eye was on the watch, he took her by the shoulders, and, although she was exposing him to serious risk of prison, or torture in Cuzco, twirled her round three times. Then, deeming she had become disorientated, he led her down some steps into a concealed vault in, or under the fortress. He removed the bandages, and Doña Maria's tongue for once was silenced. She stood on the dusty, stone floor of an ancient vault cluttered with gold and silver ingots, exquisite jewellery, and temple ornaments. Round the walls, ranged in fine gold, were life-size statues of long dead and gone Inca kings. Alone, the golden image of the Sun, on which the old Incas set the greatest store, was missing; but the lovely goldsmiths' work was of the same artistic creation as the gold and jewelled plants and flowers which the Peruvian workers made for those wondrous gardens on the isle of Puna, in the northern part of the old Empire (modern gulf of Guayaquil), where the Incas retired to hear the melancholy music of the Pacific combers on the beaches below.

Don Carlos was the custodian of the secret, and from him it passed to a successor. As Mr. Squier, one time U.S. Commissioner in Perú, said in 1870: "All I can say is if that secret chamber she had entered has not been found and despoiled, it has not been for want of digging. . . . Three hundred years have not sufficed to eradicate the notion that enormous treasures are concealed within the fortress of Cuzco. Nor have three hundred years of excavation, more or less constant, entirely discouraged the searchers for *tapadas*, or buried treasure mounds."

Even today, in 1945, the secret of that vault under the Sachsahuaman hill may still remain locked up in the breast of some descendant of the Inca. The last man of whom I heard in search of these treasures, was one, Tito Cusi Ticcapato, said to have Inca blood in his veins. It was in 1928, and he planned to accompany an American expedition to quarter another ancient hill near Cuzco, where he said the lost caches lie. He was also an inventor and sought for Inca gold to promote and exploit his creations. What struck his imagination, as he said, was "the fact, *señores*, that the old Incas wall-papered their houses with thin sheets of beaten gold".

None of the old secrets of the land of the Incas have really perished. There are native societies of the underworld who, age by age, keep them inviolate. Their members are sometimes wandering Catholic priests who, on one day of the year, revert to the celebration of their *real* religion: the rites of the sun, that Central mystic Sun of the pre-cataclysmic ancient world, symbolising the unknown Divinity and not an anthropomorphic demi-ourgos.

Perú is a very ancient country. All who sojourn there are, or soon become deeply impressed by the mystic atmosphere hanging over this strange land. There may, and probably does, still remain in some Quichua breast, the sub-conscious perception of the cyclic notions of the ancient world: that what has been will be again, when the wheel comes full circle and the life-forces rise in an ascending arc. Ancient glories will be restored, and men play again the part that was played by others whom they never knew, not even in the most shadowy ghost of a dead tradition. *Quien sabe?* says the gentle and brooding-eyed Peruvian who knows that he is still ruled by the descendants of the old Spaniards, for all the political revolution that was accomplished by Simon Bolivar more than a century ago. Be sure, then, that in some Andean village in a lone vale, lives some man who still guards this secret of untold millions.

It was in 1925 that the Tito Cusi Ticcapato, the Inca descendant, we mentioned above, told someone in old Cuzco that he had had a vision of the night in which he saw the life-sized statues of gold-armoured Inca emperors of the sun, who had been buried, perhaps in the wild and lonely hill of Guanacauri, in sight of their sun-temple city, old Cuzco.

Don José Eusebio de Llano Zapata, writing in Lima, in 1760, in the time of Señor Don Carlos III (King of Spain), tells of a number of these finds—some of them happening in his own day.

Says he:

> "In our America, men who use sorcery and divining rods to find hidden treasures, have been brought before the tribunal of the Holy Inquisition, and I have seen various *autos da fé* celebrated in Lima, where they punished severely those who persuaded others to engage in this harmful art."

Zapata gives a list of gorgeous finds of hidden gold, both in his own day, and in the preceding (seventeenth) century:

> "In the days just after the conquistadores, gold and plate worth more than 800,000 pesos were found where the last cacique of Pasmanga—Chimo-Ccapac, who was also lord of Paita and Tumbes, whose capital is Trujillo—had buried it. In another *entierro* (cache) a quarter of a league from Trujillo, which is called Tasca, and is on the high road (*camino*) of Guanchacho, Escobar Corchuelo and another *compañero* found over 600,000 pesos, and Gomara tells of a certain Spaniard who found in a *huaca* plate which he sold for 50,000 *castellanos de oro*. Moreover, late at the end of the past (seventeenth) century, in the vale of Late, in the jurisdiction of Lima, Francisco de Lorenzana found a great earthen jar (*gran tinaja de oro*) of gold (about $2\frac{3}{8}$ gallon capacity) and he bought the site of the cache, and gave his name to the *hacienda* and the manor-house he erected there. In our days, it is common talk in Lima that Alférez José de Surzo found in a pueblo of the Magdalena, half a league from Cuzco, a treasure of great worth. The news has the living appearance of truth. Surzo, born in Lima of poor parents, was, in his early years, a soldier of infantry. Afterwards, he settled himself in the same pueblo, where he became a rich merchant,

and when, in 1754, he died, he left over 200,000 pesos, which he got in less than ten years; so that the presumption of the source of his riches is not improbable."

I, myself, possess an old Spanish map made by a Jesuit missioner, in the year 1800. It is *un plano del Obispado del Cuzco* (map of the bishopric of Cuzco), and shows the route from *la Parte de la Laguna de Titicaca* through this mysterious river-*cañon* of the Huatanay—a wild, unearthly region of mountainy grandeur, where the gloomy rock-walls hem in a stream which roars and booms over the boulders, cluttering the bed, and hears no sound "save its own dashings", from age to age.

The trails through this unexplored region, where the Incas maintained, for more then eighty years, resistance to the Spanish penetration, after the murder of their last emperor, are, even today, full of dangers. As one goes through the winding gorges, far up the precipices, eyes unseen are on the watch, in eyries one cannot discern. Though all one's laden burros may carry be a load of ancient bones, or archaic pottery and artifacts of an ancient culture, that will not stay the hands unseen from sending great boulders dashing from the heights on to the narrow track on the side of vertiginous precipices. The word of the coming of strangers into these wild and gloomy regions passes with the quickness, almost, of radio. And down on the lower hot slopes westward of the great cordilleras are always *los bandidos* (the bandits)!

Indeed, this route into the unknown recesses of the Azangaro is as perilous as that to another mysterious old Inca ruin which, today, shrouded in bush, lies high up in the hills along the upper reaches of the Rio Ene, about 150 miles into the Cerro de Pasco, reached by rail from Lima. A haggard and half-crazed white adventurer, dying in a dirty hovel back of the wharfside of Callao, some years ago, told an Englishman about this mysterious Inca ruin.

"Its walls are plated with pure gold. I came very near it, one day, on the side of the mountains. The Serrano Indians alone have penetrated the *montaña* where it lies. They shoot dead, at sight, all intruders. . . . They shoot *straight*, too, *señor*."

Wonder is heaped on wonder, alp on alp rises, till, in the mystic atmopshere of the snowy cordilleras, one comes on a queer and shadowy clue to the existence of an immense treasure greater than any that has gone before. The story, which has about it that strange quality of unearthliness which reminds one, once again, that this is a very ancient land, goes back to the melancholy days of passing grandeur of an old civilisation, in the year A.D. 1533, when the last queen of the Incas, despairing of her unhappy country and murdered imperial consort, committed suicide. The last hopes of an ancient people had faded into the setting sun behind the peaks of the blue and misty Andean cordilleras—a people of whom the remorseful *el Conquistador*, Don Mancio Serra de Leguisamo wrote, on September 18, 1589, in old Cuzco:

"The Inca Peruvians were so free from crimes and excesses, the men as well as the women, that the Indian who had 100,000 pesos of gold and silver in his house, left it open, merely placing a small stick across the door as a sign that the master was out, and no one could enter or take anything that was inside. . . . When they found we put locks and keys on our doors, they supposed it was for fear of them that they might not kill us, not because they believed that anyone would steal the property of another. So, when they found we had thieves among us and men who sought to make their daughters commit sin, they despised us. But now they have come to such a pass, in offence of God, owing to the bad example we have set them in all things, that the natives, from doing no evil, have changed into people who now do no good or very little. . . . But I do what I can to discharge my conscience . . ."

Somewhere about the year 1844 an old Catholic priest was called to shrive a dying Quichua Indian (direct descendant of the Inca Peruvians). It is the strange sequel to the closing of the subterranean, of which I spoke, above.

"Bend your ear down to my mouth, *taita*," said the dying Indian, whose face was lined like an old parchment, "for I have something to tell you which is not for other ears."

The story was about a mystery of a labyrinth and a series of amazing tunnels going back far beyond the days of the Inca emperors of the sun. It was told under the inviolable seal of the confessional and could not be divulged by the priest under pain of hell fire; and it would probably have remained a secret had not the old priest, in a trail of the mountains, come into the company of a sinister Italian, who was on his travels to Lima. This Italian, with very dark, piercing eyes, and a hypnotic stare, talked to the old priest, who, unwittingly, let drop a hint about a long-sought hidden and very ancient treasure. The sinister gentleman, said to have come from Naples, somehow managed to hypnotise the old priest, who was a native Quichua, into telling him the story the priest had learnt, under confession, from the dying Peruvian peasant. The latter had said that this strange secret was known to many pure-blooded Quichua Indians, descendants of the old Incas, but not to the half-caste mestizos, who were deemed unreliable.

"*Taita*," said the dying man, "I will reveal to thee what no white man, be he Spaniard, or American, or English, knows."

The story he told was what I have related of the closing of the amazing tunnel-labyrinths, by the high priest of the sun temple of old Cuzco, and the magicians, under the eye of the imperial consort of the last emperor, Atahualpha. The old priest added that, about 1830, rumours of this tunnel had somehow reached the ears of the Peruvian authorities, for they had sent out emissaries to hunt for the concealed opening. These emissaries were disguised as scientists and archaeologists, but so well had the secret been hidden, that they went back to Lima and La Paz no wiser than they set out.

Between the years 1848 and 1850, the well-known Russo-American mystic, Madame Helena Petrovna Blavatskaya, was travelling in Perú, which was as badly—or, perhaps, worse—infested with brigands than it is, in some regions, today. She was told something of this curious story by a Peruvian she met on a mountain trail, in the Andes; and in Lima she rather curiously encountered the very Italian who had hypnotised the old priest into breaking the seal of the confessional. The Italian said he had since visited what he believed to be one of the entrances to what suggests to the imagination a great cave of Aladdin and the wonderful and very mysterious labyrinth of ancient kings, seen by Herodotus, on Lake Moeris of the Western Nile, and already ancient, even in his far-off day.

"However, I had neither the money nor the time to make a personal verification, and this I hope to do some time later," he added.

Madame Blavatskaya herself journeyed southwards from Lima to Arica (which, at that date, was not part of extreme Northern Chili), near the Peruvian frontier. It was a year or so after the story had been corroborated in her hearing, in different parts of Perú, and by people entirely unconnected.

"We reached Arica, near sunset, and at a certain point on the lonely coast we were struck by the appearance of an enormous rock, nearly perpendicular, which stood in mournful solitude on that shore, and apart from the cordillera of the Andes. As the last rays of the setting sun strike the face of the rock, one can make out, with an ordinary opera-glass, curious hieroglyphics inscribed on the volcanic surface.

"When Cuzco was the capital of old Perú, it contained a Temple of the Sun, famed far and near for its magnificence. It was roofed with thick plates of gold and its walls were covered with the same precious metal. The eaves troughs, carrying off the rain-water, were also made of pure gold. In the west wall, the architects had contrived an aperture, in such a way that, when the sunbeams reached it, it caught and focused them inside the temple's nave and sanctuary. Stretching inside the temple, like a golden chain, from one sparkling point to another, the rays encircled the walls, illuminating the grim idols, and disclosing certain mystic signs, at other times invisible."

Madame Blavatsakaya does not mention one curious fact about this mystic Sun Temple of old Cuzco—a fact found only in a very rare MS. chronicle of the conquistadorian age. It enshrined a mystic white stone—called by the Incas *Iuracrunu*—which seems to have combined the functions of an oracle with that of a crystal in which visions and pictures were seen. In some ways, it recalls the mystic Urim and Thummim and the shining light on the breast-plate of the high priest of the old Jewish Temple, themselves probably derived by Moses from the ancient Egyptian breast-plate of the goddess of truth *Thmèi* (identical with Greek goddess, Themis). The monks in the train of Pizarro felt impelled to make an end of this mystic stone, on which the rays of the rising sun also shone through the aperture. They alleged it had done great damage to native converts to Catholic Christianity, "espantandolos con tãs estreñas Crueldades, que algunos perdian la Vida" (frightening them with such extreme cruelties that some lost their lives). The Padres determined on a given day to destroy the white stone . . .

> "They first read prayers with the Indians, then round about the house of the Sun (*Casa del Sol*), and the white stone (*piedra blanca*), they laid much firewood and set fire to it in different parts, exorcising the spot beforehand, and when the fire was bigger there was heard great cries and horrid howlings, that they were persuaded were those of the Devil (*el Demonio*) that had been exorcised by our holy Mother Church."

Probably, in the old Cuzco Temple of the Sun, there may have been thaumaturgists among the priestly corps, who must have had much curious and secret knowledge about the origin, history and purpose of the amazing, labyrinthine tunnels of ancient Perú, and of other arcana of a very ancient race. The sun-emperors these priests served were men of a very different type of feature from the down-trodden Quichuas one may meet, today, on the Andean trails. There are pictures still to be seen in the old colonial church of Santa Ana, north of Cuzco, which portray the Incas as men of royal dignity, of a much lighter colour, as kingly as any Pharoah of old Egypt, and their priestly aristocrats were also men with a high forehead, slightly aquiline nose, thin mouth, firm chin, and refined and intellectual face of much majesty, or serenity.

It was only, says Madame Blavatskaya, by interpreting the mystic signs, invisible except when the sun's rays struck them at a certain angle, at a certain hour of the day, in the old Sun Temple of Cuzco, that one might learn the secret of the tunnels and how and where they might be entered.

One of the approaches to the great tunnels lay, and still lies, near old Cuzco, "but it is masked beyond discovery". This hidden approach leads directly into an immense "subterranean", which runs from Cuzco to Lima, *as the crow flies, a distance of* 380 *miles*! Then, turning southwards, *the great tunnel extends into what, until about* 1868, *was modern Bolivia, around* 900 *miles*! At a certain point the tunnel cuts into and is intersected by a royal tomb, inside which, with all the ingenuity employed by the old priestly architects and engineers of ancient Egypt, when they wished to trap tomb-robbers of the Pharaohs, thousands of years ago, the ancient Inca (?) engineers had contrived two cunningly arranged doors, consisting of two enormous slabs of carved stone, pivoted to turn and close so tightly that one can see not the faintest sign of crack or join. In fact, their position can be discerned on the sculptured walls of the royal subterranean mausoleum only by reading secret signs whose key is in the possession of hereditary custodians.

(It is whispered that the old caste of custodians of these wonderful tunnels and their secrets has not died out, even today, in 1945).

One of these pivoted, turning slabs, so cleverly sculptured and invisibly hinged, conceals the southern mouth of the branch of the tunnel leading to Lima. The other masks the southern entrance to the great tunnel to the former Bolivian end. This former Bolivian corridor (today located in Chili) runs southwards, passing through Tarapaca and Cobijo, which are in modern Chili. It must then turn eastwards, passing through or under the cordillera and, skirting the mysterious Atacama desert, of Northern Chili—itself, this Atacama desert, the home of curious remains of subterranean type, and even in the late seventeenth century rendezvous of a gang of pirates who called themselves "Brethren of the Black Flag", used five languages to hide their movements, and who left a bundle of musty and faded documents in code, found in 1934, in Santiago, about a cache they made here, in this weird desert.

The southern end of the tunnel is, thus, lost somewhere in this mysterious salt desert of Atacama, a thirst-stricken waste of llanos and alkaline deserts, out of which flow only scanty runlets of brackish water, so that coastal ports in this region rely on sweet water brought from long distances. May be, when the mysterious tunnel was made, perhaps thousands of years ago, the climate was very different from today, and the landscape one of beauty and fertility. *Quien sabe, señores?* Over this mysterious tunnel crosses a *carretera*, cart-track or high road, which runs across the northern edge of the great desert to the aptly named Rio de Mala Agua (de Loa), or Bad-Water river, passing *Indio Muerto* shacktown (Dead Indian Gulch), and ending up at old Potosi. Truly is this *Desierto de Atacama* one of strange secrets!

When Bolivia had a port at Cobijo, her government, about 1850, heard rumours about this mysterious tunnel of gold and lost secrets, and, secretly, sent out agents to try to locate it. Alas for success, the quest met with exactly that attending the seekers of other old Inca caches! All in vain! Probably, the Chilenos are too matter-of-fact and unimaginative to waste time on such a quest, in what is now their territory; and, perhaps, they may know nothing about it, in which case this book will bring to their bureaucratic knowledge a very rare secret!

Arica, a port now also in Chili, but in Perú in the 1860s, stands not far from a mysterious bluff, into which are cut the hieroglyphics seen by Madame Blavatskaya, about 1851, or 1853, and which denote—for those who can interpret them!—the signs and the key to the secret entrance. Not far inland is a little river, the Payquina, or Payaquina, a name also given to a cerro in that region, which, remarks Madame Blavatskaya, is so named from the little waves which used to drift *chispas* of gold from the old land of the Brazils. If that be so, the tunnel-makers may be men of that same lost white Atlantean race, the mantle of whose high culture and science undoubtedly fell on old Perú, ere Hy-Brazil vanished into the land of shades, leaving behind only a faint memory in wild, South American Indian traditions. She says the Incas derived their gold from this little river; but, of course, even so, it was merely one source of the supply. (Actually, it must be said that no Latin-American military or diplomatic map of the years 1840–1880, shows any rivulet, Payquina or Payaquina, running into the Pacific near Arica.)

"We found a few specks of gold in a handful of sand from this little river, the Payaquina, which we brought back to Europe," says Madame Blavatskaya, writing of a time somewhere between 1851 and 1853, when she is believed to have visited South America as well as Mexico. She is thought to have visited both lands twice, between 1851 and 1855. At the date when she visited Perú, she says the "little river Payaquina was the boundary between Perú and Bolivia". But here the mystic's memory must have been at fault.*

Madame Blavatskaya went a little way inland towards the cordillera of the Andes when she came in sight of three curiously formed separate peaks—a landmark specially, as it seemed, contrived by nature for some singular purpose of man. These peaks formed a very curious triangle. Behind, ranges the mighty cordillera

---

*AUTHOR'S NOTE: Madame Blavatskaya's memory *must* have been at fault; for, as a succession of military and topographical maps of Perú, between 1840 and 1890, show, the boundary between Bolivia and Perú, in the years 1840–1860, when Bolivia had an outlet to the Pacific (whose loss she has never ceased to deplore, though never making it a *casus belli*, as European dictators and nationalists would do), was the Rio de Loa, Pay'quina being a hill a good way inland and distant from the actual border when Madame Blavatskaya was there. The *key* to the riddle of the lost entrance of the amazing tunnel lies in the decipherment of the strange hieroglyphs cut into the enormous rock, on the shore near Arica. The rock is called the "tomb of the Incas". But the actual entrance, revealed by the key, lies somewhere in one of the three peaks, in a triangle, close to the Rio de Loa, the old Peruvian-Bolivian boundary, in 1840–1860. Payquina of the gold is, today, actually not a rivulet, but a district inland, back of the *quebradas* and pampas, on this nearly waterless coast of former Perú, near the mouth of the Rio de Loa, the old boundary with Southern Bolivia.

of the Andes, of which they are outposts. One mysterious Quichua, in a neighbouring village, whispered that the only practicable entrance into the tremendous subterranean leading northwards is somewhere cut like an adit into one of these queer peaks. Yet, lacking the secret of the landmarks which can be unriddled only by those who can decipher the meaning of a certain row of "hieroglyphics", or inscriptions cut into the rocks and visible only when the sun's rays strike the cliffs at a certain angle, a regiment of Titans, equipped with tri-nitro-toluol, or amatol high explosive, or dynamite cartridges, might even, today, rend the rocks in vain and then not unmask the mystery.

(There are, it may be mentioned here, spots along the *cañon* of the Rio Colorado, where arrows cut deeply into the face of the sheer walls can be seen in certain lights and incidences of the solar rays. They are, by roamers who go hunting treasure westwards across the Gila Desert and unpeopled, thirst-stricken and heat-crazed Arizona, believed to be pointers towards ancient caches of unknown and extremely ancient races, and, it may be, are memorials of the unknown race whose buried temples, lofty stone pyramids, seven of them within a mile square, and massive granite rings and dwellings, circular walls round venerable trees, and blocks of hieroglyphics speak of ruins of some very ancient Egypt, or Phoenicia of the wild region, at the head of the Gulf of California, "a day's march from San Diego", in 1850, when they were discovered.)

Yet, even were some one to discover the hidden entrance into the subterranean and explore the vast bore until he came as far as the wall bounding that inner sepulchre of some long-dead, Inca (?) King of the Sun, he would still lack the open sesame to the treasure tomb itself. How would be cause the great slab to turn on its pivot? If he could not find the hidden mechanism controlling the slab, and tried to blast his way into the great tomb, the old, unknown architects have been before him and his like. Almost exactly in the manner of the makers of the tombs of Thebes and Memphis along the hills of the dead, by the banks of the Nile of ancient Egypt—who, in their day, thousands of years ago, foresaw the ghoulish tomb-robber for whom no Pharaoh's *Kha* was sacred, and who tore the jewels from the brow of the royally dead and smashed the elaborately painted mummy-case, in order to filch the ceremonial vessels of carved and chased gold and remove the sheets of pure gold swathing the dead Pharaoh—the Incas (or the unknown architects) anticipated the robber-intruder. They have arranged the superincumbent rocks so that, if force be applied, the mass will fall and bury sepulchres and contents in common ruin.

A mysterious Peruvian told Madame Blavatskaya, nearly a century ago: "A thousand soldiers, were they in that tunnel, would be forevermore one with the dead, did they attempt to force their way into the treasure-tomb of the dead Inca. There is no other access to the Arica chamber, but through that hidden door in the mountains near the Rio Payquina, Arica. Along the entire length of the immense corridor, from Bolivia to Lima and royal Cuzco, are smaller hiding-places filled with treasures of gold and gems and jewels, that are the accumulations of many generations of Incas. The aggregate value of the treasures is beyond the power of man to estimate."

A plan of this fantastic tunnel* existed some years ago, and, probably, still exists until the owner judges the time has come to put his plans to the proof. (Meantime, in this book, I have given a remarkable and graphic chart based on my own secret information of this mystery. *Vide:* the end paper.)

"We had in our possession," said Madame Blavatskaya, nearly a hundred years ago, "an accurate plan of the tunnel, the sepulchre, the great treasure chamber and the hidden, pivoted rock-doors. It was given to us by the old Peruvian; but if we had ever thought of profiting by the secret it would have required the co-operation of the Peruvian and Bolivian Governments on an extensive scale. To say nothing of physical obstacles, no one individual or small party could undertake such an exploration without encountering the army of brigands and smugglers with which the coast is infested, and which, in fact, includes nearly the entire population. The mere task of purifying the mephitic air of the tunnel not entered for centuries would also be a serious one. There the treasure lies, and tradition says it will lie till the last vestige of Spanish rule disappears from the whole of North and South America."

Possibly, that time is nearer at hand today, when the last vestiges of Spanish caste rule in the western states of Central and South America—the bureaucracies and cabinets of the *gente decente*—are being threatened by the rising parties and socialising movements, representing the *peónes* of old Mexico and the down-trodden, land-less disinherited Quichua Indians of old Perú.

A word about this mysterious engineering of an antediluvian world is by no means out of place here. Again we have the shadow of old Atlantis and Hy-Brazil projected into our own era.

Tunnels and labyrinths have played a mysterious part in ancient civilisations in regions of what may wrongly be called the older worlds of Asia and Europe and Africa. Who can say what the ancient priest-emperors of old Perú knew of, or had inherited, from these vanished civilisations which are not even a name, or more than a faint and ghostly shadow? An ancient tradition of Brahmanic Hindostan

* My information is that Madame Blavatskaya's chart of the tunnel is now in the Theosophical archives at Adyar, Madras; but my own chart, in no way derived from that of the late mystic lady, is based on independent sources of Peruvian information, checked by my own original researches. Until I had nearly completed this book, I did not know that her chart was still in existence.—AUTHOR.

speaks of a large island of "unparalleled beauty" which, in very ancient times, lay in the middle of a vast sea in Central Asia, north of what is now the Himalayas. A race of *nephilim*, or men of a golden age, lived in the island, but there was no communication between them and the mainland, except through tunnels, radiating in all directions, and *many hundreds of miles long*. These tunnels were said to have hidden entrances in old ruined cities in India—such as the ancient remains of Ellore, Elephanta, and the Ajunta caverns in the Chandore range.

Among the Mongolian tribes of Inner Mongolia, even today, there are traditions about tunnels and subterranean worlds which sound as fantastic as anything in modern novels. One legend—if it be that!—says that the tunnels lead to a subterranean world of Antediluvian descent somewhere in a recess of Afghanistan, or in the region of the Hindu Kush. It is a Shangri-la where science and the arts, never threatened by world wars, develop peacefully, among a race of vast knowledge. It is even given a name: Agharti. The legend adds that a labyrinth of tunnels and underground passages is extended in a series of links connecting Agharti with all other such subterranean worlds! Tibetan lamas even assert that in *America*—it is not stated whether North, South, or Central—there live in vast caves of an underworld, reached by secret tunnels, peoples of an ancient world who thus escaped a tremendous cataclysm of thousands of years ago. Both in Asia and America, these fantastic and ancient races are alleged to be governed by benevolent rulers, or King-archons. The subterranean world, it is said, is lit by a strange green luminescence which favours the growth of crops and conduces to length of days and health.

Ferdinand Ossendowski, in his *Beasts, Men and Gods* (Edward Arnold, London, 1923), also mentions this strange Kingdom of Agharti, which, he says, he has been told by learned China lamas and Mongolian princes, has many men and tribes of incredibly ancient races, long vanished from the kingdoms of day. He mentions an old Brahman of Nepaul who, on a mystic pilgrimage, met a fisherman, apparently in the interior or on the coast of Siam, or Thailand, or, may be, another part of Indo-China, who ordered the Brahman to take a place in a boat, and obey the will of the gods by sailing with him on the sea to an Arabian Nights' island where live people "having two tongues" which "can separately speak different languages". He landed in the mysterious island, which—Monsieur Ossendowski does not say—might very well be located somewhere in the rock-pinnacle and coral-studded China Sea, a region shunned and unexplored today, off the main steam lanes, and not even charted by the Admiralty, who advise navigators to stick to the well-known sea lanes. But wherever it might be, these strange islanders showed the old lama a bird with teeth that caught sea fish and an unknown animal with sixteen feet and one eye. The islanders said: "We come out of the subterranean kingdom, where, in cars of type unknown to Western races, men rush through the subterranean world through cleavages in the earth."

Clearly, this story is of the believe-it-or-not type; but it would be wisdom not to dismiss the story as pure fantasy. There is no smoke without fire, nor are all the Eastern wandering mystics necessarily romancers of the Baron von Munchausen type, nor men whose imaginations have been over-strongly impressed by the fantasy and most entertaining novels of the H. G. Wells of a more youthful day! I say gently, again, reader, remember the Komodo dragon; and I could also add, of my own curious knowledge, the strange parchment charts of the China Sea of the year 1669, left by Captain William Kidd, the pirate-privateer, whose originals are now in a house in Sussex.

For what purposes, however, were these amazingly long tunnels of old Perú intended? What mysterious cults did they serve?

Quien sabe, señores?

A startling clue, gained in a very peculiar and romantic manner, to one of the purposes of these mysterious tunnels, and which is directly concerned with the mysterious stone city in the Lancandones territory, of which I have written elsewhere, came in the course of a chance talk between a very old Peruvian—a Quichua Indian—and the same well-known mystic and American woman traveller, the late Madame Helena P. Blavatskaya, who, as one sees, was journeying through the mountains of Perú, in 1851 or 1853. The old Peruvian had passed all his life vainly trying to conceal his hatred towards the official Peruvians, and the Spanish conquerors. He called them *brigands*.

"I keep friends with them, these *bandidos*," he said, "and their Catholic missioners, for the sake of my own people. But I am as much a worshipper of the sun as if I had lived in the days of our murdered emperor, the Inca Atahualpha. Now, as a converted native and missionary, I once took a journey to Santa Cruz del Quiché (in Western Guatemala), and, when there, *I went to see some of my people by a subterranean passage leading into a mysterious city behind the cordilleras*. Herein, it is death for any white man to trespass!"

Said Madame Blavatskaya:

> "We believe his story, as it is corroborated, elsewhere, by Stephens in his *Travels*. Besides, a man who is about to die will rarely stop to invent idle stories."

Similar strange tunnels of incredibly ancient date, and unknown origin, in the West Indies, were brought to the attention of Christopher Columbus, when he visited Martinique. No doubt, the white,

Atlantean race built splendid cities in what are now West Indian islands, but which, at the far-off date, may have formed part of a now submerged, middle American continent, whose name is commemorated in the word: "Antilles". A curious tradition of the old world of Asia, is that old Atlantis had a network of labyrinthine tunnels and passages running in all directions, in the day when the land-bridge between the drowned land and Africa, on one side, and old Brazil, on the other, still existed. In Atlantis, the tunnels were used for necromantic and black magic cults. Anyway, it is curious that the Caribs, in 1493, told Columbus that, in the old kingdom of the Amazon women warriors, anciently existing in Madanino, or Martinique, there were great subterraneans, and when the women were likely to be pestered, out of due season of love, orgasm and rutting, by periodical, cannibal lovers, the women went down to the great tunnels and hid themselves. If the lovers, not to be put off, still followed them, their ardent passions were cooled with showers of well-aimed arrows from Amazon bows, and many a cannibal beau was brought to an untimely grave, in this way, by the fierce Venuses of old Martinique.

Fuentes, who lived about A.D. 1689, and wrote an unpublished MS. history of Guatemala, speaks of the amazingly large and ancient towns (inhabited by an unknown and long vanished race) found there by the conquistadores.

He says:

> "The marvellous structure of the *tunnels* (*subterranea*) of the pueblo of Puchuta, being of the most firm and solid cement, runs and continues through the interior of the land for the prolonged distance of nine leagues to the pueblo of Tecpan, Guatemala. It is a proof of the power of these ancient kings and their vassals."

He gives no hint of the uses to which these amazing tunnels, more than thirty miles long, on the basis of the old Castilian league, were put by these ancient races of old America.

It may be, too, that the great tunnel of the Incas had a branch, underground way leading under the forests, eastwards of Cuzco, in the very direction taken by Inca Tupac Amaru, his army and his host of camp-following refugees, in the late sixteenth century? May be, the fleeing Peruvians vanished into these mysterious tunnels and left only the whispering leaves of the trees of the dense green forests, as mute witnesses of their secret exits?

The Inca fled to the mysterious "White House" of the elusive South American empire of *Gran Paytite*, about which I shall write in another book. It is evident that the men of this mysterious land of *Paytite* must have had contacts with the Incas long before the Spanish conquistadores overran the Peruvian empire.

At intervals of about forty years—the last being in 1942!—there come rumours about the existence of men of a lost Mayan, or Aztecan race who fled before the faces and horses of Don Hernando Cortes's cavalry. From time to time, strange, elusive Indians appear in the market-places of lonely frontier pueblos in the provinces of Chiappas and Western Guatemala. They contact only with Indians, barter goods, and vanish as suddenly as they come, no Mexican or Guatemalan official being any the wiser. They are emissaries from a lost city of the ancient, civilised race that once governed old Mexico. No white man has ever penetrated the region of this wilderness, where, it is rumoured, these lost-world men live as did their fathers, erect or maintain the same majestic stone buildings, palaces and temples, large courts and lofty towers with high terraces of stone staircases, and are still carving in stone the mysterious hieroglyphics that no modern scholar can decipher in the ruins of old Yucatan.

At intervals of half a century the story is revived. It was first told to the American traveller, J. Lloyd Stephens—traveller mentioned above by Madame Blavatskaya—by a Spanish priest he met at Chajol, or Chajul, a pueblo in Western Guatemala, in 1838–9. The priest swore to Stephens that he had seen with his own eyes a mysterious lost city, and so earnest was the old priest's manner, that Stephens believed him. Said Stephens, in London and New York, in 1839 and 1840:

> "The padre of the little village near the ruins of Santa Cruz del Quiché, had heard of this unknown city when he was in the village of Chajul (Chajul lies in the mountains, in Western Guatemala, close to the headwaters of the Rio Usamacinta). The priest was then a young man, and with much labour, climbed to the naked summit of the topmost ridge of the sierra of the Cordillera. When arrived at the height of ten or twelve thousand feet, he looked over an immense plain extending to Yucatan and the Gulf of Mexico. At a great distance, he saw a large city spread over a great space, and with turrets white and glistening in the sun. Tradition says that no white man has ever reached the city; that the inhabitants speak the Maya language, know that strangers conquered their whole land, and murder any white man who attempts to enter their territory. . . . They have no coin; no horses; no cattle; mules, or other domestic animals, except fowls; and the cocks they keep underground to prevent their crowing being heard."

One may, parenthetically, point out that it was down this mysterious river, Rio Usamacinta, marked on the most recent War

Department maps of the U.S. Army, unknown as to a greater part of its tortuous course and cut up by gorges and hilly jungle, that Wodan, or Votan, the Phoenician, travelled to the splendid stone cities of Palenque, Uxmal, Copan, and the mysterious stone city visited by the old Peruvian sun priest, in the nineteenth century, A.D. Of course, in Votan's far and legendary day, these cities hummed with life and high civilisation, being far from dead or lost! It is also known to the bush Indians that on a bluff over this Rio Usamacinta is the mound-tomb of Guatemotzin, last prince of Aztecs, whose body with regalia and much treasure was taken there and buried by sallow-faced Aztecan priests in Cortes's days. Any greaser or gringo seeking to cut into this royal *huaca* is sure of warm attentions from the bush Indians and the dangerous and dwarfish "white" Lancandones, who must be survivors of a once highly and ancient civilised race of old Central America.

The learned Americanist and scholar, Abbé Charles Etienne Brasseur-de-Bourbourg, when he was ecclesiastical administrator in the Mexican frontier state of Chiappas, about 1858, heard the story again with the addition that men of this lost stone city suddenly appeared and vanished in frontier pueblos and townships, where they came to barter. An English filibuster and adventurer claims he heard a similar story in 1935.

In March 1942, President Roosevelt invited to the White House two Californians named Lamb (husband and wife) who seem to have made contact in the bush of Chiappas with a degenerate tribe of Lancandones, or other Indians, who are hereditary guardians of a lost Mayan city wherein is a temple containing, on gold plates, the hieroglyphical history of the race and the world, and predicting, it is said, Great War No. 2. One gathers that the Lambs were not allowed to see this lost city, which lies behind a pass in high mountains. May be, there is more than one lost or dead city in this dense and unexplored jungle territory. According to the Lambs, the degenerate Indians go to the lost or hidden city to worship in its Mayan temple, on certain days, and they told them of the "Great Things of the Old Ones", written on sheets of solid gold, and telling of a Great Deluge.

The story above is derived from a West country evening newspaper extract cabled from a New York daily newspaper in summer 1940; but I may add that an English engineer whom I have mentioned in another part of this book as having spent many years of his life in both Mexico and the Argentine, and who died in Gloucester Royal Infirmary, in 1938, told me that, in the state of Jalisco, somewhere in the little-known southern extension of the great range of the Sierra Madre, about 121 kilomètres (about 75 miles) east of the Cabo de Corrientes, are prehistoric ruins known to the Indian *peónes*. The region is one that is never visited by Mexicans, unless in times of insurrection when a band of *revolucionarios* has sought to escape the Government troops by fleeing to the recesses of the savage mountains. Jalisco is, of course, a province well known as one of the centres of the Aztec race, just as is the valley of Anahuac in the territory round the capital.

The *Aztecos Indiós* in Jalisco state say that these ancient ruins were once the home of a people who were civilized and benevolent. Whether they were of the Mayan race or some even more ancient people with Atlantean connections derived from the Hy-Brazilian pioneer and civiliser Quetzalcoatl, only exploration by competent field workers can decide. The dead city lies on a *mesa* (plateau) and from it, at certain hours of the day, or at dawn, comes the sound of an eerie, vibrant drumming. The sound is heard from afar, even on the Pacific! The Indians declare that the drumming emanates from *los Espiritós* (ghosts), and comes from stone vaults of a great temple where there was once worshipped "the ruler of the Universe". One day, say the Indians, the wheel of life, or cycle of events, will come full circle, and the ancient people will return and re-introduce a golden age. (As one has seen, millennial prophecies of this kind are common all over the regions where the Atlantean Central and South American empire once held sway.)

The dead city is said to be of stone and massively and enduringly built. Ruins of cyclopean walls surround it. On a hill above the *mesa* is another city of the dead, which seems to be a necropolis of the princes or archons of this ancient race. It is said that pyramidal structures stand on the tops of great mounds, made by man and not nature; and, as in Yucatan and Guatemala, are shrouded in jungle and trees. Great blocks of paving lead towards the dead city in whose vaults treasures or records are concealed, watched by mystic guardians from whom the drumming emanates. Needless to say, no *Aztecos* will venture into this region. It is clearly of the sort described by Mr. Masefield, in *Sard Harker*: "a place whose gods do not wish it to be known".

Ruins of dead cities—not yet reached by archaeologists—also exist, one has been told, in Mexico, on the borders of the state of Tehuantepec. In this state there is said, by Mexicans, to exist *today* a community of *dancing matriarchs*. As this is the very region wherein—as I shall speak of in a book to follow this—were those very Amazon women of whom a certain Castilian don wrote to "Kaiser Carlos V.", the Holy Roman Emperor and King of old Spain, it, probably, in ancient days had Atlantean connections; since the Amazons of the old world of Africa and Europe more than once fought with Atlanteans, if not in the island-continent certainly in a submerged North-West African colony which Diodorus, citing vanished Carthaginian records, said had been submerged by a cataclysm long before his day.

Here, again, this *Oojah*, or mysterious drumming* is heard, coming afar over the environing jungle and ranges. One such dead city stands on a *mesa* girdled by cliffs. The region is covered with shrouded pyramids to which lead ancient roadways of massive paved blocks. In vaults of this dead city, the Indians of Chiappas say there are hidden, and guarded by the ghosts of Mayan priest-rulers, "books" written on gold leaves recording the history of ancient things and races of Ante-diluvian, or later Mayan times. Competent exploration is, of course, necessary, before these riddles can be solved.

Farther south, in the unknown mountain wilderness of South-Western Darien, today, there is told by the forest Indians a similar story of a stone city in the mountains wherein tremendous treasures are hidden and priests perform sacrifices. It may be identical with the city sought by the Castilian soldiers under Vasco Nuñez de Balboa.

Old legend says this stone city (called Dahyba) had a secret *subterranean* temple at the bottom of a cavern, where strange rites of the underworld were performed. No smoke without fire in these legends of mysterious America! A native whisper in Darien says these rites are by no means extinct, nor the subterraneans, today!

In the mountains of modern Ecuador and in Colombia the traveller encounters the same whispered stories about islands in the middle of wooden mountain tarns, to which access is gained on a certain day of the year, through a secret tunnel known only to the Indians, often speaking a tongue which they will allow no others to learn. In these sanctuaries are, also, said to be wonderful treasures of gold and jewels, and sacred vessels, or gemmed insignia of some cult of the moon-goddess Chia, or of Inti, our Lord the Inca's Sun, and, on that one day of the year, the Indians, good Catholics to all appearance, on the others, worship their old goddess, or gods.

Always, the hunters, whether or no gringos or greasers, have come up all standing against enigmatic towering cliffs with no signs of a fissure, or old rifts in the sides of some lone cordillera, where, say the informants, there existed in the days just before the hoofs of the horses of Don Hernando Cortes's Castilian *caballeria*, or Don Francisco Pizarro's conquistadores clattered over the passes of the sierras and the cordilleras on to the ruin of old Mexico-Tenochtitlan and old Cuzco, *entrances to amazing tunnels and labyrinths*.

* This mysterious drumming does not seem to be akin to that found among the Eskimos or the Lapplanders, who use it to induce hypnosis and an abnormal mental state wherein telepathic messages can be received, or clairvoyant visions of the future be seen by men in whom has been produced a dilation of the normal consciousness. It recalls, rather, that heard among the *gentilars* in that prehistoric dead city close to Trujillo, in Northern Perú, where great treasures, including the "Great Gold Fish richly jewelled", have been hidden. Von Humboldt, who heard of it when he visited those regions about 1820, theorised that the sound—suggesting galloping horses or boiling waters—might originate from differences of temperature or underground waters. The noises are heard after dark, on this Chimu or pre-Chimu hill, near Trujillo, and no adequate explanation has yet been advanced of this mystery.

Today, in the wilds of South America, when you encounter these mysteries of the mountains, and, with a good pair of binoculars, pick out what looks like signs of ancient carving or hieroglyphic inscriptions sunk in the weathered rock, your guide shrugs his shoulders and does not even attempt to repeat the parrot talk about the Incas knowing nothing of writing before the Spaniards came. You may ask him if any native has the key to those strange signs cut yonder in the wall of the cliff. What do they mean; who carved them; and when, and why?

He looks up into the gloomy sky, with dark and patient face, and from his subdued eyes comes a smouldering fire overlaid and damped down by a long-standing grief, of a conquered ancient nation.

"*Quien sabe, señor?* They are long ago dead who knew, and what *they* knew was more than those *bandoleros odiosos* of Pizarro ever dreamt. No one can read those signs today. None ever will."

Nevertheless, one need not be *too* certain that no one, *today*, among these sad-faced Quichua Indians has any knowledge of these secrets of a very ancient race. The face and the mind of the soft-spoken men of the low-pitched voices whose mules and llamas and burros pick their way so quietly through the hushed, narrow streets of old Cuzco, with no street cars and hardly any modern traffic, is not an open book for any foreigner or modern descendant of Spanish creole to read. People who have lived for any time in Central America or Perú, Yucatan, Guatemala, Chiappas, or Ecuador, suspect that these ancient tunnels and mysterious caves are still, today, in 1945, playing their secret part in the hidden life of the modern descendants of these ancient races. The secret rites and memories of the old man-god, Quetzalcoatl, of the Aztecs' murdered emperor, Montezuma, and Inti, the sun-god of the assassinated Inca Atahualpha, die hard, as hard as Votan of the Quichés of old Yucatan.

Indeed, this question is forced on the attention of the thoughtful guest of these countries! Is there, today, as in the past, some mysterious central organisation of a native, theocratic character, existing in the Peruvian *montaña*, or behind the Central American cordilleras, which still keeps in touch with the down-trodden Indians, giving them orders, keeping alive the flame of old culture and race, preserving sacerdotal cults and magical rites among men who, though nominally *Cristianos* and good Catholics, and good subjects of Mexico or Perú, are, yet, not *quite* what they seem? Even today, nagualism, or the worship of Montezma or Quetzalcoatl, is still practised, in subterranean vaults, and secret and very ancient caves and tunnels, by both *peónes* and, in some cases, men of old Spanish descent who live in remote pueblos of old Mexico, Yucatan, or over the border in Honduras and Guatemala. Nor can the Roman Catholic Church stop, or even trail it!

People who have never lived in these lands and who derive their ideas of them from films or travel books—by no means always written by devout worshippers of the George Washingtonian ideal of truth at any cost, whether self-advertising or not!—or even from the orthodox professors and unteachable academicians, too often blind leaders of the blind, may smile at these "fantasies". Yet, the fact remains that authorities such as Dr. J. J. von Tschudi, the Peruvian historian, and the famous American, William Hickling Prescott, believed in the existence of an organisation of this secret sort, about the middle of the nineteenth century.

A bold or ignorant man would he be who asserted that no such secret, native organisation, of a native, theocratic character, exists, today, either in Western South America, or old-modern Mexico, or Guatemala! If early Christians, in old Rome, had their catacombs and their pass-words, why may not this much more ancient world of South and Central America possess its mysterious tunnels and amazing labyrinths, which put in the shade any catacomb, or maze, existing in any time from old Thebes and the Minotaur of Minos to those of the lamas of the mystic land of old and modern Tibet?

CHAPTER VIII

TIAHUANACU AND THE GIANTS

"There were giants in the earth, in those days."—*Genesis.*

Tropical South America, including, as it does, the most ancient land in the world never submerged by the ocean, and never ground under the tremendous glaciers of the Ice Ages, may very well have been the cradle of the earth's civilisation, from which it spread outwards to Europe and Africa, on the one side, and Asia on the other. We cannot yet say; and yet, what has become known in the decades since 1920 is a mere, tantalising peep at amazingly ancient and unknown worlds sunk in the night of time, and still shrouded in opaque clouds of darkness and mystery. From time to time, the wind of a freakish time spirit blows the rack aside and lets an urchin shaft of starlight—it is hardly a sunbeam!—glance through the rift; then, before more than a momentary glimpse is given, the clouds coalesce and the crack closes up again.

In Guayaquil museum, on the coast of Ecuador, I have seen

strange stone arm chairs, which look as if they had come across broad seas from those wild moors of old Cornwall, in the neighbourhood of St. Just, or the pixie-haunted ruins of Chapel Carnbrea, where the ancient kings of Cornwall or the white-bearded arch-Druids sat in granite seats and drank from great golden goblets of mead, whilom sky-blasting notes were blown from bronze-golden trumpets, upraised under the ancient, mystic moon! Yet, these strange stone chairs come from the northern border of the state of Ecuador, where there is a large field encircled by similar chairs. What nation of ancient South America met in strange conclave and sat in these mighty stone seats as if they had been meeting on the Wiltshire plain at Stonehenge, or down in La Vendée, or in among the grey cromlechs of Brittany?

No one knows; nor, up to date, has any South American pre-historian been able to form even a theory, about the origin or identity of this stone-chaired race.

Again, in the same country of Ecuador, on the sea-shore, close to a place called Esmeraldas, queer relics have been found which are not only pre-Incaic, but seem even to have preceded the old European stone age! The *haciendadero*, Señor Muñoz, points out that these sub-marine relics, which include fine statuettes and busts of almost Tanagra type, and both men and women, are of almost every race (white, yellow and black) in the world, including Japanese, and of some that no longer exist. This race, in its unknown day, perhaps 100,000 (!) years ago, may have ranged right across old Brazil; for, in Marajó island, a prehistoric graveyard at the mouth of the Amazon-Marañon, one finds, in a series of amazing ceramics, exactly the same varied types of human beings, represented on funerary urns. (Esmeraldas has also *Karian* statuettes!)

The artifacts of this unknown nation, whose city is below sea off Ecuador's shores, are singular. Besides fine obsidian mirrors, carved like lenses in a way to suggest that the race had a knowledge of optics, there are queer, oblong-shaped prisms, on whose facets are carved animals, hieroglyphs, or symbols. They may have served the same purpose as the *chop* or personal seals which every Chinese mandarin used formerly to affix to documents, which were not legal without such a seal. (I note that Colonel Braghine has also reached this conclusion in his fine book on Atlantis.)

An imaginative man or woman might, therefore, have some warrant for theorising that the queer remnants of old races met in out-of-the-way or dangerous regions of this continent are survivors from some post-palaeolithic, or antediluvian age of the world's history. They are oddments dragged out of the dusty lumber-room of evolution and dawn-history and *not* popular with world-historians whose encyclopædic views will, when this latest evidence is weighed, corrected and accepted, need some adjustment, especially as regards notions of the age of human civilisation, which, possibly, did not start *after* the Ice Ages!

My friend Mr. Richard Oglesby Marsh, former U.S. *chargé d'affaires*, who has travelled over the Andes to the Amazonian head-waters' country, finds that the ancient Hy-Brazilians of the Matto Grosso's dead cities, 20–40,000 years ago, used the same names for the Zodiacal constellations as we use today! Lieut. W. Smyth met the Sencis of the Rio Ucayli, of Northern Perú, in 1836, and heard them "name the planets Mars and Jupiter and ten constellations". They are a tribe of primitive Indians, and the knowledge could *not* have originated with them. Col. Fawcett, D.S.O., said in 1921: "I have lived among South American tribes who have a name for every planet, barring Neptune, and although far from Inca influence, know the sun by the name of *Vira-Vira* and sing hymns to its rising." Neptune, it will be observed, is the most recently discovered planet, the outermost known one of the solar system, found in 1846 as a result of the calculations of Leverrier of Paris and Galle of Berlin. (*Vide:* p. 146 *supra.*)

Again, the pre-Vedic *sun*-god of Brahma was called *Vira*-dj, and according to Manu, the law-giver, was the *demi-ourgos*, or Jahveh of old Hindostan. The queerly Sanscritian sound about words in some of the South American Indians' tongues, or dialects, may cause one to wonder whether ancient South America had colonists from some long since drowned land in the Pacific, who settled on her western coasts, and, in a far day, when the Andes had not been violently upheaved, spread inland. According to Louis Jacolliot, in his *Histoire des Vierges: Les Peuple et les Continents Disparus*, this drowned Pacific continent was known as *Rutas*, in the traditions of the *goparams*, or India's pagodas, the root *Ru* meaning war, as the people were redoubtable militarists and imperialists. Their language, called *Sansar*, was said to be the parent of Sanscrit.

The mystery, again, of the origin or identity of the unknown and very ancient and highly civilised race, once ruling over what is now the comparatively unknown and still largely unexplored region of *montaña*, *cerro*, and highlands in modern Colombia, is no nearer solution, today, than in 1840. In one detail this race unknown suggests a comparison with the other unknown, North American people who ranged from the Aleutian land-bridge to the River Columbia of Oregon and Washington, across the Rockies, through Central America to old Perú. This latter race, though on a lower plane of civilisation and culture than the unknown in old Colombia, yet, like them, constructed systems of irrigation canals. They also left a trail of petroglyphs over about 5,000 miles of country.

In summer 1931, Monsignor F. Lunadi, of the Apostolic Nunciature of Santa Fé de Bogotá, organised an expedition into this unknown region, which lies in the little-explored jungles of San

Agustin. He found traces of a very ancient, South American empire extending about sixty miles along the banks of the Rio Magdalena, a gold-river so well known to the old British buccaneers of the seventeenth century. This unknown race not only built irrigation canals; but erected colossal statues, cut from solid rock, and transported them by unknown means over great distances. Many of the colossal statues had been created in the faces and figures of the great men over whose tombs they stood. In this wild region, a village named San Agustin has houses filled with curious antique statues which are also set up in the plaza, four of these great statues of a race unknown combining to uphold the marble form of El Liberador, Simon Bolivar.*

There is a suggestion of Easter Island, and of Malden, Pitcairn, the Marquesas, and Ponape about these ancient megalithic ruins in the recesses of the unknown Andes. In the Rio Negro, tributary of the mighty Amazon, are rock-pictures, two of which strike the imagination. They are of tall men (*Vide* sketch, page 139 *supra*) of archaic type, wearing long robes, one figure with arms extended, the other grasping a long baton; but what is most striking is the remarkable head-dress like an extended halo! Sir Robert Schomburgkh, in 1838, saw colossal haloed figures of just this sort† in the rock of Timeri (Dutch Guiana), and along the cataracts on the upper waters of the Rio Corentyn, borders of British and Dutch Guiana. It is curious that head-dresses of this strange type are found in some of the monuments of Tiahuanacu, the pathetic remnants of that city in the Andean clouds, in rarefied air, a long dead city which must have been raised to a great height by titanic forces of vulcanism, perhaps reinforced by some appalling, cosmic catastrophe of the sort which, I have hinted, utterly destroyed the great civilisation of white Hy-Brazil, some 11–12,000 years ago.

Colonel Fawcett advanced a theory which, breath-taking as it must be to many people, and even ridiculous to the orthodox archaeologist who still holds that civilisation is hardly older than 5000 B.C., is seen by the unprejudiced and thoughtful observer who has calmly weighed the available evidence of tradition, folk-lore and geology to be near the incredible truth. It also suggests that when native races in South America speak in their tribal and national "legends" of old and civilised races existing in a day *when mountains*

* The Guarari Indians have a tradition that these ancient races of Colombia "made fire and light by strange means". Had they a knowledge of electricity, or some form of radiology? (See Chap. 3, pp. 83-4 *supra.*)

† Poor Sir Robert was beset by peculiar difficulties in his zeal to copy these strange inscriptions. On November 25, 1838, he was about to climb great granite boulders twelve miles south-east of Mount Marua, Guiana—of which one boulder was 400 feet high and covered with hieroglyphs—when an Indian, bitten by a snake as he fished in a brook, insisted that Sir Robert procure for him a small cup of milk drawn from what an American acquaintance of mine called "mammy's titties". So, stifling an oath, Sir Robert was forced to send for an Indian woman, chafe the Indian's leg, and abandon the rubbing or copying of the strange inscriptions.—AUTHOR.

were not, they are not talking what the modern American called "childish baloney".

He said:

> "These megalithic ruins of Tiahuanacu were never built on the Andes at all. They are part of a great city submerged ages ago in the Pacific Ocean. When the crust of the earth upheaved and created the great Andean cordilleras, these ruins were elevated from the bed of the ocean to where you now see them."*

This, if accepted, at once shatters a theory of some South American *Indianistas* who advance a story that Tiahuanacu was an outport of the Atlantean-Brazilian empire of old Brazil, and was partly swept away in the catastrophe that overwhelmed Atlantis. Moreover, fantastic as Colonel Fawcett's theory may seem, it must be remembered that Lake Titicaca, close to Tiahuanacu, has a chalky deposit of ancient seaweeds, with lime, about two yards deep, which indicates that the ridge where it is found was once an ancient seashore. In fact, modern geologists say that the actual shore of *Titicaca was once immersed in the ocean*, and more than *two miles lower* or a great deal below modern sea level of the Pacific! If Tiahuanacu sprang from the bed of the ocean—the Pacific—where a terrible catastrophe had sunk it, under tidal waves released by vulcanism and stimulated, perhaps, by some cosmic forces, then civilisation must be much older than many modern archaeologists and historians are ready to concede. Collateral evidence about the catastrophic alteration in the height of Tiahuanacu exists in the "Giants' Field", near Bogotá, in modern Colombia. This strange field *is on the same level as Tiahuanacu*, and it is covered with fossilised or petrified bones of mastodons, overtaken by catastrophe, withering of pasture grounds, once, near the sea, and dead of cold and rarefaction of air. Extinct animals figure on ceramics dug up in the plain of modern Tiahuanacu, and geologists and biologists assert that these animals were extinct thousands of years ago. In fact, their fossil remains have been found in this same strata of Tiahuanacu.

The great heaps of hewn stone, once found at Tiahuanacu, abandoned by their ancient builders suggest, as in Easter Island, sudden catastrophe. (Alas, the modern Governments of Bolivia have used these ruins merely as a quarry for ballasting the road-bed of the railroad!)

Even the astronomers do not altogether resolve the riddle of the

* One other theory, raising the still unsettled problem of the age of the Andes, is that Tiahuanacu may have been a port, or outpost of some long-vanished *Pacific* continent, *standing at sea level* at a time when the Andes had not been upheaved from the ocean bed. This would account for the sea-horses (hippocampi) and flying fish images found among the prehistoric ornaments of the structures. It may also suggest some vanished link in the shape of some land, sunk by cataclysm in the Pacific, where *giraffes* were of the fauna. (*Vide* p. 189 *infra*.)

age of Tiahuanacu. They say that the great Kalasasaya—a name which, again, has a queerly Sanscritian sound and suggests a connection with some drowned continent in the Pacific—or sun temple, in the vast stadium of modern Tiahuanacu, was built some time between 21,600 B.C. and 2800 B.C.—a range of 18,800 years. This calculation is arrived at by using data connected with the obliquity of the ecliptic, or wobbling of the earth's axis in the polar spin. German astronomers from Potsdam Observatory used signs found in this stadium and calculated that the Kalasasaya was left unfinished about 9550 B.C. But there is some agreement—outside the ranks of "conventional" and academic archaeologists—that ruins of an ancient port are found near the stadium of Tiahuanacu, suggesting that it was once near the sea-shore, and that cast-down builders' tools, found in the ruins in the sixteenth century of our own era, also suggest a hurried abandonment, in a far day. Obviously, however, these evidences are by no means inconsistent with a catastrophe that occurred ages before the great upthrust of the crust of the earth that raised the Pacific shore and heightened the Andes, say geologists, about 12–13,000 years ago.

Suppose Fawcett is right?

Then, perhaps, 100,000 years ago Tiahuanacu was a "recent" colonial outpost—still in the building—when cataclysm overtook it and drowned the great motherland of Mu, or Lemuria. It is significant that, in this connection, there stands in the plain of the bleak paramo on the Andes, at Tiahuanacu, a colossal statue, wearing a strangely inflated skull-cap, one hand clasping to his breast a sceptre of a condor-head, the other a tablet with hieroglyphics. The guide told me, when I was gazing at this colossus whose thick, tightly closed lips, square and powerful jaw are those of a man of a master-race, that he is called *Ra-mac.*

Ra-Mac is singularly like the name of the sun-god, which the old Sanscritian traditions say, in the drowned Pacific continent of Mu-Lemuria, was called *Ra-Mu.* And *Ra,* of course, was the sun-god of old Egypt.

The old Peruvians told Cieza de Leon, who visited Tiahuanacu in a day—about A.D. 1540—when immense walls were still standing, and there were two colossal figures in stone, with long robes reaching to the ground and with ornamental caps on their heads:

> ". . . Some of the natives told me . . . that all these marvels sprang from the ground in a single night. . . . There are not such stones in any of the hills around."

The natives may have been alluding not to necromancy, but to tremendous volcanic action resulting in the upthrust of the Himalayas and the Andes, after the cataclysm that sank the great land of Mu into a pit of fire and then poured the raging ocean into the inferno.

The place has suffered terrible modern vandalism at the hands of modern railroad and permanent-way makers. But even before that modern day the old *misionero*, Diego de Alcobaso, tells us of what he saw in the sixteenth century of our era:

> "I saw a vast hall carved on its roof to represent thatch. There were the waters of a lake which washed the walls of a splendid court in this city of the dead, and, standing in its fine court, in the shallows of the water, on the platform of a superb colonnade were many fine statues of men and women. So real they were that they seemed to be alive. Some had goblets and upraised drinking-cups. Others sat, or reclined, as in life. Some walked in the stream flowing by the ancient walls. Women, carved in stone, dandled babies in their laps, or bore them on their backs. In a thousand natural postures, people stood or reclined."

Of this host of life-like statues, not one is left today! And yet they existed in the days of Atahualpha, the last murdered Inca emperor.

> "These are the words of Fray Diego de Alcobaso who hath been visitor and preaching friar among the Indians in many provinces of this kingdom."

One of these statues *wore a beard.* And the Indians or *Indianistas* of South America are, and were, beardless and glabrous.

When the early Inca emperors entered Tiahuanacu, in the second century A.D., they found it had long been a deserted city. Its streets were still beautifully paved and splendid temples still stood in its deserted plazas. There were also remains of fine aqueducts, and fine statues graced the bed and sides of ancient waterways. Among the ruins of megalithic buildings stood heaps of hewn stones, ready to place *in situ*, perhaps, when sudden calamity dispersed the ancient builders. That this city of the dead—probably the oldest in the world—was *originally* built in the clouds, in rarefied air, where breathing is a torture, and in a waste of scrub, on a bleak paramo, where nothing grows that is edible, or can grow, is *most* improbable. There are also remains of what looks like an unfinished *port* off the field of the Kalasasaya, and ports are not usually built on the tops of high plateaux.

When Pizarro's conquistadores entered Tiahuanacu they committed terrible vandalism in its ruins. Thousands of fine statues were smashed with hammers wielded by soldiers hungry for gold, or set on by fanatics with fires of madness and intolerance burning in their monkish eyes. One man, standing by a great monolith in a square of the dead city, noted that a mammoth silver bolt riveted the stone. He called up other *bandidos* and straightway there began an orgy of iconoclasm. The monoliths were broken up in order to extract the silver bolts, which weighed from half to three or more tons.

Yet, I do not believe that this dead city of Tiahuanacu was ever an outport of the bearded men in black who ruled Hy-Brazil's Atlantean civilisation, some 20,000 or more years ago. The Inca-Quichuan tradition was that the man in black, Viracocha—*vira* meaning the *sun*—who brought to the primitive Peruvian tribes the elements of civilisation from the east of the cordilleras, *entered the city of the dead*, *Tiahuanacu*, when already it lay in grey, deserted ruins. Tiahuanacu may, then, have been a city of an even earlier civilisation dominating the Pacific, perhaps that called *Rutas*, in the early Brahminical traditions of old Hindostan. The men depicted on its statues are really, I think, too archaic in type to be compared with the beautiful youths and maidens and the men of Grecian characteristics carved in stone in the dead Hy-Brazilian city entered by the *bandeiristas* in A.D. 1750.

They were a reddish-skinned race, though among them, as remarkable statuary, dug up from the ruins shows, were also black men, with prognathic features. One splendid piece of terra cotta depicts in beautiful colours a high priest of the sun, with remarkably Egyptian eyes and having on his fine, large forehead a mitre and the sign of evolution, called by Bolivian archaeologists, *el simbolo escalonado* (the stairway sign). Only a race that had attained a very high degree of civilisation, perhaps more than 25,000 years ago, would have reached such a concept of descent from some mystic Central Sun, symbolising the Great and Unknown God-head of the cosmos. There was a college of surgeons who in bronze age Tiahuanacu trepanned with bronze knives!

The great Sun Temple of ancient Tiahuanacu was built on the top of a gigantic truncated pyramid, one more pointer towards the probable or possible fact that the ancestors of the ancient Egyptians of the Pharaohs came from some lost land far out in the Western Pacific. The astronomers of Tiahuanacu had all the elements of the modern telescope: reflectors and *lenses*! They do not seem to have known the Moon—which certainly suggests that that planet was captured by the Earth, about the time the great catastrophe destroyed their civilisation, and possibly that of Easter Island and the lost land called Mu, or Lemuria. Another remarkable piece of statuary is the head of a *giraffe*.

That animal, as we know, is not found in South America. From over what lost land-bridge, then, came this piece of evidence to Tiahuanacu, off the western shore of archaean South America?

All the signs on the ruins of Tiahuanacu point to a great earthquake, accompanied by tremendous vulcanism. The sea, sweeping inshore in gigantic tidal waves, engulfed the great city. Then came a second appalling disaster, which buried the smoking ruins under a great heap of muck, alluvium, mud and sand. Everything was reduced to chaos. Fragments of skeletons of men and animals lie anyhow among the broken, massive stones of megalithic proportions. Bits of pottery depict prehistoric animals which must have been familiar to the old Tiahuanacuans. Pottery, jewels and implements of engineering and architecture are inextricably mixed in utmost confusion. The heaps of blocks of masoned stone bear every evidence of having been abandoned by men fleeing for their lives, and taken by surprise.

Look inside the great ruins, today. Some of the pillars were obviously decorated in colours, like the interiors of old English naves of cathedrals of pre-Reformation days. There are remains of great drainage systems—cloaca maxima, such as were found in old Rome. But what strikes the imagination so vividly are the coverings of extremely ancient volcanic ash and powder which overlay the ruins of this city of the great unknown and mighty dead. Decomposed felspar—itself a volcanic rock—lies at the bases of massive walls that it seems giants must have heaved into place. How long did it take this felspar to rot?

Ages and ages, say geologists.

Standing in niches of the powdered walls were finely carved images of the men of this great city. One of them has been found. It is carved out of *human bone*, and depicts a man of strong face, wearing a queer turban. He has a perforated ear and carries a sceptre in one hand, and a bundle of inscribed slabs in the other. So far back is his time that he and the images found in the muck of ages are fossilised and petrified. . . . Very suddenly, like a thief in the night of time, came disaster on this colonial outpost of a Pacific continent at the doors of ancient South America. Only men engaged, probably, in mining in the *proto* Andes, then, on this theory, not part of archaean South America, and far lower in altitude, then, than now, escaped. And, even so, they could not have carried away any of the civilisation; for the subsequent violent and sudden elevation of the Andes would have wiped even them out.

Two mighty continents vanished, apparently almost in a day and a night and at the same time: most part of Mu, or Lemuria in the Pacific, that had survived an earlier catastrophe, and Atlantis in the northern tropical part of the Atlantic Ocean. Alike with these ancient lost continents, this riddle of a city of Tiahuanacu—of incredible age, perhaps even 30,000 years old—has suffered cataclysms separated by great intervals of time, and probably in the far-off day before what are *now* the Andes arose, *for the second time, from the bed of the Pacific Ocean.*

One may be forgiven, when contemplating the amazing command of these ancient engineers and masons over vast masses of rock in a way that can hardly be rivalled by modern engineers with all their wonderful technique and power appliances, for speculating whether they were a race of giants *in stature*?*

If they were a race of "the giants in the earth, in those days", who built this strange city, it is clear that when they vanished from the earth—whether by inundation and vulcanism, in some Pacific lost continental-island, or on the Andes themselves—they left behind them degenerate men who, too, were master-builders in stone. This is no fantasy of mine. It is a story of very ancient Peruvian tradition; for, in the reign of the Inca Ayatarcó Cuso (Inca XII), *giants* entered Perú from the sea. Fernando Montesinos, native of Osuña, in old Spain, probably derived this story from the lost MSS. of the famous Blas Valera, whose mother was a Peruvian lady and father a conquistadorian soldier.

These giants arrived in boats made of reeds, or a sort of rushes, and they landed from the Pacific off the Point Santa Elena, close to Puerto Viejo, in the old empire of Perú. The times were extremely remote, say the Indians, "and we had the tradition from our parents".

Here was the peculiar story told by the Quichua-Peruvian Indians to Don Cieza de Leon, the old Spanish soldier-priest, in A.D. 1545. "These giants from the sea were so great in stature that from the *knee down, they were as tall as a tall man*. It was amazing to see how the hair hung from their great heads to their shoulders. Yet were they beardless. They ate more than fifty ordinary men. Their eyes were big as plates (*como pequeños platos*). Their arms and legs were proportionately huge. Some were clad in skins of animals; others quite naked. No women came with them. Going inland, they ravaged the country, and, finding no water, these builders in great stones set to and sank an immensely deep well in the living rock" . . . "and today (in A.D. 1545), the water of this ancient well is so clear and cold and wholesome that it is a pleasure to drink of it." This well the giants lined with masonry, from top to bottom—"and so well are these wells made that they will last for ages".

The giants overran all lowland Perú, beat down the puny resistance of the Indians, and took their women to wife. "But they ruined the women; for they were too big for them, and the women were ruptured and died."

Cieza de Leon also tells how in Cuzco, in A.D. 1560, in the days of the viceroyalty of Don Antonio de Mendoza, a tomb was found containing large human bones, and says that similar bones were already found in Mexico City. Let none suppose these were bones of dinosaurs, or other prehistoric mammoth mammals, any more than were the bones of giants "of huge greatness" which, says

* The Montagnais Indians of Canada have a tradition that God was angry with the Giants and sent an inundation upon them.

another old Spanish missioner and historian, Padre Acosta, were found round Manta, Perú, in A.D. 1560. (This Manta is identical with the Manta of the Central Railroad of Ecuador, where bones of similar human giants were found, in a cave, in 1928, behind great stalagmites on the petrified floor. The remains found in this cave were of *ancient men* over eight feet in height! And the stalagmites, testifying to the remote age of the bones, were of immense size. Scientists know how long such stalagmites take to grow.)

Similar remains of giant men have also been found on the Pacific shores of modern Mexico. In his Eighth Decade of *de Orbe Novo*, Peter Martyr de Anghiera tells a queer story of that Diego de Ordaz who, subsequently, went out on an El Dorado quest into the interior of Eastern South America. Diego was he who, according to Las Casas, in his *Historia de las Indias*, climbed the high volcano of Popocatepetl, near Mexico City.

Says Peter Martyr:

> "De Ordaz found in the sanctuary of a temple the thigh bone of a giant, which had been cut and half-gnawed away with age. This bone was brought to Vittoria to be sent to Rome to the Pope. Said Ordaz: 'I have preserved this bone, which measures from the neck to the knee-cap (*patella*) five cubits (about 8 feet 4 inches!) Its width is in proportion.' Men sent by Cortes to the mountains of the south, later discovered the country inhabited by these giants. In testimony of their discovery they have brought back several ribs torn from the dead bodies."

This race of giants entered Mexico, in some far distant day. Near Tepic, Señor de Valda, in 1938, found a series of very ancient grave-mounds wherein were seven skeletons of men *and women* lying under thin slabs of grey stone of slaty-blue colour. The skeletons were all from eight to nine feet tall. No trace of metal was found in these ancient Mexican graves, but there were fragments of unglazed pottery, and bowls with a pattern of painted Greek-line Meander design, in blue and red lines. Señor de Valda took a foot and arm each of the skeletons and showed them to Dean Cummings of Arizona University.

It has been found that giants ranged far south in South America into what is now Patagonia. Years ago, indeed, Charles Darwin, landing in a fjord at Ultima Speranza, entered a cave where he found dung-balls of chewed grass lying close to the gigantic bones of a monstrous prehistoric type of mylodons. Only giant men, it may be, could have tamed such huge animals at that far time of day and used them, as they did, as beasts of burden.

It may, or may not be, that those were descendants of this incredibly ancient race of giant men who overwhelmed the warm lowlands of old Perú, as the Ayar-Inca traditions tell, and forced the ancestors of the early Incas to retreat to walled mountain cities 12,000 feet up in the cordilleras and paramos above old Cuzco, where the city of retreat hung like a fly on a ceiling, and was reached by men toiling painfully up 536 hand-hewn masoned steps past tiers of white granite walls with a gradient of 50 degrees. The ruins of this ancient refuge city were found, in 1940, by the Axel Wenner-Gren expedition led by Dr. Paul Fejos. (The Peruvian authorities at Lima intend to make an automobile road to this strange dead city.)

One may theorise, with probability, that lack of oxygen and the rarefied air at these great altitudes were the more potent guards against the irruption of these giants, used to the warmer lowlands.

At one time of day, and not long ago, either, these and all such stories would have been dismissed as "mistakes" by or naïveté of men who knew not the difference between the bones of men, prehistoric saurians, or giant mammals. Today, one is not so positive that that is *always* the explanation!

If one may believe the queer stories that, from time to time, come from the North-West territory of Canada, giants still exist! There is the story told by trappers and Indians, as recently as A.D. 1938, that, in the unexplored recesses of British Columbia's rugged hinterland, a race of hairy giants, called locally "The Sasquatch", are to be found, today. The Indians say these hairy giants are eight feet tall, and covered, except round the eyes, with short woolly hair of simian character. J. W. Burns, Indian agent in Chehalis Indian reservation, says these modern giants are very shy men, descendants of an ancient primitive tribe, and meet in secret conclave atop of the Morris Mountain. The Indians say they have met the giants, and an article on them appeared, quite recently, in the Victoria *Daily Times*, British Columbia.

At Pachacamac, where, today, exist ruins that have received much attention from the archaeologists of U.S. and British museums and the Carnegie Institution, the giants, mentioned (as we have stated above) by Blas Valera and Fernando Montesinos, repeating ancient records of the Inca priestly caste, built a sumptuous temple with *iron tools*. This, as already stated, was in the time of the Ayar-Inca emperor (the twelfth), Ayatarcó Cuso, about 500 B.C., the time when one British authority suggests that only savages inhabited South America! (Here seems to have been a case where a stone age race were also workers in iron).

This curious passage seems also to import that the giants remained in the land for a long time after their landing on the coast, though it is odd that the Incas are said never to have used iron tools! Did the giants bring such tools with them? Later on, the giants became homo-sexual, according to the story and traditions of the Peruvians;

"for they had no women with them, and, one day, when they were publicly polluting the market-place with these practices, the fire from heaven rained down on them, and consumed them".

But not all were burnt in this Sodom-Gomorrah holocaust—either of some immense aerolite, which, before now, and as recently as 1932, has devastated hundreds of square miles of Brazilian jungle, or from vulcanism. Some of the giants ascended the cordilleras, and, outside old Cuzco, were met by the armies of Inca XII (Ayatarcó Cuso) and dispersed.

That giants of this sort existed in ancient Perú is a fact depicted on some ancient pottery, dug up near Pachacamac, which shows them engaged in these perverted amours. And giants must, at one time, have ranged very widely over the equatorial belt of South America—not to speak of the ten-footer Goyazes, or Brazilian Curiù-queanos, of the Amazons, in quite recent times, who were adorned with gold; or the ten-footer Marquitas, who fought under women chieftains.

Whoever these giants of old Perú were, they were clearly makers of megalithic structures as were the men of mysterious Tiahuanacu. Were they an outlying colony whose remote ancestors had escaped the cataclysm that drowned a great land and great cities formerly located well out in the ocean off the western shores of ancient South America, and which, as to one ancient city, was later upthrust from the sea-bed to below the peaks of Andean cordilleras as we see them today?

Old Europe had also giants.

Homer's Lestrygones were giants. Some have supposed that the land they inhabited was ancient Norway, where in caves have been found tremendous human arm, leg and head bones, long antecedent to any Aryan invasion. It will be remembered that these giants of old Europe, allied to the Cyclops, fed on human flesh, and that when Odysseus, or Ulysses came on their coasts, they sank his ships and ate his companions. Homer does not name their country, but says their capital city was called Lamus. One Lamus led a colony of these giants—or so said ancient authors—into Italy, where they built the town of Formiae.

A discovery made in a field in the Jalpaigur district, near Simla, in June 1938, suggests that old Hindostan had, too, *her* giants. Many footprints, apparently human and of unknown date, were there found in a field. The footprints are said to have been two feet in length and eleven inches wide, and it was reckoned that those who made them must have been at least eighteen feet tall.

I have, for a very good reason, alluded to the world-wide provenance of these giants who, said the Babylonian priests, corroborated by Eupolemus, built ancient Babylon after escaping the Great Deluge. They were said to have erected a tower of Babel, and were great astrologers who received from their fathers, "The Sons of God", all secret learning which they imparted to the ancient priests of Babylon, according to Eusebius (*Vide*: the *Praeparatio et Demonstratio Evangelica*), and desposited in the Babylonian temples records of the periodical cataclysms they themselves had witnessed.

Some have been tempted to euhemerise these Giants of the pre- and post-diluvian eras as leaders of a lower Atlantean caste in that old island-continent, who had revolted against the ruler-castes, as the Titans did against the Gods, or Lucifer against the Ruler of the Heavenly Fields. It is, however, evident that Giants in the ancient world cannot *all* be allegorised away in this fashion. They certainly existed, unless the reader be prepared to dismiss all these evidences from South America, old Europe or old Asia. Who they were, whence they came, and what relation they bore, if any, to the lost world-races of Atlantis or Rutas-Mu-Lemuria are still enigmas. The legends of the Fomorians in old Ireland, of Gog Magog in ancient Britain, and of Albion, the giant-god of old Britain, seem to enshrine ancestral memories of such people.

Some light may have been thrown on the riddle by the discovery in Western Missouri forests, in 1875, of conical mounds, on high bluffs overlooking the Missouri river, which were the tumuli of skeletons with head bones of monstrous size. The lower jaw of one skeleton was double the size of that of a civilised man. The thigh bone looked like that of a horse; but the receding human or anthropoid frontal bone indicated a low order of intellect. These skeletons were found in sitting posture with flint knives and scrapers. Are they, then, of palaeolithic age?

Once more we grope dimly through the mists and darkness of very mysterious ages in the world's most mysterious continent, perhaps at a time before the ice ages had gripped our planet, and when glaciers, still existing above the level of 12,000 feet, reached as far south as the Sierra Nevada, including a large glacier about 250 miles north of Los Angeles, California. The last great ice age is said to have ended some 15,000 years ago, leaving, as echo soundings made with dynamite recently indicated, a continental ice sheer, in the interior of Greenland, which is over a mile deep. (Thousands of years hence, much of the ice may return to the sea, and the polar zones become what they have been before: lush, warm lands with tropical vegetation reaching as far north as the Canadian border.)

Scientists have arrived at the conclusion that the mystery of the cause of the (last) ice age is that volcanic activity, with heat and fire, touched off the ice age. This theory, one of others, seems true, perhaps, in a way not quite appreciated, in view of what one has written in this book. Man, it is said, arrived in the North American continent, about 15,000 years ago, at a time when an animal trap existed in what today are the McKittrick tar seeps in the San Joaquin Valley. An earlier prehistoric animal trap is found in the La Brea tar pits of Los Angeles, contemporary with a day some 25,000 years ago, when imperial mammoths, thirteen feet high at the shoulder, huge wolves, sabre-toothed tigers, *camels*, *horses*, sloths and bears roamed the North (and South) American lands.

The reader may remember the *camel* found carved in a pottery statuette in the ruins of Tiahuanacu, and also the figure of a horse in a pre-Incaic inscription existing ages before the conquistadores introduced the Castilian jennet into the "Spanish Indies". All that has gone before may suggest to *some* that a rectification of a chronological and palaeontological character seems long overdue in relation to the remote date when *civilised* man appeared in America. May be, in the pre-cataclysmic ages, not 15,000, but 25,000 years is nearer the truth in relation to man's appearance in America.

We may now return for a last glance into the dimmed mirror of pre-history in which is reflected a hazy picture of "the age of giants" whose work was the cyclopean city of Tiahuanacu, the great and the mysterious. It is a riddle of the "dark backward and abysm" of Time upon which, probably, no last word may ever be said.

In a preceding part of this chapter, concerning the problem of the age of Tiahuanacu, I referred to the astronomical calculations of the Potsdam Observatory staff who used certain data, in part furnished by the remains of the Kalasasaya, or Sun Temple at Tiahuanacu, to determine the date of this extremely ancient civilisation. I have left to the last some comments on the very interesting theories advanced by Mr. H. S. Bellamy, in his fascinating book: *Built Before the Flood* (Faber and Faber, London, 1943). He visualises a heaping up of the tides, swelling from northern and southern hemispheres, in a great girdle roughly corresponding with the zones between the tropics of Cancer and Capricorn. He appears to suggest this phenomenon occurred some quarter of a million years ago, under the pull of a disintegrating satellite that preceded the capture of the present moon. His interesting theories are inspired by the glacial cosmogony and "Welteislehre" studies of the late Hans Hörbiger, "Maschineningenieur" of Atzgersdorf, near Vienna. According to Mr. Bellamy, the dead city of Tiahuanacu was surrounded by a rampart of the Andes, which barred off the rising waters of the Pacific, until, under increasing pull and pressure from the disintegrating satellite, those waters spilled over and drowned the city. Twice the city was drowned, while, on the "inter-Andinian plateau", lived races who had sought refuge there from the catastrophes that had, in the north and south hemispheres, drowned populations. The final cataclysm happened, he says, about 13,500 years ago, when the ancient metropolis was to have formed a source of building materials, or to be repaired. Before the final disaster, there had been no satellite accompanying the earth, the first "moon having been disintegrated, and its débris thrown on to the earth." After the "lunar interregnum," our present moon had approached near the earth and been attracted into its gravitational field. The survivors lapsed into primitivism and the ruins were henceforth avoided, and put under taboo.

We are asked to believe that this interregnum—time between the death and disintegration of No. 1 satellite and the capture of our present moon—lasted about 230,000 *years* and that in all this immense stretch of time survivors from the cataclysm that ruined "classic" Tiahuanacu were living in the lush, warm lowlands on the paradisial coast of Western South America! When the present moon threatened them with another inundation, they sent pioneering "scouts" to view the uplands where stood the ruins of Tiahuanacu, which was merely a dim memory or myth among them—as well it might be after more than 200,000 years! All one can comment is the famous remark of the celebrated dominie in Scott's novel: "Mon, 'tis *prodeegious*!" A race whose paradise on the Pacific littoral lasted 230,000 years!

I say nothing about this theory existing in a vacuum that apparently has no relation to the cataclysmic loss of a continent or continental islands in the Pacific Ocean.

In its second prime, under a bronze age race which had developed a lost technique of tempering bronze that could cut and shape the very hard stone used—andesite—their world was very different. Frequent vulcanism shook the country, and the tremendous megalithic structures were deeply embedded in the ground in order to withstand tellurian shocks. At that time, he says, the climate of the Andean Altiplano, on which the ruins stand, must have been tropical.

It is, however, I suggest, very difficult to understand how at a *height of over* 12,000 *feet*, conditions such as these prevailed, where, as Mr. Bellamy points out, the great structures of Tiahuanacu—in Quichua, meaning "city of darkness or waning light"—were built unroofed and open to the sky as assembly places for great multitudes. Nor, unless the region of the dead city, the Altiplano, once stood at a far lower level in a day before the rise of the Andes to their present elevation, can one comprehend how prehistoric animals, existing only in lush, warm regions and unable to withstand glacial temperatures, could have ranged these regions, or how fossil fishes of tropical type can be found in the strata round the dead city.

Even if, as Mr. Bellamy, following Hörbiger's glacial theory, urges, the pull of the disintegrating satellite, that preceded in earth's skies the capture of our present moon, caused the belt of our atmosphere to be drawn off from the poles and northern regions into a relatively thicker blanket over this region of archaic South America as well as over other sectors environed by his girdle tides of global-cincturing range round "the waist" of our earth, then this denser belt of air could hardly have created lush tropical conditions at the height of 12,000 feet in the clouds at which Tiahuanacu even then, he presupposes, was situated. (One has a comparable state in the highlands of Kenya Colony on the equator; where, despite the fact that the region is on the equator, the cold at great heights is not lessened in the fact that, below, is an atmospheric belt of relatively greater density.)

Mr. Bellamy, too, is opposed to the theory of scientists that there occurred about the end of the Tertiary Age a catastrophically sudden and unbalanced rise of South America out of the waters of the ocean, which elevated the continent more strongly in the north than the south. When this occurred, say scientists, the Andes must have been jerked up more than 12,500 feet on an average. This catastrophic movement—by the way, not confined to this region of our world—exposed a continental shelf which is now the arid lowlands of Perú and North Chile, and raised into regions of rarefied air this dead city of Tiahuanacu as well as the mountain ramparts girdling it, all of which, prior to their sudden elevation by tremendous forces of both tellurian and cosmic origin, had been submarine mountains with a paramo, or plain set in their crests, also under sea.

When this happened, some 13,500 years ago, say, the dead city of Tiahuanacu had simply risen *dead* from its watery tomb under the old Pacific Ocean, and what are now the Andean cordilleras with it. The problem is, clearly, one of chronology and resolves itself into one main question: just how old are the Eastern and Western cordilleras of the Andes? That question has not really been resolved. The remarkable unevenness of the forces would account for the curious fact that shore or strand lines, found on mountain slopes and walls on the Bolivian Altiplano, and denoting the beaches of ancient seas, or ancient sea levels, are not level either with the present level of Lake Titicaca or with that of the modern Pacific Ocean.

One other point may be noted: the mitre of the high priest in terra cotta, found under the earth at Tiahuanacu of today—it is depicted in pages 90, 132 *supra* of my own book. This archaic and very beautifully made and designed statuette bears, on its polychrome cap, 4 quadrants of symmetrical symbols which are in the form of *el simbolo escalonado*, with a black crosslet and orb in the centre of the design. They are the subject of a rather fantastic suggestion by Mr. Bellamy, who says that the pictograph on the cap of this mitre of a Tiahuanacu high priest denotes "a highly conventionalised map of the world, known to the inhabitants of the Andinian Life Asylum, which also features certain magical (or religious) elements".

But is this not a far-fetched notion? Surely, the world, as known by these very ancient races, could not have been so symmetrical in the shape of all its continental outlines as to be capable of representation in this way? I advance the theory—and I am not alone in it—that the *simbolo escalonado*, found also on later Mayan glyphs, on artifacts all over South America, and, today, in native non-Christian wayside altars at Carangas, and in the form of a sacred volute at Chimbote, Perú, was the sign of evolution from the godhead; denoted by the Central Mystical Sun of the universe: the unknown God, or *Dyas*, of whom, in old Hindostan, Brahma was the demi-ourgos.

As for the black crosslet and yellow orb in the middle of the cap of the mitre, with the stairway signs on all four sides, which Mr. Bellamy calls a heaven-pillar magically warding off lunar dangers from the earth—denoted, he says, by the hierographs of the four stairway signs—that crosslet is identical in origin with the Venus sign of reproduction—the phallic symbol of coition, the cross, or Egyptian *tau*—found on glyphs in Mayan Guatemala and Yucatan, and on tombs of the Etruscans in old Italy.

If this interpretation of mine be correct, the yellow orb in the middle of the black crosslet, denotes not Mr. Bellamy's "evil" yellow, former tellurian, pre-Luna satellite of the earth, but the Mystic Central Sun of the universe, which the sun of our own planetary system symbolised. After all, these ancient men of Tiahuanacu were *sun-worshippers*, and so, far more likely to set *his* sign on the dome of a mitre, than a yellow disk of merely "evil" significance. One might as well have expected a mediaeval abbot to set the horns, tail and trident of the Evil One not on a gargoyle but on the topmost turrets of a minster or abbey, rather than the Christian cross! I hope Mr. Bellamy will forgive me for my constructive criticism of a part of his very interesting and illuminating book. Many of us are faced by the danger of pressing our theories too far.

BIBLIOGRAPHY

ADAIR, James. *History of American Nations* (1735–75).

AELIAN, Claudus. *Varia Historia* (A.D. 140).

ALCEDO, Antonio de. *Diccionario geográfico-histórico de las Indias occidentales ó America.* (Madrid, 1786–89.)

ALCEDO Y HERRERA, Dionisio. Captain-General of Quito. Died A.D. 1777.

ARCHEOLOGIA BRAZILEIRA ARCHIVOS (Rio de Janeiro). Various volumes from Museu Nacional, Rio.

ARCHIVO GENERAL DE INDIAS (Sevilla). *Papeles pertenencientes á los Generales y Almirantes de Armados, años* 1520–1624, *y* 1705–80.

ARCHIVOS DE LA ACADEMIA DE HISTORIA (Madrid).

ARISTOTLE (384–322 B.C.). *Meteorologica.*

Pseudo-ARISTOTLE. *Aristotelis Liber de Mirabilibus Auscultationibus explicatus a Ioanne Beckmann.* (Edn.: Gottingae, 1786.)

AUDIENCIAS (*Cartas* and Reports of, in *Archivo Gr̃l de Indias*, relating to El Dorado and El Gran Paytite, sixteenth to early eighteenth century.) (Many of these reports are, for the first time, translated into English in this and a subsequent book.)

ST. AUGUSTINE. Latin citations in *De Civitate Dei* from lost Roman Greek and other authors, relating to the Great Cataclysm, called the Deluge, and also referred to in Plato's dialogues from Solon and old Egyptian temple records at Sais and Heliopolis.

AVIENUS, Rufus Festus. *Ora Maritima.* (Early Phoenician and Carthaginian voyages into the Atlantic.)

AZTEC CODICES. *Chimalpopoca, Telleriano Remensis, Dresden, and Mexicanus Vatican.*

BACH, Dr. *Articulos*: *Revista do Museo Paulista.*

BACH, Johann Nicolaus. *Solonis Atheniensis carminum quae supersunt* (Ed. A.D. 1825).

BALDWIN, John Denison. *Ancient America* (1872).

BARAZA, Fray Cypriano. *Relación Sum̃aria de la Vida . . . del U.P. Cyp*[r]. *Baraza . . . muerto á manos de Barbaros en la Mission de los Moxos de la Provincia del Perú.* (Lima, *Imprenta Real de Josef de Cofriras*, 1704.) Very rare, blackletter vol. S. Americana.

BEDE, The Venerable. *Historia Ecclesiastica.*

BENALCAZAR, Sebastian (de Moyano). Conquistadorian eye-witness of affairs in the Popayan, and Nueva Andalucia y Nueva Granada (modern Colombia. S.A.). (Died at Benalcaz. A man of action, he is not known to have left any MSS., or diaries.)

BERREO, Antonio de. (*See* DE BERREO.)

BLAS VALERA, Fray. Lost sixteenth-century Latin MS. histories of Peruvian antiquities, cited in Fernando Montesinos's *Memorias Antigas, historiales y Politicas de Perú.* (Only one MS. known to exist, and (No. 3) published anonymously by Señor Ximinez de la Espada at Madrid.)

BOAS, F. Report on N.W. Tribes of Dominion of Canada. (Brit. Asscn. meeting at Bath, September 1888.)

BOECK (German Hellenist). The Panathenaean Festival (ancient Athens) on Atlantean memories.

BRASSEUR-DE-BOURBOURG, Abbé Etienne-Charles. *Popul Vuh* (Quiché reprint, with French translation); *Histoire des nations civilisés du Mexique et de l'Amérique centrale.* (Owner, in 1874, of very rare and valuable MSS. on obscure Central American races, Spanish and native writers.)

BRAZILIAN ARCHIVES (Museo Nacional, Rio de Janeiro, and Archivos, São Paulo.

BUEHLER, Georg. *Grundriss der Indo-Arischen Philologie und der Altertums-künde.*

BUFFON, Comte Georges L. L. *Histoire Naturelle.*

BURTON, Sir Richard Francis. *Travels in the Brazilian Highlands* (1869).

BUSTAMENTE, Carlos Maria. Mexican Historian, 1774–1848.

CALMET, Dom Augustin. *Dissertorum Hebrorum Ritu Phaenicio de Urbe West Capell* (*circa* A.D. 1710).

CARVAJAL, Fray Gaspar de. *Descubrimiento del Rio de las Amazonas según la Relación de Fr. G. de C.* (Various sixteenth and early seventeenth century MSS.).

CASTELNAU, Comte Michel de (Sieur de la Mauvissière, Touraine). *Expédition dans les parties centrales de l'Amérique du Sud* (6 tomes, Paris, 1850–1).

CEDRENUS, Georgius. *Compendium historarium ab urbe condito ad Isaac Comnenum* (eleventh-century work).

CENSORINUS. *Liber de die Natali* (*circa* A.D. 238).

CHARLEVOIX, Père François Xavier de. *Histoire et description générale de la Nouvelle France* (1744).

CIEZA DE LEON, Pedro. *La Crónica del Perú* (*circa* A.D. 1555).

CLAVIGERO, Francisco Javier. *Historia del Mexico* (1781); *Storia Antica del Messico* (Cesena, 1780).

COCHRANE, Captain Charles Stuart, R.N. *Journal of a Residence in Colombia* (London, 1825).

COLUMBUS, Christopher. *Viages.* (*Vide:* NAVARRETE, and PETER MARTYR DE ANGHIERA.)

CONGRÈS DES AMERICANISTES. Various reports and conferences in European capitals.

COSMAS INDICOPLEUSTES. *Topographia Christiana* (sixth century, A.D.).

CRANTOR. Philosopher of Soli, of First Academy of Platonists. References from Egyptian temple records, *re.* Atlantis.

CUNNINGHAM, Sir Alexander. *Corpus Inscriptionum Indicarum.*

CURTIN, Jeremiah. *Creation Myths of Primitive America.*

DA ROCHA PITTA, Sebastião. *Historia da America Portugueza* (Lisboa, 1880).

DARWIN, Charles. *Voyage of the Beagle.*

DA SYLVEIRA. Capitão Symão Estacio. *Relação Sumaria das Cosas do Maranhão* (Madrid (?), 1624. Very rare vol.).

DAVIS, Rev. Edward. *Mythology of the British Druids* (London, 1807).

DE ACOSTA, Fray José. *Historia natural y moral de las Indias.*

DE ACUÑA, Fray Cristobal. *New Discovery of the Great River of the Amazons* (Eng. trans. of the Madrid edn., 1641).

DE BERREO, Don Antonio. Letters to Carlos V. (in Archivo Gral de Indias, Sevilla-Simancas).

DE BRY, Theodore. *Historia Americae.* (Rhine edn., 1596, with fine "iconae".)

DE CARDENAS, Don Gabriel. Prologue to Garcilasso de la Vega's *Comentarios Reales de los Yncas* (Madrid, 1723).

DE CHARENCEY (*Rivae Americanae*, 2e série, No. 2).

DE GARCIA, Fray Pedro. *Origen de los Indiós del Nuevo Mundo* (Valencia, 1607).

DE GUSMAN, Don Nunno. Letters to Carlos V., on the Mexican Amazons. (*Vide*, also, *Ramusio.*)

DE HERRERA, Antonio. *Historia General de los Hechos de los Castellanos en las Islas de Tierra Firme del Mar Oceano.*

DE LA CONDAMINE, Charles Marie. *Voyage from the South Sea to Brazil and Guiana* (Paris, 1754).

DE LAS CASAS, Fray Bartoloméo. *Historia General de las Indias.*

DE LEON, Don Juan Recio. *Breve Relación . . . de las Provincias de Tipuane Chunchos . . . y otras muchas . . . del grñde Rey del Paytite*, (Madrid, 1626.) (*Papeles Varios de Indias.* Lord Kingsborough's Library.)

DE LLANO ZAPATA, Don José Eusebio. *Memorias Historicas-Fisicas-Apologeticas de America Meridional.* (Lima, reprint of eighteenth-century edn. in Biblioteca Nacional del Perú, No. 388.)

DE MAGELHAES, General Conto. *O Selvagen: seus costumes, suas origems*, etc. (Rio de Janero, 1876.)

DE MOLINA, Alonso. *Arte de la lengua mexicana y castellana, en casa de Pietro de Ocharte* (A.D. 1571).

DE ORDONEZ Y AGUIAR, Don Ramón. MS. *Historia del cielo y la tierra . . . relación de los ritos y costumbres de los Culebras.* (Concg. Votan and the Phoenicians in Central America.)

DE ORTIGUERA, Toribio. *Noticias y relación de Quito y del rio de las Amazonas*

DE RIBEIRA, Don Hernando. Conquistador and follower of Cabeza de Vaca, in Paraguay, A.D. 1541. Testimony about the Amazon women.

DE RIVERO Y USTARIZ, Mariano. *Antiguedades Peruanos.*

DE SAMPAIO, Xavier Ribeiro. *Diario da viagem no anno de 1774 e 1775* (Lisboa, 1826 edn.).

DE SAN VICENTE, or VINCENTE, Fray Marcelino. MS. *Relación de modo de decobrir el Dorado.*

DE VALLENCEY. *Collectanea de Rebus Hibernicis.*

DE ZAMORA, Fray Alonso. *Historia de la Provincia de S. Antonio del Nuevo Reino de Granada, del Orden de Predicadores, compuesta por el M.R.P.M. F. Alonso de Zamora, su Provincial Qualificador del Santo Officio y Examinador Sinodal de su Arcobispado. Dedicada a la Milagrossa Imagam de N. Señora del Rosario que se venera en su Conuento de la Ciudad de Santa fé.* (Barcelona: Em la Imprenta de Joseph Llopis, Año de 1701.)

DIODORUS SICULUS. Works.

"Enciclopedia Universel Illustrada Europeo-Americana" (Barcelona).

Eusebius, Bishop of Caesarea (A.D. 267–340). *Praeparatio et Demonstratio Evangelica* (edition Vigerus, fo. 2 vols., Rothomagi, 1628).

Fawcett, Colonel P. H., D.S.O. References to lectures at Royal Geographical Society, London, and to letters.

Ferghil, or Vergil, or Virgil (Bischof Vergil von Salzburg). Irish monk who was threatened with excommunication for asserting the existence of the Antipodes, and of America!

Gaffarel, Professor Paul. *Études sur les rapports de l'Amérique et de l'Ancien continent avant Christophe Colomb* (Paris, 1869).

Gandavo, Pero de Magalhães de (Peter Magellan). *Historia da provincia de Sačta Cruz.* (Very rare volume on the colonial history of Lusitanian Brazil, edition 1576.)

Gerhard, Eduard. *Ueber die Kunst der Phoenizer.*

Gesenius, Guil. *Scripturae Lingaeque Phoeniciae monumenta quotquot supersunt* (Lipsiae, 1837).

Gottfried, J. L. *Newe Welt und Americaniche Historien* (edition 1631); *De Aanmerkenswaardigste Zee-en-Landreizen*, etc. (edition 1727). The South American section is based on De Bry's *Historiae Americae* whose "iconae" Gottfried reproduces.

Graham, R. B. Cunninghame. *Gonzalez Jiminez de Quesada.*

Gregory, Professor J. W. *Physical and Comparative Geography of South America* (1896). (Gregory was drowned, in an overset canoe, in 1932, while crossing the Pongo de Mainique rapids on the Rio Urubamba, Perú, when leading a geological expedition to settle the problem of the age when the Andes were upheaved from the bed of the Pacific.)

Gumilla, Fray Joseph. *Histoire naturelle, civile, et géographique de l'Orénoque.* (Eidous's translation into French of the Spanish edition. Paris, 1848.)

Hakluyt, Richard. *Principal Navigationes.*

Hanno. *Periplus* (fifth century B.C.).

Harris, John. *Moral History of the Spanish West Indies* (London, 1705).

Herodotus. *Melpomena.*

Herrera, Antonio (*see* De Herrera).

Homer. *Odyssey.*

Hornius, George. *De Originis Americanis* (Hague edition, 1652).

Huc, Abbé Evariste-Régis. *De la Tartarie et du Tibet.*

Hull, Professor. Geological works on South America.

Humboldt, Baron Friedrich Alexander. *Ansichten von Natur* (3 Ausgabe); *Vue de Cordillères et Monuments*; *Monuments and Ancient Inhabitants of America*; *Researches concerning the Ancient Inhabitants of America.*

Ixtlilxochitl, Fernando de Alva Cortes. *Historia de los Chichimecs.* (edition 1658 (?)).

JEFFERSON, Thos. (ex-President U.S.A.). *Notes on the State of Virginia* (1784).

"JENAER LITERARZEITUNG" (1874).

JORDANES (JORNANDES). *Getica* (sixth century A.D.).

JOSEPH, F. L. (of Trinidad). *History of Trinidad* (1840, very rare volume).

JUVENAL. Roman satirist's references to frog-worship and augury.

KAETZER, Doktor Friedrich. *Grundzüge der Geologie des unteren Amazonas gebietes* (Leipzig, 1903).

KINGSBOROUGH, Viscount (Edward King). *Antiquities of Mexico* (1830–48). (He tries to prove a Hebrew migration to Mexico; but it is no more convincing than the rumour that there are Irishmen suffering, in Jerusalem, owing to Anglo-Saxon persecution.)

KIRCHER, Athanasius. *Oedipi Aegyptiaci Theatrum Hieroglyphicum.*

LERY, Jean de. *Histoire d'un voyage au Brésil en* 1556–58.

LESCARBOT, Marc. (French traveller to North America). *Histoire de la Nouvelle France* (1651).

LOCH, Captain Erskine, D.S.O. (Letters to author of this book).

LORENZANO, Francisco. *Documentos Mexicanos.*

MARCELLINUS, Ammianus. *Historia Rerum Gestarum Libri XXXI* (Paris, 1680). (Only surviving book of 30 others, lost.)

MARCELLUS. *Tois Aithiopikos* (lost work cited by PROCLUS).

MARCOY, Paul (*pseudonym:* Saint-Cricq-Laurent). *Voyage à travers l'Amérique du Sud* (1869).

MARKHAM, Sir Clements. *Expedition into the Valley of the Amazons*; numerous works on Perú; and introductions to translations of Spanish-American chroniclers and historians, in the Hakluyt Society's series.

MARTINI, Fray Martin, or Martinius. *Historia Sinensis* (very rare volume).

MARTYR, Peter (PETER MARTYR DE ANGHIERA, or ANGLERIA). *De Orbe Novo* (edition 1526).

MAWE, John. *Viagem ao Interior do Brasil* (Lisboa, 1812).

MEANS, Philip Ainsworth. Introduction to Fernando Montesinos's *Memorias Antigas Historiales del Perú.* (Means considerably underestimates the great antiquity of South American civilization.)

MOCQUET, Jean. *Voyages* (editions 1645 and 1655). (A Rouen, chez Jacques Caillove, dans le Cour du Palais.)

MOLINA, Avila. *MS. Tratado y Relación de las fabulas y ritos de los Ingas* (Madrid, *Archivos*).

MUNTER, Frederick. *Religion d. Karthäger* (1827).

MUSEO NACIONAL (Rio de Janeiro). *Archeologia Brazileira Archivos.*

NAU, E. *Histoire des Caciques d'Haïti* (Port-au-Prince).

NAVARRETE, Martin Fernandez. *Viajes de los Españoles.*

NEPOS, Cornelius, Citations from his lost books.

NUÑEZ, H. B. Archaeological works on Venezuela (Caracas, 1925).

NUÑEZ DE LA VEGA, Fray Francisco. *Constituciones diaecesanas del obispado Chiapas* (Roma, 1702). (Very rare volume not in British Museum, but of sections of which I have obtained photostats from the Bibliothèque Nationale (old French Royal Library), a few months before the Germans entered Paris, in 1940.)

OAKENFULL, J. C. *Brazil, Past, Present and Future* (1919). A carefully written account of modern Brazil.

ORDONEZ Y AGUIAR, Ramon de. MS. in Museo Nacional, Mexico City; *Historia del cielo y la tierra . . . y relación de los ritos y costumbres de los Culebras.*

PAUSANIAS. *Periegesis.*

PAUW, Cornelius de. *Récherches philosophiques sur les Américains* (1768–70).

PHILO JUDAEUS. *Of the Indestructibility of the World* (Paris, 1640).

PIEDRAHITA, Don Lucas Fernandez. *Historia General de la Conquista del Nuevo Reyno de Granada.*

PLATO. *Dialogues*, and *Scholiast ad Plat. Rep.* (*Politeian*), referring to memories of Atlantis.

PLINY (The Elder). *Historia Naturalis.*

PLUTARCH. *De Facie in orbe Lunae.*

POCOCK, Roger. *Chorus to Adventurers.*

POLYBIUS. Fragments of lost works of, *re* Amazons, Atlanteans and old Carthage.

"POPUL VUH" (The Bible of the Quichés of old Yucatan).

POSIDONIUS. Lost book (fragments of), on Atlantis.

POSNANSKY, Professor Arturo. *Thesaurus ideographiarium americanarum* (in Spanish and German: Berlin, and La Paz, Bolivia, 1913). Also, *La Guia general ilustrada . . . de Tihuanacu é Islas del Sol y la Luna* (*Titicaca y Koaty*. La Paz, Bolivia, 1925).

PROCLUS. *Commentary on the Timaeus.*

PROCOPIUS. History, with references to expelled Hivites, Canaanites, or Phoenicians, and their colonies in North Africa.

RALEIGH, Sir Walter. *Discouerie of the Empire of Guiana*; also MSS. attributed to him, in the Sloane Collection.

RAMUSIO, Giovanni Battista. *Raccolta di Navigazione et Viaggi* (1550–63).

RANKING, John. *Historical Researches concerning Perú* (London, 1827).

RAWLINSON, Sir Henry Creswick. *Cuneiform Inscriptions in Central and Western Asia.*

REMESAL, Antonio de. *Historia de las provincias de Chiapa y Guatemala* (Madrid, 1619).

RIVAE AMERICANAE. *Traditions Américaines sur le Déluge.*

RIVERO, Mariano Eduardo (and VON TSCHUDI, John James). *Antigüedades Peruanas.*

ROBLEDO, Capitan Jorge. *MS. Relación de lo que sucedio al Magnifico señor capitan Jorge Robledo, en el descrubrimiento que hizo de las provincias de Antiochia.* (The time for the publication of this valuable MS., which is in the archives of the Academia Reale de Historia, Madrid, is considerably overdue, unless it is intended that it be left to *mañana*!)

ROOSEVELT, ex-President Theodore. *Trails through the Brazilian Wilderness.*

SAHAGUN, Fray Bernardino. *Historia General de las Cosas de Nueva España,* with Bustamente's Commentary on old Mexican antiquities.

SALLUST, C. S. Crispus. *Historiarum Fragmenta.*

SALVADOR, Fray. *El Dorado cartas* (letter-reports) to the Council of the Indies (*Archivo Gral*, Sevilla).

SARMIENTO, P. *Apology* for Padre Feijoo's *Theãtre Critique* (on the South American Amazon women).

SCALLON (the late), General Sir Robert Irvine, K.C.B., K.C.I.E. Letters to the author of this book on Arabo-Sabaean Inscriptions and old Indian antiquities.

SCHNIRDEL, Hulderike. *Travels in The Twentie Yeeres' Space, from* 1534–54 *in South America.*

SCHOMBURGHK, Sir Robert Herman. *Journals of Travels in Guiana and North Brazil.*

SCHUCHERT, Professor. *Geographical Review*, Vol. III, 1917.

SCHWENNHAGEN, Professor Ludovico. *Antiga Historia do Brazil, Imprensa official, Theresina,* 1928.

SCYLAX, Caryandenis (*flor.* 550 B.C., commissioned by Darius Hytaspes, King of Persia, to make discoveries in the East). *Periplus* (Amsterdam, 1639).

SENECA, L. Annaeus (4? B.C.–A.D. 65). *Medea.*

SENECA, M. Annaeus (The Rhetor, father of the above, 61 B.C.–A.D. 30). *Suasoriae et Controversiae.*

SHORT, John T. *North Americans of Antiquity* (1880).

SMITH, George (English Orientalist, A.D. 1840–76). The Story of the Akkadian Deluge, from the bricks of the cuneiform library at Nippur-Nineveh.

SMYTH, Lieutenant W., and Mr. F. Lowe. *Journey from Lima to Paraguay* (1835).

SOCIÉTE DES ANTIQUITÉS DU NORD (Kobenhavn). *Journals,* 1839–40.

SOLON (The Athenian) (639?–559 B.C.). Lost Poem: *Atlantikos,* to which Plato, as a relation, had access for the Platonic dialogues *Timaeus* and *Critias.* The poem was written somewhere between 570 and 560 B.C.

SOUTHEY, Robert (A.D. 1774–1843). *Commonplace Book; Travels in Brazil;* and *History of Brazil* (1817–22).

SPANISH DOCUMENTS *re* THE AMERICAS. (*See* ARCHIVO GRAL DE INDIAS.)

STEPHENS, J. Lloyd (American author and traveller, A.D. 1805–52). *Travels in Central America,* 1838–39.

STRABO (Greek Geographer, 63 B.C.–post-A.D. 20). *Geography.*

STRAHLENBERG, Philip Johan. *Description of Northern and Eastern parts of Europe and Asia* (Siberia and Great Tartary) (1738).

SYRIANUS (teacher and master of PROCLUS, the Neo-Platonist of fifth century A.D.). Taught that Atlantis had actually existed.

TE PITO TE HENUA (or Easter Island). Paymaster Wm. J. Thomson, U.S. Navy (Smithsonian Institution, Washington, D.C., 1891)

THEOPHRASTUS (Greek philosopher, who died *aged* 107, denouncing Nature and the gods for granting longevity to the crow and the stag! Born 395? B.C., died 288? B.C.). *History of Plants.*

THEOPOMPUS of CHIOS. Greek historian. (*flor.* 354 B.C.). Lost books cited by AELIANUS.

THEVET, André. *Les Singularités de la France Antarctique* (Paris, 1558). *Cosmographie Universelle.*

THOMSON, Paymaster W. J., U.S. Navy. (*See* TE PITO TE HENUA.)

TORQUEMADA, Fray Juan (Franciscan monk). *Monarquia Indiana* (edition 1723).

VALLANCEY. (*See* DE VALLANCEY.)

VARRO, M. Terentius (Roman scholar and writer, 116 B.C.–A.D. 27?). *De gente Populi Romani* (lost book cited by St. Augustine).

VELASCO, Fray Juan de. *Historia del reyno de Quito.*

VENEZUELA DOCUMENTS (British Government: *Guiana Boundary Commission*, MSS. Dept., British Museum).

VIRGIL. (*See* FERGHIL.)

WALLACE, Alfred Russel (English naturalist, A.D. 1823–1913). *Notes of a Botanist on the Andes.*

WALLIS BUDGE, Sir E. *On the Sumerians.*

XIMINEZ, Fray Francisco (Dominican missioner in Yucatan and Mexico). *Vocabulario del lengua Quiché.*

ZAMORA. (*See* DE ZAMORA.)

ZAPATA. (*See* DE LLANO ZAPATA.)

ZARETE, Agustín de (Spanish Historian, A.D. 1492?–1560?). *Historia de la Conquista del Perú.*

INDEX

Page numbers marked with an asterisk (*) refer to footnotes in the page numbered.

A

B

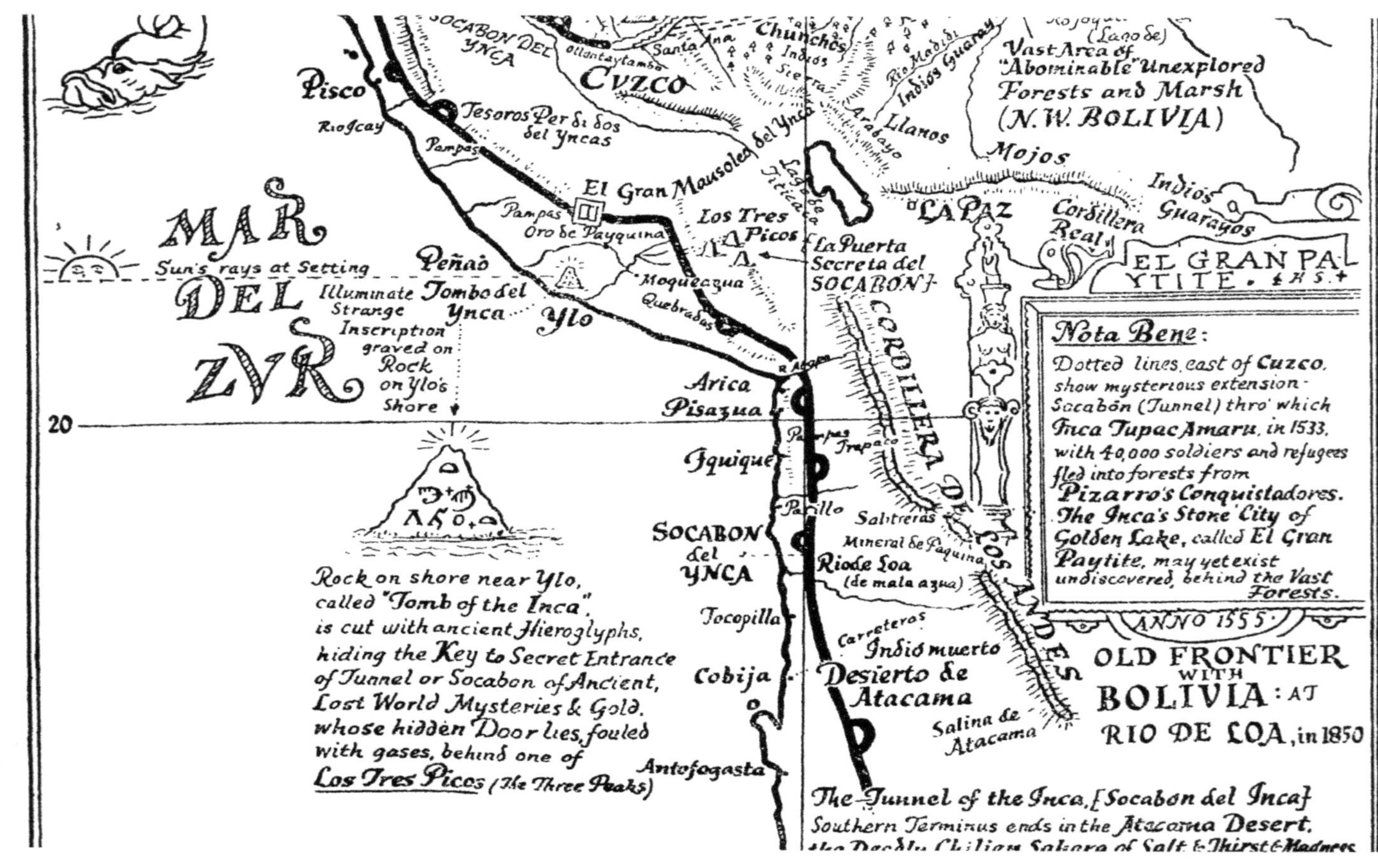
Vast Area of
"Abominable" Unexplored
Forests and Marsh
(N.W. BOLIVIA)
Mojos
Llanos
Indios Guarayos
Cordillera Real
LA PAZ
Pisco
Rio Icay
Tesoros Per di dos del Yncas
Pampas
SOCABON DEL YNCA
Ollantaytambo
Santa Ana
CUZCO
Chunchos
Indios
Sierra
Arabayo
Rio Madidi
Indios Guaray
El Gran Mausoleo del Ynca
Lago de Titicaca
Los Tres Picos
La Puerta Secreta del SOCABON
Pampas
Oro de Payquina
Moquegua
Quebradas
Ylo
Peñao
Tombo del Ynca
MAR DEL ZUR
Sun's rays at Setting Illuminate Strange Inscription graved on Rock on Ylo's Shore
20
Arica
Pisazua
Iquique
Tarapaca
SOCABON del YNCA
Pabillo
Saltreras
Mineral de Payquina
Rio de Loa (de mala agua)
Tocopilla
Cobija
Antofogasta
Carreteros
Indio muerto
Desierto de Atacama
Salina de Atacama
CORDILLERA DE LOS ANDES
EL GRAN PAYTITE • IHS +
Nota Bene:
Dotted lines east of Cuzco, show mysterious extension Socabon (Tunnel) thro' which Inca Tupac Amaru, in 1533, with 40,000 soldiers and refugees fled into forests from Pizarro's Conquistadores. The Inca's Stone City of Golden Lake, called El Gran Paytite, may yet exist undiscovered, behind the Vast Forests.
ANNO 1555
OLD FRONTIER WITH BOLIVIA: AT RIO DE LOA, in 1850
Rock on shore near Ylo, called "Tomb of the Inca", is cut with ancient Hieroglyphs, hiding the Key to Secret Entrance of Tunnel or Socabon of Ancient, Lost World Mysteries & Gold, whose hidden Door lies, fouled with gases, behind one of Los Tres Picos (The Three Peaks)
The Tunnel of the Inca, [Socabon del Inca] Southern Terminus ends in the Atacama Desert,

www.ingramcontent.com/pod-product-compliance
Ingram Content Group UK Ltd.
Pitfield, Milton Keynes, MK11 3LW, UK
UKHW021127260726
13994UKWH00001B/23